W9-BMA-741

Ancient China in Transition

先秦社會史論

許倬雲著

葉公超署

Cho-yun Hsu

Ancient China in Transition

An Analysis of Social Mobility, 722–222 B.C.

Stanford University Press, Stanford, California

Stanford University Press
Stanford, California
© 1965 by the Board of Trustees of the
Leland Stanford Junior University
Printed in the United States of America
Cloth ISBN 0-8047-0223-3
Paper ISBN 0-8047-0224-1
Original edition 1965
Last figure below indicates year of this printing:
80   79   78   77

To My People

Preface

This work is an effort to provide Western readers with a general social history of ancient China from the beginning of the Ch'un Ch'iu period to the unification of China under the First Emperor of Ch'in (221 B.C.). Social mobility was chosen as the focus of this work partly because it is a built-in index of the stability of a stratified society, partly because the highly fluid social mobility in the Chan Kuo period (463–222 B.C.) is worth careful study in itself. The societies of these two periods, the Ch'un Ch'iu and the Chan Kuo, are compared in order to disclose the trend of change and its dynamics.

The major source for my research on the Ch'un Ch'iu period is the *Tso Chuan*. For the Chan Kuo period I used the *Chan Kuo Tse*, a collection of assorted materials of the period, and a number of works by Chan Kuo scholars. I have also relied heavily on the *Shih Chi*, a general history of China written in the second century B.C. The dating and authenticity of these and other sources used in this study are discussed in the Appendix.

The dates of persons used in this study, unless otherwise stated, are largely based on Professor Ch'ien Mu's *Hsien Ch'in Chu Tzu Hsi Nien K'ao Pien*. Romanization of Chinese names is according to the Wade-Giles system, but diacritical marks are omitted with the exception of the umlaut on "u." Names used in quotations from translations are changed in accordance with this system, and English translations cited are sometimes revised in other minor details.

I should like here to express my deep debt to Professor H. G. Creel, under whose guidance I prepared the first draft and who has so often corrected my errors. I would like to thank Professors Han-sheng Ch'uan, Bert F. Hoselitz, Milton B. Singer, and John A. Wilson for reading my draft. Professor Edward A. Kracke, Jr. and Professor T. H. Tsien have read my draft and suggested a number of substantial revisions. For Professor Tsien's advice on the design of the charts, I am especially grateful. My special acknowledgment should be given to my teacher in the National Taiwan University, Professor Tsung-t'ung Li, who first led me into the field of social history of ancient China. I am indebted to Professor James T. C. Liu, whose guidance in many regards through the year 1963–64 has given me the most rewarding experience of intellectual activity. I owe a great deal to Professor P. T. Ho for his encouragement and to Professor Wolfram Eberhard for his thorough criticism. I also would like to thank Miss June Work, as well as staff members of the Far Eastern Library of the University of Chicago and of the Library of Academia Sinica, for their kind help. My friends E. Buote, S. P. J. Chen, William J. Lyell, H. P. Shih, T'ien-yi T'ao, Lehnert and Nancy Riegel, and Lawrence and Phyllis Kessler have helped me with the editing, typing, and proofreading of this work; I give my thanks to them. My gratitude also goes to His Excellency, Dr. George Yeh, who honors this volume with an elegant Chinese inscription.

CHO-YUN HSU

April 1, 1965

Contents

Ancient China in Transition

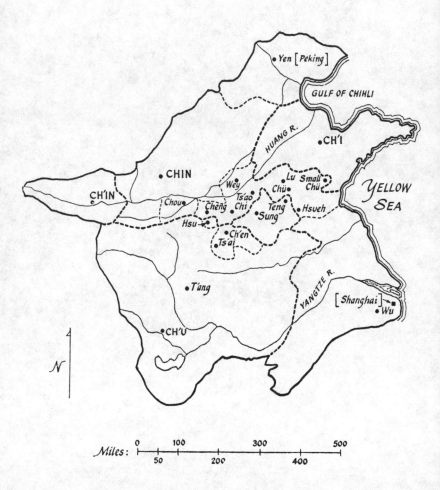

Political Boundaries of China about 560 B.C., Showing the Spheres of
Influence of Ch'u and Chin

Chapter 1 Problems and Background

I propose to write a history of the Chinese societies of the Ch'un Ch'iu and Chan Kuo periods, dating from the end of the eighth century B.C. to the close of the third century B.C., with special emphasis on social mobility. Before the Ch'un Ch'iu period China was ruled by feudal lords and her society was rigidly stratified. After the Chan Kuo period China was a unified nation in which social strata were not as sharply defined and freer movement between strata was permitted.

The transition of an individual from one social stratum to another was easier during the Chan Kuo period than during the Ch'un Ch'iu.* In trying to ascertain why, one must ask several questions. First, how free was social mobility during these periods? Second, did this mobility occur within an unchanged social structure? Third, if the social structure remained unchanged, what caused the greater mobility of individuals within it? Fourth, if there were changes in the social structure, what were they, when did they occur, and how were they related to the changes in social mobility?

The society of the Ch'un Ch'iu period is characterized by a structure of "familial relationships," i.e., a structure based on families rather than individuals.[1] In such a society, the individual is fixed within a ramified kinship structure that provides a conventionalized pattern for all social relations. By Chan Kuo times this pattern was changing. In investigating social mobility in the Ch'un Ch'iu and Chan Kuo periods we shall see the pattern of social relationships change from Max Weber's "communal" to his "associative" relationships, the authorities from Weber's "traditional" to his "rational-legal."[2]

* The Ch'un Ch'iu period begins in 722 B.C., the first year of the *Ch'un Ch'iu* annals. The Chan Kuo period ends in 222 B.C., the year the Ch'in unification was completed. Usually the end of the Ch'un Ch'iu period is considered to be 481 B.C., the last year of the annals; and the beginning of the Chan Kuo period is variously given as 475 B.C., 468 B.C., and 403 B.C. In this study 464 B.C., the last year of the *Tso Chuan*, is taken as the end of the Ch'un Ch'iu period, and 463 B.C. is accordingly taken as the beginning of the Chan Kuo period.

We shall use the term "familialistic" to describe the Ch'un Ch'iu society. The familialistic relationship was manifest in the familial concept of the state, the strong clan organization, and the system of self-sufficient estates or "manors." Kinship ties maintained social stratification in terms of heredity; hence social mobility was restricted. However, when the familialistic relationship broke down, family ties disintegrated and a social vacuum appeared in which men moved upward or downward as a result of their own actions. Before the end of the Chan Kuo period a system of contractual relationships started to emerge: bureaucracy, employer-employee relations, and commercial exchange all came into existence. Such a society must continuously redistribute the membership of its social strata. In other words, freer social mobility develops.

The old values and moral concepts changed during the transition period. There seems to have been a change in social structure rather than simply more mobility within the society. Conceptual evolution is often the consequence of a change in social structure; yet, in turn, conceptual change often paves the way for the emergence of a new society. The association of Protestant ethics and the development of capitalism in western Europe is a classic example.[3]

The various political, economic, ideological, and social changes were so interwoven that no distinction can be made among them in terms of cause and effect. In this study, vertical social mobility is treated as an indicator, and other changes are investigated from this perspective. It is not cause and effect that will be sought after, but the correlations or functional relations of the different changes. In the following chapters, the phenomena of social mobility, the struggles for power inside and outside the state, economic progress, and the evolution of concepts will be discussed. The question is: what happened during the process of reshaping Chinese society, and how did it happen?

Ruling Elements of the Feudal Society

Western Chou feudal society had changed greatly by the beginning of the Ch'un Ch'iu period. Since historical records directly concerning Western Chou are lacking, we must reconstruct its history from scanty data in such ancient materials as the *Shih Ching*, some bronze inscriptions, and such accounts of the Ch'un Ch'iu period as the *Tso Chuan*.[4]

The Chou feudal system was established just after the Chou overthrew the Shang states of the eastern plain in the closing years of the twelfth century B.C. During the long struggle with the people of eastern China, the Chou developed a garrison system to control that vast and populous plain with a comparatively small number of warriors from the Wei valley to the west, which was then the site of the Chou capital (Map 1). This system was built up by the installation of Chou princes and royal kinsmen as feudal lords in the lower Yellow River valley among their former enemies.* By integrating familial relations with the feudal system, the Chou kings identified political leaders with family heads. The terms of address used by the king to his dukes and vice versa are those of the family. Dukes possessing the same surname as the royal house were addressed by the king as paternal uncles; dukes with other surnames were addressed as maternal uncles. Not only these classificatory kinship ties, but also the enfeoffed dukes' need for support from home for security amid a hostile people, ensured their loyalty to the Chou king.†

As time passed, local hostility toward the dukes decreased and their kinship ties with the homeland, drained of the affection which was essential for the structure to work, inevitably lost importance, the more so since the royal house was preoccupied with barbarian attacks from the west. In 770 B.C., the Chou capital in the west was lost to the barbarians after internal disturbances, and the ruling house was forced to move to the east. The earliest historical data from the *Tso Chuan* show the Chou king no longer a universal ruler. The chronicle recounts the defeat of the king's troops in 707 B.C. by the state of Cheng, which had been established by a royal prince, and the ex-

---

* HT, 4/13; TCCI, 15/9-10, 52/14. Whether the Chou conquerors differed ethnically from the conquered has provoked some debate. Eberhard says yes, while Bodde, Creel, and Lattimore say no. See Bodde, "Feudalism in China," p. 52; Creel, *The Birth of China*, pp. 135-36; Eberhard, *History*, p. 25, and *Conquerors*, p. 4; Lattimore, pp. 307-8. (Full titles and publication data are given in the Bibliography, pp. 221-29.) I tend to agree with Eberhard's theory of super-stratification, yet I also agree with Bodde, who argues that ethnic difference was not a necessary condition, that such a super-stratification could be created by cultural differences as well. See Eberhard, *Conquerors*, p. 10; Bodde, "Feudalism," p. 82. Also compare Granet, *Chinese Civilization*, pp. 175-77.

† LC, 1/22. For example: Duke Huan of Ch'i, upon being presented with a royal gift, was addressed as a "maternal uncle" of the royal house (TCCI, 13/6), and Duke Wen of Chin was called "paternal uncle" under similar circumstances (*ibid.*, 16/2). Concerning such classification of persons as relatives of the same kind even though no actual genealogical tie is known, see Radcliffe-Brown, p. 49, and esp. p. 62. At this point we can see the distinctive features of Chinese feudalism; its counterpart in western Europe, according to Marc Bloch, differed significantly because in Europe the feudal ties developed when those of kinship proved inadequate, though the fundamental features of European feudalism discussed by Bloch seem generally congruent with the picture of our present study. Bloch, pp. 443, 446.

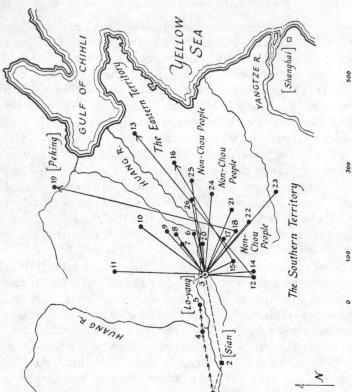
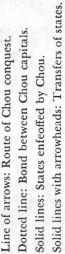

1. Chou homeland
2. Chou western capital
3. Chou eastern capital
4. Jui   5. Yü
6. Tso   7. Fan
8. Wey   9. Ping
10. Hsing   11. T'ang (Chin)

12. Lü	13. Ch'i
14. Sheng	
15. Lu	16. Lu
17. Hsu	
18. Yen	19. Yen

20. Tsi   21. Ch'en
22. Ts'ai   23. Chiang
24. Sung   25. Mao
26. Ts'ao

Line of arrows: Route of Chou conquest.
Dotted line: Bond between Chou capitals.
Solid lines: States enfeoffed by Chou.
Solid lines with arrowheads: Transfers of states.

MAP 1. The Early Chou Expansion

change, thirteen years earlier (720 B.C.), of a son of the Chou king and a son of the duke of Cheng as hostages.[5] By the end of the century, Chou had sunk to the level of her former vassals, though nominally she still ruled over all China.

Thus in the Ch'un Ch'iu period all the states enjoyed *de facto* sovereignty,[6] and their rulers were equal in this key respect despite differences in their titles, e.g., *kung* (duke), *hou* (marquis), *po* (earl), *tsu* (viscount), and *nan* (baron).* For convenience we shall often use the term "dukes" to refer to all rulers of states, including the Chou kings.† These rulers of course stand at the top of the social scale. Since the decline in power of a ruler is difficult to detect directly, the positions of rulers' sons will be used to delineate such changes. During the Ch'un Ch'iu period a ruler often installed his brothers in dominant positions as ministers. Although this practice led to some sharing of power among brothers, brothers so appointed apparently remained subordinate to the ruler in all matters of state.

Next in the descending social scale were the ministers. The relation of a state ruler to his ministers was like that of the Chou king to his dukes. There were two ranks of ministers, the *ch'ing* and the *tai fu*; there were usually only a few (rarely more than half a dozen) of the former, who were the chief administrators of each state. In some states the most powerful *ch'ing* was the eldest; in other states, he might have been the head of the strongest noble house. *Ch'ing* posts were normally hereditary; the first-generation *ch'ing* were generally rulers' sons who had been enfeoffed and had therefore established noble houses.‡ Other sons of rulers, along with younger sons of *ch'ing*, usually became *tai fu*, or "great officers," officials inferior in rank to the *ch'ing* and functioning as their assistants. Within the rank of *tai fu* there were two or three grades, although the classification is not entirely clear. Heirs apparent of *tai fu* of the upper grades apparently

---

* The translations of these titles are the customary ones. The Confucian school used these five titles as if they implied a descending scale of importance from *kung* to *nan*, but it is doubtful whether they were used in so orderly a manner in Ch'un Ch'iu or even Western Chou times. See *LWTC*.

† Ministerships of the royal house were all filled by nobles with the title of duke or other noble titles. Some of them were installed in tiny fiefs inside the royal domain, but they were not independent, and will therefore be dealt with as ministers of state rather than as rulers.

‡ Here a problem of great importance is touched upon: whether Chou feudalism ever developed sub-infeudation. Maspero thought not; see his "Le Régime féodal," pp. 133, 143–44, summarized in Bodde, "Feudalism," pp. 53, 57–58. But I have found explicit evidence that sub-infeudation was practiced in the Western Chou dynasty in a bronze inscription reproduced in *LCCW*, p. 85.

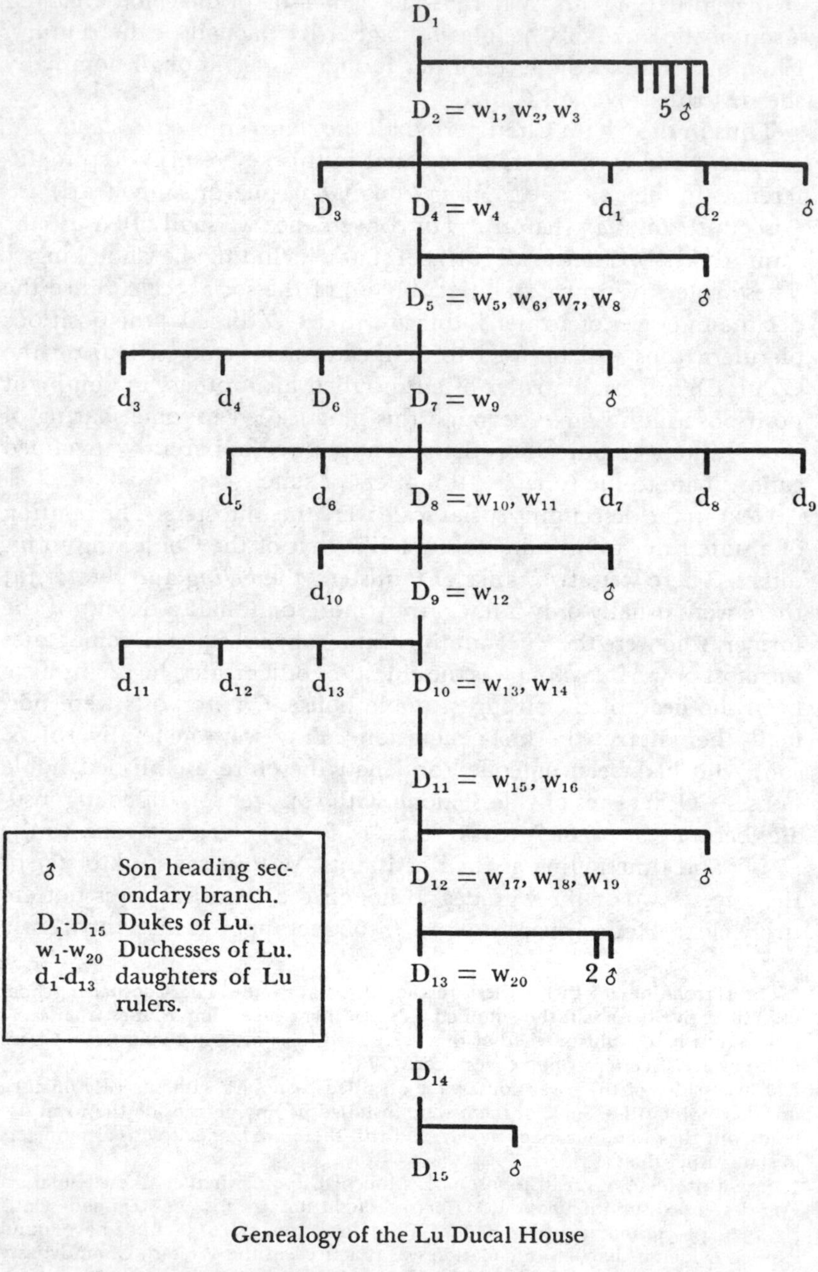

Genealogy of the Lu Ducal House

could inherit their government posts; other sons of such *tai fu* seem also to have held *tai fu* offices. The younger son of a *tai fu* of a lower grade in some instances held the lower rank of *shih*, often translated into English as "knight."[7]

The accompanying genealogy shows the relationships that linked the noble ministerial houses of the state of Lu with each other; all of these families were either descended from the ducal house or connected with it by marital ties. The table shows the multiple marriages that linked the ducal family of Lu, surnamed Chi, with ruling houses having other surnames in other states; the rulers of Lu took wives from these other families, and sent daughters in marriage to them.

TABLE OF LU MARRIAGES

Surnames and states of Lu rulers' wives and sons-in-law	Wives from other states	Daughters to other states
Tzu (state of Ch'ü)	—	d_4
Tzu (state of Sung)..............	W_1, W_2, W_3	d_5, d_{10}, d_{11}
Chiang (state of Ch'i)............	W_4, W_5, W_6, W_9	d_8, d_{12}
Chiang (state of Chi)............	—	d_1, d_2
Ssu (state of Ch'i)...............	W_{14}, W_{20}	d_3, d_6

Note: Data based on *CCST*, I, 14–16, and *CCST*, Appendix, pp. 2–4. Two different states named Ch'i are listed. The one with rulers surnamed Chiang was large and important; the one with rulers surnamed Ssu was relatively small and insignificant.

Just as the younger sons of dukes established branch families of high-grade ministers, so the younger sons of these ministers established branch families of low-grade ministers and *shih*, who served the ministers roughly as the ministers served dukes. This process of familial subdivision was conceived as a strengthening of the family, since each new branch remained a subordinate part of the main familial group.[8] A noble, in general, yielded to his feudal master not only as his superior in the lord-vassal relationship, but also as the head of the family from which his own branch sprang. The familial network embraced all of China, with the feudal structure as the political counterpart of the family structure.

The ruler and his ministers of various grades constituted the power group in a state. They will be collectively referred to as aristocrats or nobles, although this class will sometimes not include the ruler. The class inferior to the power group was the *shih*, whose forefathers were *tai fu*, *ch'ing*, or even state rulers, yet whose own position lay somewhere between the power group and those who were ruled. The *shih*, like the *ch'ing* and the *tai fu*, received training as warriors, participated in religious sacrifices and other rituals, and, as literati, were conversant with basic learning and history.* A *shih* might be himself a small landlord with tenants to till his land, or merely an employee in the government or in a noble household. Some *shih* were stewards; some were officers in charge of fief-towns, manors, or estates; some were minor government officials.† Some of them seem to have had to work the land themselves; when his age was asked, a *shih* answered formally that he had been able to till the land, if he were an adult, or to carry firewood, if he were still young, for so many years.[9]

A moral code developed among the *shih* which may have been the basic code of the entire feudal society.[10] One of its tenets was loyalty to one's master; after a *shih* submitted himself to a master, neither father nor ruler could force him to renounce the relationship.[11] A *shih* was proud of his status and derived strong self-respect from it. Improper favors to *shih* were not to be accepted even in matters of life and death.[12] The code of the *shih* was adapted and given new moral content by Confucius and his disciples in the Chan Kuo period, by which time *shih* had come to mean an educated man, a bravo, or both. The new Confucian code became the standard of conduct of the new *shih* class.

The Labor Service of Peasants

When the Chou king invested his dukes with fiefs, the dukes enfeoffed their ministers, who in turn enfeoffed their subordinates. Each received tribute from below and presented part of his revenue to his superior; the only real producers were the peasants and the *shih* who tilled the land. Like the medieval European serf, the *shu jen* or peasant was obligated to work in the field to support his superiors.[13] He

---

* The *shih* was acquainted with six arts or skills: propriety of conduct, music, archery, chariot driving, writing, and arithmetic.
† A noble in Chou China, like his counterpart in feudal Europe, possessed one or more estates inherited from the past or bestowed by an overlord. We do not know the precise organization of these estates, or their relationship to villages, which were often coterminous with manors in western Europe (Bloch, pp. 241ff). Towns were often established by nobles to serve as fortified strongholds or as sites for ancestral temples (Granet, *Chinese Civilization*, pp. 237–46). A single noble house might have as many as several hundred "manors"; on one occasion 300 towns were given to a noble by the Duke of Ch'i (bronze inscription in *LCCW*, pp. 202–3). A manor or estate often seems to have been an independent unit bearing the name of the locality in which it was situated; there is a good example in Maspero, "Le Régime féodal," p. 118. Bodde, "Feudalism," p. 57, compares an estate to a villa.

did not own the land, but was attached to it and given with it as a vassal.[14] He was probably assigned a piece of land to cultivate for his lord, and another piece to support his family.[15] Confucius once told his disciples that in ancient times "fields were taxed on the basis of labor service, and adjusted according to the distance."[16] The word "distance" here probably refers to the distance from the peasant's house to his assigned field. There was also the saying, "Dukes live on tribute, ministers on their estates, *shih* on the land, and peasants on their own toil."[17] The life of a peasant is depicted in the following lines from the *Shih Ching*:

> In the seventh month the Fire Star passes the meridian;
> In the ninth month clothes are given out.
> In the days of [our] first month, the wind blows cold;
> In the days of [our] second, the air is cold.
> Without coats, without garments of hair,
> How could we get to the end of the year?
> In the days of [our] third month we take our plows in hand;
> In the days of [our] fourth we make our way to the fields.
> Along with wives and children,
> We eat in those south-lying acres.
> The surveyor of the fields comes and is glad.
>
> In the seventh month the Fire Star passes the meridian;
> In the ninth month clothes are given out.
> With the spring days the warmth begins,
> And the oriole utters its song.
> The young women take their deep baskets
> And go along the small paths,
> Looking for the tender [leaves of the] mulberry trees.
> As the spring days lengthen out,
> They gather in crowds the white southern wood.
> The girl's heart is wounded with sadness,
> For she will soon be going with one of the young lords.
>
> In the seventh month the Fire Star passes the meridian;
> In the eighth month are the sedges and reeds.
> In the silkworm month we strip the mulberry branches of
>   their leaves,
> And take axes and hatchets
> To lop off those that are distant and high;
> Only stripping the young trees of their leaves.
> In the seventh month the shrike is heard;
> In the eighth month spinning is begun;
> We make dark fabrics and yellow,
> "With our red dye so bright,
> We make robes for our young lords."

In the fourth month the small grass is in seed;
In the fifth the cicada gives out its note.
In the eighth harvest is done.
In the tenth the leaves fall.
In the days of [our] first month we go after badgers,
And take foxes and wildcats,
"To make furs for our young lord."
In the days of [our] second month we have a general hunt,
Practice for deeds of war.
The boars of one year we keep,
Those of three years we offer to the lord.
In the fifth month the locust moves its legs;
In the sixth month the spinner sounds its wings,
In the seventh month in the fields,
In the eighth month under the eaves,
In the ninth month about the doors;
In the tenth month the cricket
Enters under our beds.
Chinks are filled up, and rats are smoked out;
The windows facing [the north] are stopped up.
"Come, wife and children,
The change of the year is at hand.
Let us live inside the house."

In the sixth month we eat plums and cherries;
In the seventh month we boil mallows and beans.
In the eighth month we knock down the dates;
In the tenth month we reap the rice
To make with it the spring wine,
With which we toss for longevity.
In the seventh month we eat the melons;
In the eighth we cut down the gourds;
In the ninth the hemp seed is gathered:
Also gathered are bitter herbs and fetid trees for firewood.
Those we husbandmen take as food.

In the ninth month we prepare the stockyard,
And in the tenth we bring in the harvest.
The millets, the early and the late,
Together with paddy and hemp, beans and wheat.
My husbandmen have put together our harvest.
Now we go up to work in the manor.
"In the day you gather the thatch-reeds;
In the evening twist them into rope;
Go quickly on to the roofs;
Soon you are to sow the grain."

In the days of [our] second month we cut the ice with
    tingling blows;

In the days of [our] third month [it is] stored in the icehouse.
In the days of [our] fourth month, very early,
A lamb with scallions is offered in sacrifice.
In the ninth month are shrewd frosts;
In the tenth month the stockyard is cleared.
With twin pitchers we hold the feast,
Killed for it is a young lamb.
Up we go into the lord's hall,
Raise the cup of buffalo-horn;
"Long life for our lord; may he live for ever and ever!"[18]

In the relatively self-sufficient community of the estate or "manor," the peasant provided his lord with food and cloth and worked in both field and house. He was heavily burdened not only with year-round field work but also with occasional compulsory labor services such as building a new wall or repairing a palace. In this feudal society there was no clear distinction between the public affairs of a state and the private business of a lord; a subject might be called upon to work for both.[19] A passage in *Mencius* says: "If a common man is called to perform any service, he goes and performs it."[20]

Thus the peasant of ancient China: bound to and transferred with the soil; the sole source of food and labor for a self-sufficient manorial community; a man of few rights, few opportunities, and few pleasures. He is almost at the bottom of the social scale.

Merchants and Artisans

Until late in the Ch'un Ch'iu period, trade amounted to little more than the exchange of local materials for materials that were not produced locally. The aristocrats, provided by the peasants with food, clothing, and labor, wanted only a few items, such as jewelry and salt, that were produced in other areas. In the circumstances there was little demand for the services of merchants. In time, however, the demand increased, and merchants and artisans came to be maintained in manorial communities as a group distinct from the rest of the rural population, and distinct also from urban businessmen.[21] There is no trace of organization similar to the guilds of medieval Europe (i.e., organizations partially independent of the feudal lords), but merchants in ancient China were nonetheless often dealt with as a group. For instance, the state of Chin once demanded that the state of Wey send its artisans and merchants to Chin as hostages in order to guarantee the submission of Wey.[22] Though the people of Wey preferred to fight rather than comply, it would seem that the merchants and artisans composed a specific professional group capable of being moved en masse, a difficult operation if the merchants were scattered. In another case, an agreement between a Chin envoy and a Cheng merchant was reported to the Cheng government. The same passage mentions an agreement formerly made between the Cheng merchant and his own government,[23] which suggests that the merchant may have represented a collective body of merchants. In the end, it seems clear, the merchants became a professional class whose members were distinct from both the commoners and the nobles. Yet this class remained under the full control of the state and the feudal lords, the relation being that of retainer to master.*

A prerequisite for a prosperous merchant class is active commerce, and three factors that vitalize commercial activities—a good market, abundant commodities, and a widely adopted monetary system—seem to have been lacking before the later part of the Ch'un Ch'iu period. From very early times there were small fairs and local markets, at which some sort of barter system was used.† But the commodities available for trade on such occasions were restricted largely to the excess production of the peasants, which would be limited in quantity and possibly in quality. The professional handicraftsmen of the time seem to have numbered no more than a few hundred per state. One hundred each of mechanics, embroiderers, and weavers were sent from Lu to Ch'u as hostages in 588 B.C.[24] In several states there was an office in charge of handicraftsmen.[25]

As for money, it existed as early as the Shang dynasty,[26] but it was by no means common even in Ch'un Ch'iu times. Wealth was still measured in terms of livestock.‡ In the time of Confucius, salaries

---

* The agreement between the Cheng ruler and the merchants has been used as evidence for the theory that merchants were independent of the state; see CKFC, pp. 201–2. However, we know from the context that the forefathers of the Cheng merchants were from the old royal capital of Chou in the west, having moved when that city was lost to the barbarians. The state of Cheng, also originally in the west, had reestablished itself in the east, seemingly aided by the above-mentioned merchants. Since these were from the capital, and presumably belonged to the royal house, the ruler of Cheng could not keep them in his state, nor could he establish his overlordship through feudal rights because the merchants were not a part of the feudal structure. A practical way to establish this overlordship would have been to conclude an agreement with them in order to legalize the protector-retainer relationship. This may well have been the background of the agreement in question, although no other historical accounts record such use of an agreement.

† The Meng Tzu, though a late work, contains an interesting passage about the origin of commercial enterprise that reads: "In old times, the market dealers exchanged the articles which they had for others which they had not, and simply had certain officers to keep order among them." See Legge, Mencius, 2.2.10.

‡ Duke Wen of Chin owned 80 horses when he was in Ch'i. See TCCI, 15/5; KY, 10/2. The chancellor of Ch'u was so generous with his favorites that they became famous for the numbers of horses that they owned. See TCCI, 35/3 (Hsiang 22).

were paid in grain,[27] and commodities were often used as objects of barter.[28] Money was apparently not in wide circulation until late Ch'un Ch'iu or early Chan Kuo times. Large amounts of various denominations have been found in the archaeological strata of the Chan Kuo period.

It is accordingly impossible to imagine a prosperous and powerful merchant class in the early Ch'un Ch'iu period.* Neither merchants nor artisans could yet rise from their low position in feudal society.

Servants and Slaves

According to the *Tso Chuan*, eight occupations, including house servants, grooms, and herdsmen, occupied the bottom of the social scale.[29] Female members of this class included housemaids, women artisans, and dancers.[30] It appears that a slave was valued by his owner about as much as a dog. On one occasion, a slave was ordered to test some poisoned meat after a dog had been killed by it.[31] A servant of the duke of Chin was buried with the duke in order to serve him in the next world.[32] A large family might possess many slaves; a thousand families of barbarian captives were bestowed upon a Chin general by his duke as a reward for merit in battle.[33] A bronze bell of Ch'i tells of three hundred families, a fief of three hundred towns, and four thousand other persons granted by the duke to the owner of the bell.[34] Slaves were purchasable; an inscription records the price of five male slaves as being one hundred units of metal,[35] and also tells us that slaves, along with land, grain, and silk, could be used as part payment in an agreement.[36] A passage of the *Tso Chuan* relates that the self-exiled Duke Chao of Lu sold the messengers sent by his usurping chancellor.[37]

The above accounts tell us something of the fate of slaves, but we do not know whether they participated widely in productive work or served mainly as house servants. There is no evidence that the economy of ancient China was based on slavery like the economy of ancient Greece.

Upper and lower strata of the feudal society during and before the Ch'un Ch'iu period were widely separated, but the gap was not unbridgeable. Confucius once resented the performing of the royal dance in the home of a chancellor of Lu,[38] which indicates that the clear social distinctions of earlier times had become blurred in the

---

* Merchants in ancient China, though socially distinct from common peasants, do not seem to have evolved into tribute collectors or officials, as some venture to infer. No trace of such status has been found in ancient texts as far as I know. Cf. Eberhard, *Conquerors*, p. 11.

later multi-state system. The rich *shih* lived more comfortably, while the poor *shih,* having to earn a living, lived more and more like a peasant. Dukes occupied the top social stratum and slaves the bottom, but Duke Hui of Chin named his son "Slave" and his daughter "Female-Slave" because a diviner had predicted that the children were doomed to become slaves.[39] Both the duke and the diviner apparently considered such an event possible, though no doubt only remotely so.

The Concept of Nobility

During the Western Chou period and most of the Ch'un Ch'iu, the economic and political stratification of the feudal society was justified and guaranteed by the familial concept and the beliefs associated with it. The Shang oracle bone inscriptions record that kings occasionally brought problems and offered sacrifices to deceased kings and queens who "were godlike, if not gods, and wielded about the same powers as those of Ti, in about the same manner in which he wielded his."[40] Since most of the ruling houses of the Ch'un Ch'iu period claimed descent from ancient dynasties, and most nobles were kin to the ruling houses, the nobles could justify their privileged status by maintaining that their ancestors were deities, a claim found in many cultures. The kings of ancient Egypt claimed to be sons of the sun god Re, and the king of Sparta traced his descent from Zeus.[41]

The ruling houses in the Ch'un Ch'iu period can be classified into three general groups. The first is the house of Tzu of the defeated Shang dynasty, which ruled only the state of Sung. The second group consists of the ruling houses of the states originally given to Chou princes as fiefs in the Chou empire; the clan name of these was Chi. The third group is the ruling houses of the states that had existed before the Chou conquest. Rulers of these pre-Chou states usually claimed descent from ancient emperors, who, whether historical or legendary, are little more than names to the historian. More significant than names or legends is the relationship claimed by various tribes to ancient deified figures, since it was this relationship that endowed the overlords, and in turn their kinsmen, with the power— the *ming,* the *teh,* the charisma—that made their overlordship legitimate and inevitable.[42]

The Shang imperial house also claimed descent from gods.[43] According to the epic of Sung, the Shang power was established by the commission of Ti, the supreme god. The *Sacrificial Odes of Shang* in the *Shih Ching* reads as follows:

> Heaven commissioned the swallow
> To descend and give birth to the [father of our] Shang.
> [His descendants] dwelt in the land of Yin and became great.
> [Then] long ago Ti appointed the martial T'ang
> To regulate the boundaries through the four quarters.
>
> . . .
>
> From the four seas they come to our sacrifices,
> They come in multitudes; . . .
> The state has the He [River] for its outer border.
> That Yin should have received the appointment [of Heaven]
> Was entirely right . . .
> [The sovereign] sustains all its dignities.⁴⁴

In short, the god gave world rule to the founder of Shang, who was born of a swallow at the god's command. Another myth from the *Shih Ching* about the founding of the Shang empire reads:

> Profoundly wise were [the lords of] Shang,
> And long had there appeared the omens [of the dynasty];
> When the water of the deluge spread vast abroad,
> Yü arranged and divided the regions of the land.
>
> . . .
>
> Then the daughter of the Jung offered sacrifice.
> Ti raised up the Tzu house and founded [the family of] Shang.
>
> . . .
>
> The favors of Ti did not leave Shang,
> And in T'ang was found the subject for its display.
> T'ang was not born too late,
> And his wisdom and virtue daily advanced.
> Brilliant was the influence of his character [on Heaven] for long
> And Ti appointed him to be a model to the nine regions.
>
> . . .
>
> Formerly in the middle of the period [before T'ang],
> There was a time of glory and accomplishment,
> But truly did Heaven deal with him as its son,
> And sent him down a minister,
> Namely A-heng,
> Who gave his assistance to the King of Shang.⁴⁵

The female ancestor of the Shang offered sacrifices so piously that Ti made her son T'ang the head of a great kingdom and had him received by heaven as its own son. Ti blessed the Shang and kept them, and sent down help when they were in need. (Many generations after the conquest of Shang, a scion of the Sung ruling house serving in the court of Ch'i inscribed in bronze his prayer to his remote ancestor T'ang.)⁴⁶ The house of Shang thus had ample justification for exercising its noble prerogatives.

Even more important, for our period, is the ancestry of the Chi family of Chou. Early Chou documents emphasize that Chou was able to conquer Shang because heaven deserted the wicked Shang ruler, and transferred its blessing and mandate to the leader of the Chou. It is moreover suggested that the heavenly mandate had been shifted in the past whenever the reigning dynasty ceased to be deserving of it, as a master might switch servants.[47] The odes show the first Chou leader begotten by the holy spirit of the god, as follows:

> The first birth of [our] people
> Was from Chiang Yüan.
> How did she give birth to [our] people?
> She had presented a pure offering and sacrificed
> That her childlessness might be taken away.
> She then trod on a toe-print made by Ti,
> And was moved,
> In the large place where she rested.
> She became pregnant; she dwelt retired;
> She gave birth to and nourished [a son],
> Who was Hou Chi.[48]

The name of Hou Chi, the founder of the Chou royal family, suggests that he was probably an agricultural deity, since *hou* means "ruler" or "sovereign" and *chi* is millet.[49] Like many legendary heroes, he faced and passed a number of trials:

> When she had fulfilled her months,
> Her first-born son came forth like a lamb.
> There was no bursting, no rending,
> No injury, no hurt; . . .
> Showing how wonderful he would be.
> Did not Shang Ti give her the comfort?
> Had he not accepted her pure offering and sacrifices,
> So that thus easily she brought forth her son?
> He was placed in a narrow lane,
> But the sheep and oxen protected him with loving care.
> He was placed in a wide forest,
> Where he was met with by the woodcutters.
> He was placed on the cold ice
> And a bird screened and supported him with its wings.
> When the bird went away,
> Hou Chi began to wail.
> His cry was long and loud,
> So that his voice filled the whole way.[50]

The ode then tells of the wonderful works achieved in agriculture by Hou Chi. It is said that his abundant sacrifices pleased the god and were reverently continued by his descendants.[51]

The Chou sovereigns not only were ancestrally related to the deity, but also had been given the heavenly decree to replace the Shang in ruling the world.[52] The mandate of heaven was to be extended to the Chou successors: "Truly will the king preserve the appointment."[53] Past kings were believed to dwell in heaven at the side of Ti and were naturally expected to ensure heavenly blessings for living rulers of their line. Thus another poem reads:

> King Wen is on high;
> Oh! bright is he in heaven.
> Although Chou was an old country,
> The [favoring] appointment lighted on it recently.
> Illustrious was the house of Chou,
> And the appointment of Ti came at the proper season.
> King Wen ascends and descends,
> On the left and the right of Ti.[54]

Another poem tells us:

> Successors tread in the steps [of the predecessors] in our Chou.
> For generations there had been wise kings;
> The three sovereigns were in heaven;
> And King Wu was then the worthy successor in his capital.
> King Wu was their worthy successor in his capital,
> Rousing himself to seek for hereditary virtue,
> Always striving to accord with the will [of heaven];
> And thus he secured the confidence due a King.[55]

Now and then the deities sent down ministers to the Chou king to aid him in carrying out his holy appointment. The dukes of Fu and Shen, for instance, were given birth by a spirit sent down by the mountains that reach to heaven. These two dukes were praised as "the support of Chou, screens to all the states" and "diffusing [their influence] over the four quarters of the kingdom."[56] A minister named Chung Shan Fu was born because

> Heaven beheld the ruler of Chou,
> Brilliantly affecting it by his conduct below;
> And to maintain him, its son,
> Gave birth to Chung Shan Fu.[57]

Relying upon his divine ancestry, the heavenly mandate entrusted to his house, his forefathers dwelling at the side of Ti, and Ti's affectionate protection, a Chou king could have no doubt of his fitness to rule. This feeling was shared by the nobles of the many states reigned over by the descendants of Chou princes. Thus:

> Full of earnest activity was King Wen,
> And his fame is without end.
> The bestowing on Chou
> Extends to the descendants of King Wen,
> In the direct line and the collateral branches
> For a hundred generations.
> All the officers of Chou
> Shall [also] be illustrious from age to age.[58]

The descendants were to receive the blessings of heaven as long as they walked in the steps of their forefathers.[59]

The concepts discussed above are amply documented in bronze inscriptions of Western Chou times. An inscription dating from the reign of King Wu, the sovereign during the conquest of Shang, states that the king offered sacrifices to Shang Ti with his royal father Wen looking on from heaven.[60] One from the reign of King Chao (reigned ca. 1052–1002 B.C.) contains a prayer that the deceased kings who dwell above will bless their filial successor with a long reign.[61] In another, probably dating from the time of King I (reigned ca. 934–910 B.C.), the former kings are said to exist by the side of Ti and to shower boundless blessings on their descendants.[62] Not only royal inscriptions contained tales of heaven-dwelling ancestors; even ministers could claim the same. A minister, probably of King Li (reigned ca. 878–841 B.C.), prayed to his father and predecessor, who dwelt in heaven but could influence the world of the living, to send down his benediction.[63]

We know very little about ruling houses other than the Shang and Chou. A large number of clans in the east traced their ancestry to Shao-hao, a god of the eastern peoples who was later incorporated into the "Five Emperors."[64] An inscription on a bronze vessel dating from the early Chan Kuo period traces the ancestry of a Ch'i ruler surnamed Ch'en—whose father had usurped the throne of Ch'i from the legal ruling house—back to Huang Ti, the Yellow Emperor, a culture hero of Chinese history; thus the house of Ch'en, originally from the state of the same name, claimed a more august descent than the house it overthrew.[65] The ruling houses of the Chan Kuo states Ch'in and Chao both bore the surname Ying; their legend relates that the clan ancestress swallowed the egg of a flying dark bird and gave birth to the progenitors of the Ying.[66] Two inscriptions on Ch'in bronzes of Ch'un Ch'iu times contain the following passage: "Brilliantly my ancestor received the decree from heaven to dwell in the land settled by Yü. The twelve dukes since that time are at the side of Ti, the god; duly and reverently they keep the decree of heaven and protect the state of Ch'in in order to let her be served by the barbarians and Chinese."[67]

The Influence of the Ancestors

The people of Ch'un Ch'iu China considered two things to be of paramount importance in a state: military affairs and sacrifices.[68] The living were completely in the shadow of their ancestors; for instance, the ceremony of capping, by which a youth was initiated into the adult world, was held in the ancestral temple. When Duke Hsiang of Lu was twelve years old, he participated in an interstate meeting attended also by the duke of Chin, who, according to prevailing custom, was considered to be his uncle. The latter suggested that his nephew be capped, and Duke Hsiang's escorting minister from Lu answered, "The capping of our ruler must be done with the ceremony of libations and offerings. Its different stages must be defined by the music of the bell and the musical stone; it must take place in the temple of his first ancestor. Our ruler is now traveling and those things cannot be provided. Let us go to a brother state and borrow what is necessary to prepare for the ceremony." The ceremony was then properly performed in the temple of the deceased duke of Wey, a member of the same branch of the Chou house.[69]

In time of war the expeditionary troops were given their orders in the ancestral temple; the ancestral tablets were sometimes taken along when the ruler led the troops in person.[70] Before joining battle, the officers and warriors gathered to make divinations "before the spirits of the former rulers," as at the battle of Yen-ling between Chin and Ch'u in 575 B.C.[71] A warrior's ancestors might be asked to help him win the battle:

I, K'uai-hui, your distant descendant, venture to announce to you, King Wen, my great ancestor, to you, K'ang-shu, my distinguished ancestor, and to you, Duke Hsiang, my accomplished ancestor: Sheng of Cheng is siding with the rebellious, whom Wu of Chin, in the midst of difficulties, is not able to deal with and bring to order. He has now sent Yang to punish them and I, not daring to indulge in sloth, am here with my spear in my hand. I presume to announce this to you, and pray that my sinews may not be injured, my bones not broken, and my face not wounded, but that I may succeed in this great engagement, and you my ancestors may not be disgraced. I do not presume to ask for the great appointment; I do not grudge the precious stones at my girdle.[72]

After a war was over, the victorious army was expected to report the victory, and present captives, to the temples.[73]

In times of peace, interstate treaties were ratified before the ancestors of all the participants. One such treaty ended as follows:

Should any prince break these engagements, may he who watches over men's sincerity and he who watches over covenants, [the spirits of] the famous hills and the famous streams, the kings and dukes our predecessors, the whole host of spirits, and all who are sacrificed to, the ancestors of our twelve [thirteen?] states with their seven surnames: ... may all these intelligent spirits destroy him, so that he shall lose his people, his appointment pass from him, his family perish, and his state be utterly overthrown![74]

The nobles seem to have believed that they possessed an inborn endowment which ordinary people did not have. The spirit of a minister of Cheng who had been murdered in a *coup d'état* was believed to be haunting the capital. A duke of the neighboring state discussed the matter with a Cheng envoy, who spoke as follows:

When an ordinary man or woman dies a violent death, the soul and spirit are still able to keep on hanging about men in the shape of an evil apparition; how much more might this be expected in the case of Liang Hsiao, a descendant of our former ruler Duke Mu, the grandson of Tzu-liang, the son of Tzu-erh, all ministers of our state, engaged in its government for three generations! ... His clan also was a great one, and his connections were distinguished. Is it not entirely reasonable that, having died a violent death, he should be a ghost?[75]

Several corollary concepts derive from the idea that the aristocracy was endowed with a superior charisma by its ancestors. One was that the religious duty of the ruling group was to ensure the continuation of this charisma. Another was that the individual was entirely submerged in the family, through which the divine prerogatives were handed down in the blood line. A third was that the traditions were respected because of their associations with the deified ancestors.

In the Ch'un Ch'iu period the ruler was considered to be "the host of the spirits and the hope of the people." It was said that "Heaven, in giving birth to the people, appointed rulers to act as their superintendents and shepherds."[76] Hence the ruler was considered unqualified if he ignored his duties to the people or to the spirits.[77] In general, a ruler's secular and religious duties were considered equally important. In some instances the religious prerogatives of a ruler seem more essential to his role than the actual reigning power. An exiled duke of Wey, in negotiating his return home, promised the minister who was then *de facto* ruler of Wey that he would preside only over sacrifices and leave state affairs to the minister's family.[78]

This indicates that *de jure* sovereignty was associated with the religious function.

During the Ch'un Ch'iu period, the parent-child relationship, or the relationship of a shepherd to his sheep, was used by the Chinese to describe the ruler-subject connection. For instance, a learned music master once said: "A good ruler will reward the virtuous and punish the vicious; he will nourish his people as his children, overshadowing them as heaven, and supporting them as the earth. Then the people will maintain their ruler, love him as a parent, look up to him as the sun and moon, revere him as they do spiritual beings, and stand in awe of him as of thunder."[79]

Even when a minister usurped the authority of his ruler, the nominal relationship of the ruler to his subjects remained in most cases unchanged. The members of a ruling group usually came from the same clan, and this may have lent stability to the ruler-subject relationship. Since a noble owed his status to the charisma his clan had inherited from their ancestors, it was only reasonable that the ruler, who represented the main branch of the clan, had inherited more of the holy nature than a lesser member.*

The people of the Ch'un Ch'iu period developed a moral code based on maintaining fixed relationships. Once the ruler-subject relationship was established, it was difficult to avoid or circumvent. When a minister of Ch'u returned to the state after his relatives were slain, he rejected advice to flee, saying, "If I abandon the king's commission, who will take it up? My ruler is heaven; can heaven be fled from?"[80] The code exalted the status quo; a familialistic feeling provided its ideological basis. A covenant made by the people of Wey after their exiled duke had returned home and effected a reconciliation reads as follows:

Heaven sent calamity down on the state of Wey, so that the ruler and his subjects were not harmonious and were brought to our present state of sorrow. But now heaven is guiding all minds, bringing them in humility to a mutual accord. If there had not been those who abided in the state, who would have kept the altar for the ruler? If there had not been those who went abroad with him, who would have guarded his cattle and horses? Because of the former want of harmony, we now clearly beg to covenant before

---

* The gradations of the various rituals seem to have been for the purpose of emphasizing the dominance of the ruler's holy nature. For instance, a ruler could erect a temple for the worship of remote ancestors, while a noble was allowed to worship fewer generations of ancestors and could expect to enjoy ancestral blessings and share the hereditary nature in lesser degree than the ruler.

you, great spirits, asking you to direct our consciences; ... from this time forward after this covenant, those who went abroad with the marquis shall not presume upon their services, and those who remained in the state need not fear that any crime will be imputed to them. If any break this covenant, exciting dissatisfactions and quarrels, may the intelligent spirits and our former rulers mark and destroy them![81]

Such mutual tolerance after political trouble is like the reconciliation of brothers after a quarrel. Had it not been for the familial concept of the state, this story might have ended differently.

An official held his office not because of his personal competence or choice but by hereditary tenure; he represented the joining of family and state. Once, when the position of Duke Chao of Sung became unstable, a minister-designate declined his father's office and asked to give it to his son. The post was perilous; the choice was between sacrificing a son and incurring a calamity that might extend to the whole branch of which the minister-designate was head. "My son is a second self, but by means of him I could postpone my death for a while. Although I abandon him, I shall still not abandon my kindred."[82] The family as a whole counted for more than any individual member. And as in the family, so in the state. Not only did the parts defer to the whole, but all the intrafamilial moral tenets, such as tolerance, were applied to behavior in a familially oriented state.

A final aspect of the ancient code was its respect for tradition. It was reasonable for a man to model his behavior on the past, since the past was associated with the venerable ancestors. In bronze inscriptions that describe how a noble was given office or emolument, the merits and achievements of his ancestors are cited. For instance, an inscription commemorating a royal decree in honor of an official named Yü records that Yü was told by the king of the merits of his ancestor Nan Kung, was ordered to follow the example of Nan Kung, and was given his banner.[83] Tradition was followed to such a degree that when a messenger from Chin, then the strongest state, wished to report a victory to the royal court, which was hardly more than a puppet of Chin, the king declined to receive him because his rank and mission were considered unfit in the light of traditional propriety.[84] Thus a poet, referring to the proper conduct of a ruler, sang:

> Erring in nothing, forgetful of nothing,
> Observing and following the old statutes.[85]

This chapter has depicted the feudal social structure and the concepts that served to explain or justify it. If time had stood still, the upper elements of the structure would have retained their conviction of divinely granted superiority, and the lower elements would have had to accept their lot ungrudgingly. However, time continued to flow, and change and revolution took place. The Ch'un Ch'iu and Chan Kuo periods were to witness not only social mobility but also reshaping of the social structure. Political institutions, economic factors, and ideologies all influenced, and were influenced by, the revolution in social relations and patterns. In the following chapters we shall first consider the phenomenon of social mobility in ancient China and then examine the political, economic, and ideological changes that accompanied it.

Chapter 2   Changes in Social Stratification

The social structure of the Ch'un Ch'iu period (722–464 B.C.) was that of an orderly society in which heads of state, their ministers, and *shih* (officials, warriors, and stewards of the noble households) constituted the ruling group. This stratification was not static, however, throughout these two and a half centuries. Changes over short periods of time may escape notice, but the long view discloses some remarkable transformations. Again and again we find the authority of nominal rulers usurped by ministers, rulers deposed by ministers in alliance with noble families, and even palace revolutions climaxed by the division of the state among the victors, as happened at the end of the Ch'un Ch'iu to Chin, one of the greatest states, which was split into three parts, each ruled by one powerful family.

Now also the *shih* class, which heretofore had remained unobtrusive, began to take part in the molding of history, becoming most active near the end of the period. In the state of Lu, for example, an official of one of the aristocratic families led a *coup d'état* and reigned as a dictator for a number of years.[1] A disciple of Confucius, though nothing more than the steward of a noble family, actually commanded troops in a battle against invaders from Ch'i, a neighboring state.[2] Confucius himself is the most important historical figure of the *shih* class.

That changes in the social order were being noticed not long after the Ch'un Ch'iu period is shown by statements attributed to persons of that time. Thus Shu-hsiang, an envoy of Chin to Ch'i, was told by Yen Tzu, a minister of Ch'i, that the popular Ch'en family was on the point of seizing the government of Ch'i from the ruler, who had apparently lost his subjects' affection. Shu-hsiang replied that Chin was no better off. Its administration was paralyzed, its people exhausted and starving, while its ruler squandered the state's resources on new palaces and court favorites. Many important families, he said, were becoming impoverished; other, more powerful families had taken over the administrative authority from the ducal ruling house, whose fall he expected momentarily.[3]

The scribe Shih Mo, commenting in 511 B.C. on the exile of the duke of Lu by his own chancellor, said that since ancient times relationships between rulers and ministers had never been constant; thus the poem

> High banks become valleys.
> Deep valleys become heights.

He stated that the Chi family had been in power so long—during the reigns of four dukes—that the people no longer remembered that there was a duke.[4] Shih Mo himself may not have approved of such changes, but his words show that change was considered not only possible but inevitable. The *Kuo Yü* gives similar instances. After a power struggle among six great families of Chin, the two defeated clans were liquidated; their offspring were condemned to till the soil of a foreign state and their sacred sacrificial bull of the ancestral shrine was put to work in the fields. The commentator observed that changes among people were indeed happening all the time.[5]

The high incidence of social change may be more clearly shown by an investigation of the entire Ch'un Ch'iu period. The most useful document for this purpose is the *Tso Chuan,* an annalistic history of the period. An exhaustive study of all the thousands of persons whose names appear in the *Tso Chuan* would be scarcely feasible. However, the *Ch'ien Han Shu (History of the Former Han Dynasty)* by Pan Ku contains a section titled *Ku Chin Jen Piao (Table of Ancient and Recent People)* in which 1,998 names of persons of former times have been culled from various sources and graded into nine ranks according to their moral achievements. Of these, 648 lived earlier than Duke Yin of Lu (with whose reign this study begins), and 13 lived after the unification of China in 222 B.C. (the date with which my study ends).[6] Pan Ku's list includes persons only if some information was available about them and only if the information enabled him to fit them into one of his nine classes of moral worth, which are unrelated to the problems of social mobility and stratification. Nevertheless the list is useful since it provides us with random samples for the study of other problems.

Some 1,337 names from the Ch'un Ch'iu and the Chan Kuo periods are given in Pan Ku's work; of these, the 516 whose source is the *Tso Chuan* will form my basis for the study of the Ch'un Ch'iu period, and 197 other datable persons are studied for the Chan Kuo period. Categories not included are women, persons whose dates cannot be fixed, and rulers, whose careers seldom involved social mobility. The 516 names, which make up only a small part of those appearing in the *Tso Chuan*, are divided into year-groups of thirty years each, starting with the year 722 B.C., the first year of the *Tso Chuan*.

My basic premise is that a man is unlikely to have been mentioned in the annals unless he possessed some historical significance. Although some names may have entered the historical records by chance, it is safe to assume that the larger the group is of historical personages included in each stage, the less likely it will be that those accidentally included could exceed a negligible fraction of the group. The relative significance of the various groups may possibly be determined by comparing the numbers of historical figures belonging to each group.

Three social strata of the Ch'un Ch'iu period are investigated: brothers and sons of rulers; ministers, or *ch'ing* and *tai fu*; and the groups of *shih*. Most of the 516 persons fall into these three categories, but a few are classified as clerk-scribes, servile personnel, commoners, and persons of uncertain status. These four groups are included in Table 1, but they are not discussed in the text because information concerning them is insufficient and they make up only 15 per cent of the total number of persons considered. For the first stratum, by definition, the criterion for inclusion is birth only. For the second and third strata, the criteria are more difficult to define. The status of people in these two groups is determined by the offices they held or by activities that give evidence of their position. In cases of movement from one stratum to another, the person will be classified according to his original status.

Brothers and Sons of Rulers

The son or brother of a ruler might perform the most significant political functions, such as serving the ruler as chancellor, leading a military expedition, representing the state on diplomatic missions, or deciding the succession to the throne, besides being closest to the ruler in a familial sense. The first relevant historical event recorded in the *Tso Chuan* is the quarrel between Duke Chuang of Cheng and his ambitious brother Shu-tuan.[7] Also among the seventeen sons of rulers mentioned in the first stage (722–693 B.C.) was Chou-yü of Wey, who usurped his father's throne.[8] Tsang Hsi-po, a son of the duke of Lu, probably was of some importance in the Lu court for his occasional advice to the duke.[9] Kung-tzu Hui, likewise a son of the duke, commanded a Lu expeditionary force; later he murdered the ruler and put Duke Huan on the throne.[10] Kung-tzu Chien-mou, Kung-tzu Shou, and Tai-tzu Chi, three sons of rulers of Wey, were involved in intrigues over the succession to the throne. Two sons of other former

Wey rulers played influential roles in determining the Wey succession.[11] A son of the Ch'u ruler, Tou Po-pi by name, was important in the Ch'u court.[12]

Eight sons of rulers were mentioned for the second stage (692–663 B.C.). Two sons of Ch'en rulers were Kung-tzu Wan and Kung-tzu Yü-k'ou; the former went into voluntary exile in Ch'i because he was involved in the death of the latter.[13] Kung-tzu Ch'ing-fu and Kung-tzu Ya of Lu established families that eventually eclipsed the Lu ruling ducal house. A third family was established by Kung-tzu Yu (or Chi Yu). They are called the "three Huan families" because they were all sons of Duke Huan of Lu. However, Kung-tzu Yu is here counted in the third stage (662–633 B.C.), in which period he is one of the most active sons of rulers.[14]

In the third stage, Kung-tzu Pan, T'ai-tzu Shen-sheng, and T'ai-tzu Hua, of Lu, Chin, and Cheng, respectively, were heirs apparent who were killed by their own brothers or uncles.[15] Kung-tzu Mu-i, the son of the Sung ruler, declined the throne offered to him by his father and founded a family whose members for generations occupied key positions in the Sung government.[16] Kung-tzu Yung of Chin, after being sent as a hostage to Ch'in, was recalled to succeed his father on the throne of Chin. However, the minister of Chin had a change of heart while he was on his journey homeward, and rejected him.[17] Wang-tzu Tai, a prince of the Chou royal house, expelled the Chou king but was killed when the king returned with powerful support from the state of Chin.[18]

Among the seven sons of rulers mentioned in the fourth stage (632–603 B.C.), Shu-wu, the son of a Wey ruler, was in charge of state affairs when his brother was ousted by powerful ministers. He was shot by the vanguard of his brother's troops when they returned from exile.[19] Kung-tzu Kuei-sheng and Kung-tzu Sung of Cheng were guilty of ducal murder. Kuei-sheng once commanded Cheng troops in Sung.[20] Wang-tzu Po-liao, who held the title of royal prince, appears in the *Tso Chuan* apparently as a courtier of Cheng. He might have been in exile; his true status is unknown.[21]

Eight sons of rulers are mentioned in the fifth stage (602–573 B.C.). Tzu-fan of Ch'u was the commander-in-chief of the Ch'u forces at the battle of Yen-ling.[22] Wang Cha-tzu of Chou was guilty of the murder of two ministers.[23] Tzu-liang and Kung-tzu Pan, both of Cheng, established prosperous families in that state. Tzu-liang was once sent to Ch'u as a hostage; on several occasions he commanded the Cheng army and he sometimes accompanied the duke of Cheng on visits to

TABLE 1

Social Stratification in the Ch'un Ch'iu Period

Stage number and dates (years B.C.)	Son of Ruler		Minister		Shih		Scribe		Servant		Commoner		Uncertain		Total
	No.	Pct.	No.	Pct.	No.	Pct.	No.	Pct.	No.	Pct.	No.	Pct.	No.	Pct.	No.
I (722–693)......	17	53	14	44	0	0	0	0	0	0	0	0	1	3	32
II (692–663)......	8	19.5	26	63	0	0	1	2.5	2	5	1	2.5	3	7.5	41
III (662–633)......	9	16	30	52	1	2	9	16	5	9	0	0	3	5	57
IV (632–603)......	7	10	49	70	4	6	3	4	1	1	1	1	5	8	70
V (602–573)......	8	12	51	74	1	1.5	1	1.5	2	2.5	1	1.5	5	7	69
VI (572–543)......	8	10	57	68	7	8	7	8	1	1	1	1	3	4	84
VII (542–513)......	5	6	56	70	4	5	5	6	4	5	0	0	6	7	80
VIII (512–483)......	5	9	37	66	9	16	2	4	0	0	0	0	3	5	56
IX (482–464)......	1	4	15	55	6	22	0	0	2	7.5	0	0	3	11.5	27
Total..........	68	13	335	65	32	6.0	28	5.5	17	3.5	4	1	32	6.0	516

other states.[24] Kung-tzu Hsin-shih of Ts'ao was sent to bring back the body of his father, who had died during an expedition, while another son of the ruler managed the affairs of state in Ts'ao. Upon his return, finding that his brother had slain the legal heir and usurped the throne, he planned to go abroad again; the people of the state wished to go with him in order to protest the actions of the usurper. His official position, though unknown, seems to have been quite important.[25] Kung-tzu Shen of Ch'u was one of the two ministers of military affairs in the Ch'u government.[26]

Eight sons of rulers are mentioned during the sixth stage (572–543 B.C.). Kung-tzu Chuan of Wey had an active part in negotiations with other Wey ministers to restore his brother, the exiled duke of Wey.[27] Tzu-nan of Ch'u was chancellor of that state, as was Tzu-nang.[28] Chi-cha of Wu declined the throne offered to him by his father and brothers, and served instead as envoy of Wu to several states in north China.[29] Kung-tzu Fei of Cheng, a few years after putting down an armed riot and restoring order, became the chancellor of Cheng. He slew the newly enthroned young duke and put a five-year-old child on the throne, but while serving as regent he was killed by another noble.[30]

In the seventh stage (542–513 B.C.) five sons of rulers are mentioned. Kung-tzu Chao of Ch'en, at one time a delegate from that state to an interstate conference, a few years later killed the heir to the Ch'en throne and enthroned his own candidate.[31] Wang-tzu Ch'ao, of the royal house of Chou, divided the already tiny royal domain with his brother and named himself the "Western King." Five years later he was ousted by his ministers and fled to Ch'u, where he was killed a few days later.[32] The heir apparent T'ai-tzu Chien of Ch'u, although acknowledged the legal successor to the throne, lost the favor of his father through being slandered by a favorite courtier. At first he was sent to govern a district on the northern frontier, but he was eventually forced to leave the state, and died in exile.[33]

Five sons of rulers are cited during the eighth stage (512–483 B.C.). One, the son of Duke Chao of Lu, was known as the "Duke's Uncle," although his actual importance seems not to have been in accordance with the title. A warrior with only one retainer, a neighbor lad, he died in battle while charging the invading enemy. Had he been treated as befitted his birth and title, he would at least have had some soldiers under his command.[34] Tzu-hsi was the chancellor of Ch'u, while Tzu-ch'i occupied the leading military position there.[35] Kung-tzu Ying of Wey was so favored by his father that he was nearly named successor to the throne.[36]

TABLE 2

The Increasing Importance of Ministers

Stage number and dates (years B.C.)	Total number of persons	Number of ministers	Number of active ministers	Per cent of active ministers		Activities participated in[a]						
				among total persons	among total ministers	A	B	C	D	E	F	G
I (722–693)......	32	14	8	25	57	1	4	0	2	5	4	4
II (692–663)......	41	26	7	17	27	0	0	2	0	2	4	4
III (662–633)......	57	30	16	28	53	4	7	7	2	11	7	3
IV (632–603)......	70	49	38	54	77.5	10	18	21	3	23	16	7
V (602–573)......	69	51	40	58	78	8	22	24	1	12	29	11
VI (572–543)......	84	57	35	42	61	12	18	23	2	13	24	9
VII (542–513)......	80	56	37	46	66	7	16	21	0	15	16	8
VIII (512–483)......	56	37	26	46	70	5	16	13	0	7	17	16
IX (482–464)......	27	15	11	41	75	2	5	1	0	1	7	7
Total	516	335	218	42	65							

[a] The seven categories are: A, Chancellorship; B, Military Command; C, Envoy; D, Adviser; E, Official Position of Importance; F, Family Head; G, Decisive Political Maneuver.

Only one son of a ruler appears in the list during the last stage (482–464 B.C.). This is Tzu-lu of Sung, who was killed during a riot.[37]

It is clear from the preceding survey that fewer and fewer sons of rulers held important positions in government as time went on. If we rule out Ch'u, which in many respects appears to be a special case, apparently no ruler's son served as chancellor after the thirty years 542–513 B.C. and no new noble families of political influence were founded by sons of rulers who reigned after this period.[38] Also the proportion of rulers' sons mentioned declines, as Table 1 shows. The decline starts with a steep drop at the second stage, after which it is gradual. It seems clear that sons of rulers became less active as time went on, which is to say that the center of political activity shifted toward the ministerial class.

The end of the intimate conjunction of the state and the family may be said to have occurred when brothers and sons of rulers no longer automatically, by reason of their birth alone, shared in the power to rule. At the end of the Ch'un Ch'iu period no brother or son of a ruler held the chancellorship of any state but Ch'u. The brother or son might have been given a small fief where he could live in comfort, but his importance in state affairs was far less than it would have been at the beginning of the Ch'un Ch'iu. The decline in his power marked the first step toward the time when the enfeoffment of royal relatives would be ended by the first emperor of Ch'in.

The Rising Power of the Ministers

The second class to be considered consists of ministers and state officials of the upper aristocracy. Members of this class usually held fiefs and served their rulers as vassals as well as in official capacities. Although they are traditionally divided into two groups, ministers and officials, the difference between the two categories is not highly significant. Ministers were more active and had more responsibility in government than ordinary officials. Both groups will be discussed here as one class.

Customarily a member of the aristocracy inherited both his position and his fief from his father, who was either a ruler's son or a minister. His less fortunate brothers accepted lower social positions as officials or stewards, either in the main branch of their own family or in another important clan.

As we have seen, the sons of rulers gradually disappeared from the historical forefront while the minister class became more and more active throughout the Ch'un Ch'iu period. As Table 1 indicates, of our 516 personages, 335 ministers make up 65 per cent of the whole. The proportion of ministers to the whole reached high tide during the fourth stage (632–603 B.C.) and remained around 70 per cent during the four stages from 632 to 513 B.C., after which it declined as the *shih* group gained power.

Of the 335 ministers, 218 were active (see Table 2). The proportion of active ministers to total personages reached its climax during the fourth and fifth stages (632–573 B.C.) and then declined; at the end of the Ch'un Ch'iu only 41 per cent of all personages were active ministers. It is interesting that the proportion of active ministers among the minister group itself, after a sudden drop during the sixth stage (572–543 B.C.), climbed gradually back almost to its fifth-stage peak by the end of the Ch'un Ch'iu period. This rise, together with the declining proportion of active ministers to total number, suggests that inactive ministers had less and less opportunity to enter the historical limelight in the last stages, whereas their equally moderate predecessors may well have been noticed without engaging in any significant activities. Such a change implies the decline in social function, and therefore in importance, of the minister group at large.

Another significant aspect of the predominance of ministers is their concentration within a few large families. Some of these families have been mentioned in previous paragraphs, such as the "three Huan" of Lu. Most of them were established by segmentation from ruling houses when sons of rulers established separate lineages. Furthermore, sub-lineages might split off from these lineages by a process that Radcliffe-Brown named "polysegmentation."[39] The richer or more powerful the lineage, the greater its ability to provide for its sublineages. Yet frequent polysegmentation may drain the resources even of a rich ruling house, to the point where the ruling house becomes "skimmed" and the ministerial lineages become strong enough to take over the commanding position.[40]

This seems to be what happened in the case of the Ch'un Ch'iu families. Most of these families did not exist at the beginning of the period but emerged as time went on. Perhaps a particularly favored son of a ruler or an outstanding minister would serve the government for many years, and after his death his descendants would continue the tradition of government service that he had started. A respected family would thus be established and its reputable sons could endow their family with much influence and responsibility. It might even be able to afford further segmentation. Again let us take Lu as an illustration. We see that after the fourth stage (632–603 B.C.), only one new lineage of considerable influence branched out directly from the ducal house, while several sub-lineages from ministerial houses in Lu emerged thereafter.[41]

The following are some important families of various states, some of which will be discussed individually in Chapter IV:

Chou: Chao, Shan, Kan, and Liu;
Lu: Chi, Meng-sun, and Shu-sun;
Chin: Chao, Han, Wei, Fan (or Shih), Chung-hang, Chih (or
      Hsün), Luan, and Hsi;
Wey: Shih, Ning, Sun, and K'ung;
Cheng: Hang, Ssu, Feng, Yü, Ying, Kuo, and Liang;
Ch'i: Kao, Kuo, Ts'ui, Ch'ing, and Ch'en (or T'ien);
Sung: Hua, Lo, Huang, Yü, Lin, Tang, and Hsiang;
Ch'u: Tou, Wei, and Ch'u;
Ch'en: Hsia.

Some of the families, such as Chao and Shan of Chou, and Kuo and Kao of Ch'i, are generally believed to have been established in very early times, but most of them were founded during the Ch'un Ch'iu period. If we consider our nine-stage division of the period from the point of view of these families (Table 3), we find the familiar increase in the fourth stage (632–603 B.C.). The fourth and fifth stages saw the rise of some extremely important families, among them Han, Chao, and Wei, who later divided Chin into three independent states, and

TABLE 3
Concentration of Ministers in Big Families

Stage number and dates (years B.C.)	Number of big families mentioned	Total number of ministers	Number of ministers from big families	Pct. of ministers from big families
I (722–693)	2	14	2	14
II (692–663)	5	26	5	19
III (662–633)	7	30	7	23
IV (632–603)	14	49	20	41
V (602–573)	19	51	28	55
VI (572–543)	23	57	27	47
VII (542–513)	14	56	21	37
VIII (512–483)	13	37	17	46
IX (482–464)	7	15	8	53
Total		335	135	41

the three Lu families Chi, Meng-sun, and Shu-sun, who at the end of the Ch'un Ch'iu period completely eclipsed their nominal ruler, the duke of Lu. The sixth stage, in which the largest number of families appeared, was also the beginning of a decline. For example, in this period the Luan family of Chin and the Ch'ing and Ts'ui families of Ch'i were liquidated by the combined pressure of other powerful families.[42] The struggle for survival among large clans brought some of them to power at the expense of others; finally so many had been destroyed that too few families were left to constitute a class. By the ninth stage the number of active families had been reduced to seven.[*]

As mentioned above, members of the ministerial group became concentrated within comparatively few families. Over the whole period, an average of 41 per cent of all ministers came from big families; for the last five stages the average is 48 per cent, which suggests further reasons for a shift of power into the hands of the ministers. If that power shift was part of a process of separation of family relationships from politics, perhaps ministers, in contrast to sons of rulers, obtained their positions by ability as well as by birth, being better able to move with the times.[†] That the decline of the minister class had begun even before the end of the Ch'un Ch'iu is revealed by a study of the figures given in Tables 1 and 2. The ministers kept the power only during the Ch'un Ch'iu period and were to pass it on to a group whose predecessors were already in existence: the *shih*.

Generally individual success can be attributed to personal ability or to coincidence. However, the occurrence of an unusual number of successes in the same area during a short period of time implies that not only individual qualities but also social processes must be involved. Such a clustering of successes is a highly significant phenomenon in the history of any particular area or period.

The Rise of the Shih

Although the *shih* were more numerous than other members of the aristocracy, they were almost ignored by historians. The list used here does not mention the *shih* in the first two stages; they must have been considered too insignificant to merit a place in the annals. From the third stage (662–633 B.C.) on, however, they are cited in connection

---

[*] For example, the more than ten great Chin families of Ch'un Ch'iu times dwindled to the three that divided the territory of Chin into three independent states at the beginning of the Chan Kuo period.

[†] A more detailed discussion of this process is given in Chapter 4.

with historical events. The first *shih* who enters Pan Ku's list is one Chieh Chih T'ui. Although a follower of Duke Wen of Chin during his self-exile, Chieh was not rewarded with any fief after the duke returned home and gained the throne.[43]

One of the four *shih* cited in the fourth stage (632–603 B.C.), Kung-jan Wu-jen, was a steward in an aristocratic household.[44] The other three were presumably warriors: two were bodyguards and one was sent by the duke of Chin to assassinate a minister.[45] Only one *shih* was mentioned in the fifth stage. K'uang Kou-hsü, a steward of a noble family, was assigned a fief, but resigned it to another steward who was more capable than himself.[46] Seven *shih* were mentioned in the* sixth stage (572–543 B.C.). Chih Ch'o, Ch'in Chin-fu, Shu-liang Ho, Ti Ssu-mi, Ch'i Liang, and Hua Chou were warriors of various states.[47] Tsang Chien, the scion of a ministerial family of Lu, earned a place in history by choosing death rather than maltreatment which he considered insulting to his rank.[48]

The list of the seventh stage (542–513 B.C.) includes four *shih*. Hsieh-shih, steward of a noble family of Lu, managed a city in the service of his master.[49] Nan K'uai, who managed a town for the Chi household, raised a rebellion in the town but was expelled to the neighboring state. His purpose, he said, was to restore power to the weak ducal house.[50] Tsung Lu was the bodyguard of a Wey noble.[51] Chuan Chu was a bravo who assassinated the Wu ruler on behalf of an ambitious prince.[52]

Confucius was active mostly in the eighth stage (512–483 B.C.). When he was young he served both as an accountant and as a field superintendent of livestock.[53] Later he was promoted to the rank of *tai fu* (probably the lower *tai fu* grade), perhaps because of his extensive knowledge in various fields.* Confucius devoted himself to the instruction of his disciples in Lu. Some of his followers achieved great success and importance during his lifetime, and their admiration for him no doubt contributed much to his reputation abroad as well as within Lu.[54] By the time of his death Confucius had become a highly respected scholar. Chi K'ang-tzu, the *de facto* ruler of Lu, consulted him on occasion, and the duke of Lu expressed sorrow at his death.[55]

One of the other eight *shih* mentioned in this stage was Tzu-lu (or

---

* Legge, *Analects*, 9.2. Confucius was well known for having learned much about many subjects instead of concentrating on a single career. He was apparently in the service of a government when he said that he had to maintain a vehicle because of his social status. See *ibid.*, 11.7.

Chi Lu), a disciple of Confucius of almost the same age, who came from a relatively poor family.* After studying with Confucius, he became the steward of the noble Chi family of the state of Lu. While thus employed, he played an important role in dismantling the fief fortifications of powerful noble families in Lu.[56] Tzu-lu died in an attempt to rescue the man whom he last served, a nobleman of Wey who had been captured in a *coup d'état*.[57] Although he never held an office in the state government of Lu, he was confident of his ability to run a fair-sized state.[58] Both Yu Jo and Fan Ch'ih were Confucius's disciples. Yu Jo joined a volunteer infantry task force that was given orders to raid the headquarters of the invading Wu army.[59] Fan Ch'ih was the right side man of the war chariot of Jan Yu, who commanded a part of the Lu troop that resisted the Ch'i invasion.[60] Yang Hu of Lu began his career as a retainer of the Chi family. By gaining control over this clan, for generations the most powerful in Lu, he virtually ran the state from 505 to 502 B.C., when an armed force of another noble family entered the Lu capital and drove him into exile.[61] Thus Yang Hu began as a *shih* and made his way almost to the peak of power in a state through his stewardship in an influential family. Kung-shan Pu-niu was also a steward of the main settlement of the Chi family. He was the actual ruler of his area, and he finally rebelled against a plan of Tzu-lu to destroy the fortifications of the fiefs. His troops were defeated in the Lu capital and he was compelled to flee the state.[62] Tung An-yü, a retainer of the Chao family of Chin, was killed during a feud among several noble families of Chin, some of which were later destroyed.[63] Meng Chih Fan (or Meng Chih Tse), a warrior of Lu, fought as rear guard when the Lu troop retreated in a battle.[64] Lü Chin arranged asylum for the Ch'u ruler in exile when he was serving a Ch'u noble family, after which the ruler contemplated giving him an official state position.[65]

Three of the six *shih* who are mentioned during the ninth stage (482–464 B.C.) were disciples of Confucius. Tzu-kung, an able businessman according to Confucius, apparently made a sizable fortune.[66] In studying under Confucius he specialized in argumentation, which was useful in his later diplomatic role as an aide to the Lu envoy on several missions to other states.[67]

Jan Yu, a steward of the Chi family, participated in deciding some governmental matters such as taxation. He urged the chancellor and

---

* *SCHI*, 67/3. Tzu-lu allegedly picked wild plants for food, carried his own rice bag, and dressed in rather disreputable clothing.

other nobles of Lu to resist an invasion from the neighboring state
of Ch'i, and was named co-commander of the Lu army during the
ensuing battle.[68] Tzu-kao, another follower of Confucius, was the
protégé of Tzu-lu, by whom he was appointed to manage the main
settlement of the Chi family.[69] Tzu-kao seems to have accompanied
Tzu-lu everywhere; with him he was employed by the K'ung family
of the state of Wey, but he fled when in danger of a death that he
did not feel obligated to suffer. Later he was mentioned again in the
Tso Chuan as the assistant of a Lu noble accompanying the duke to
an interstate conference. The suggestions he made at this meeting
were highly respected.[70] Hu Yen and Shih Ch'i were warriors in Wey.
It was they who killed Tzu-lu in the *coup d'état*.[71] Tung-kuo Chin was
a warrior in a Ch'i noble household. When his master was killed in
an armed *coup d'état*, the new regime offered him amnesty, seemingly
because of his popularity and reputation, but he refused, preferring
to live in exile rather than compromise his personal integrity.[72]

Though the number of *shih* in each stage is by no means impressive, the general trend shows a remarkable change, from no mention
at all to mention in somewhat active roles. There are two possible
lines of explanation: individual mobility and group mobility.[73] But
the clear decline of the ministerial class during the very period of increasing *shih* activity suggests at least a partial shift of the center of
power from the ministers to the *shih*. Consideration of the few examples given for the *shih* class reveals that historical events correspond in large measure to the trends indicated by the figures. Yang
Hu and Tung An-yü, for example, had become the focal points of
political power, while their ostensible masters played only supporting roles.

If the trends of *shih* and ministerial importance were extrapolated,
they would cross somewhere in the early Chan Kuo period; the point
of intersection would then describe the beginning of ministerial collapse and *shih* predominance. Unfortunately, however, because of the
meagerness of historical accounts the final years of the Ch'un Ch'iu
period and the beginning of the Chan Kuo are almost a blank to us.
It is accordingly impossible to extend the curves that could be drawn
from the rich and continuous account of the *Tso Chuan*.

Social Changes in the Chan Kuo Period
Starting from the point when historical information again becomes
available (although it is by no means of the *Tso Chuan* quality), we
find a state of affairs completely different from that of the Ch'un

Ch'iu period. Important changes have occurred, some of which will be investigated below.

We turn first to the personnel list of Pan Ku in an effort to determine the percentages of "newcomers," persons of obscure origin who were not connected with large families. The criteria for persons of this group are as follows: first, there must be no positive evidence that the person in question is a member of any aristocratic family; second, the person's name must not be that of any such family; and third, his name must not include any sort of title of office, because such titles often became grafted onto surnames of families that had held positions for generations and therefore could not be considered unknown or obscure. Keep in mind, however, that some persons left out because of failure to meet the second or third criterion might yet have no connection with a noble family. Even if a man had the surname of a big family, his ancestors might have long since sunk to a low social status, having been only distantly related to the rich and powerful members of their clan. All persons with noble surnames have nonetheless been excluded in order to avoid including an actual member of a noble family. The number of persons in this group is therefore a minimum. Table 4 shows the percentages of persons of obscure origin among the total number in Pan Ku's list.

Before 464 B.C., persons of unknown origin averaged 26 per cent of the total; after that time, they averaged 55 per cent, which suggests that after 464 B.C. most historical figures were self-made men who rose from obscurity. This trend, together with the decline of the minister class in the late Ch'un Ch'iu period, may indicate not only that there was more mobility between classes at the beginning of Chan Kuo times, but that the former dominant class, the ministers, had already collapsed. The disappearance of old families may be a consequence of the conquest and annexation of many older, smaller states by a handful of newer states; families from the conquered states dissolved in the agglomerative process. Nevertheless, if the old social order were still in effect, many new powerful families should have appeared in the courts of the new states. An inspection of the backgrounds of the chancellors of various Chan Kuo states indicates that there were few if any such families. In brief, what happened during the Chan Kuo period was the disappearance of the former social stratification, not merely freer mobility between strata.

The Backgrounds of Chan Kuo Chancellors

We shall next examine the backgrounds of the chancellors in the Chan Kuo period. The data were taken from various sources, includ-

TABLE 4

Persons of Obscure Origin in the Ch'un Ch'iu and Chan Kuo Periods

Period (years B.C.)	Total number of persons mentioned	Number of persons of obscure origin	Pct. of persons of obscure origin
Ch'un Ch'iu period			
722–693	32	2	6
692–663	41	13	32
662–633	57	14	25
632–603	70	21	30
602–573	69	17	25
572–543	84	19	23
542–513	80	21	26
512–483	56	16	29
482–464	27	12	44
Total	516	135	26
Chan Kuo period			
463–434	21	12	57
433–404	15	5	33
403–374	21	10	48
373–344	20	14	70
343–314	41	25	61
313–284	36	16	44
283–254	24	12	50
253–221	19	14	74
Total	197	108	55
Grand Total	713	243	34

ing the *Shih Chi* and the *Chan Kuo Ts'e,* that do not match the *Tso Chuan* for continuity and detail. The list of chancellors is by no means complete; most of the available information concerns the chancellors of Wei and Ch'in, whereas little is known about the Yen and Ch'u chancellors. Even where there is comparatively ample information, there are so many gaps and omissions that a chronologically continuous list is not possible. The names will, however, be listed generally in chronological order although they do not form a complete series.[74]

The State of Chao

Kung-chung Lien held the chancellorship around 403 B.C. in the reign of Marquis Lieh; we have no other information.[75]

Ta Ch'eng Wu took the chancellorship in 372 B.C. during the reign of Marquis Ch'eng; he also appears in 334 B.C. in the reign of Marquis Su. On one occasion he suggested to Shen Pu-hai, the chancellor of Han, that friendly relations should be maintained between their two states so that both chancellors might be of mutual help in holding their offices. This story hints that his status was not as firm as it would have been had he come from a powerful family or been related to the ruler.[76]

Chao Pao held office in 325 B.C. during the reign of King Wu-ling. Chao Pao had the title of Lord Yang-wen; his surname, the same as that of the Chao ruling house, indicates that he was a prince or a member of that house.[77]

Fei I had already gained a position of importance in the reign of Wu-ling's father, Marquis Su (reigned 349–325 B.C.).[78] He was appointed chancellor in 298 B.C. under Wu-ling's son, Hui-wen, and was killed in a *coup d'état* in 295 B.C.[79]

Kung-tzu Ch'eng, also called Lord An-ping, lived during the reign of Hui-wen and was a scion of the ruling house. He was appointed to the chancellorship after the *coup d'état* in 295 B.C.[80]

Lo I, in actuality the chancellor of Yen, was provisional chancellor of four other states when he commanded an allied armed force of five states in an attack on Ch'i in 285 B.C. He was a commoner who came to Yen in response to the invitation of the Yen king to talented persons to help in his plan of revenge against Ch'i.[81]

Wei Jan, a relative of the Ch'in ruling house, was sent by his government to be chancellor of Chao in 281 B.C. during a period of good Ch'in-Chao relations. However, the same year he left Chao and returned to Ch'in to take office as chancellor of that state.[82]

Yü Ch'ing, a poor scholar, was "walking . . . and carrying his own luggage on a pole" when he entered the state of Yen. He was presented with gifts after his first interview with King Hsiao-ch'eng (reigned 265–245 B.C), received a ministerial office after the second, and was made chancellor after the third. Not long after, in about 265 B.C., he chose to follow into exile a banished friend who had sought his aid. His old age was poverty-stricken and lonesome. He is also credited with having written a book.[83]

T'ien Tan was a general of Ch'i who belonged to the Ch'i ruling house, the T'ien family. Later he served in Chao under two kings, Hui-wen in 269 B.C. and Hsiao-ch'eng in 264 B.C. On at least one of these occasions he was chancellor.[84]

Chao Sheng, a brother of King Hui-wen, was known as one of the four hospitable Chan Kuo princes.* He was said to have been appointed chancellor three times and discharged three times. He held the title of Lord P'ing-yuan from 298 B.C. on. One of his appointments to the chancellorship was in 265 B.C. He died in 251 B.C.[85]

Lien P'o, the finest warrior of Chao, was made chancellor and ennobled in 251 B.C. after the death of Chao Sheng.[86]

About Chancellor P'i we have no information other than his surname.[87] About Chancellor Chang little information is available. He was said to have missed his mother country, Wei, which indicates that he was not native to Chao and hence not a member of any large family of Chao.[88]

Of these thirteen chancellors, three were princes and two were related to royal houses of other states. The remaining eight apparently were related neither to any ruling house nor to each other, nor is there evidence of any connection with an influential family.

The State of Ch'i

Tsou Chi first attracted the attention of the ruler of Ch'i by his talent in playing the *ch'in,* a harp-like musical instrument. The ruler was impressed by his political advice and gave him the chancellorship in 337 B.C. Hostile relations between Tsou Chi and T'ien Chi, a prince and general, caused the latter to flee abroad.[89]

T'ien Ying, the son of King Wei and a younger brother of King Hsüan, served both men. He was chancellor under King Hsüan for eleven years beginning in 311 B.C. He was eventually enfeoffed with the former small state of Hsüeh in 298 B.C. by King Min, son of Hsüan.[90]

Han Mei, a prince of Han, was sent to serve as chancellor in Ch'i (ca. 306 B.C.) during a period of friendly relations between the two states.[91]

T'ien Wen was the son of T'ien Ying and one of the four hospitable Chan Kuo princes. During the reign of King Min he was invited to go to Ch'in to take office as chancellor in 298 B.C., but he returned to Ch'i after a short, unpleasant sojourn, and received the chancellorship of his own state. In 294 B.C. he became involved in a political plot to seize and hold the king. Nevertheless he held the chancellorship of Ch'i for many years. Eventually his fief of Hsüeh

---

* There were four princes of the Chan Kuo period who were celebrated for their generosity in keeping thousands of retainers and guests. They were Lord Hsin-ling (Kung-tzu Wu-chi) of Wei, Lord P'ing-yuan (Chao Sheng) of Chao, Lord Meng-ch'ang (T'ien Wen) of Ch'i, and Lord Ch'un-shen (Huang Chieh) of Ch'u.

became a semi-independent state. He was also known as Lord Meng-ch'ang.[92]

Lü Li, a former general of Ch'in, was exiled from that state and took the office of chancellor of Ch'i under King Min (probably in 288 B.C.). The Ch'in ruler considered the appointment an insult and attacked Ch'i, whereupon Lü Li fled from the state.[93]

Nao Ch'ih was a general of Ch'u who commanded the Ch'u army sent to the aid of Ch'i when that state was attacked by an allied force of several states. The grateful Ch'i ruler made him chancellor as a reward in 285 B.C. Later he succeeded in deposing and slaying King Min, and was slain by the enraged people of Ch'i.[94]

T'ien Tan, a member of the Ch'i ruling house, commanded the forces that held the last remaining cities in Ch'i lands during the war with Yen and other states. After ca. 284 B.C., he enthroned and served as chancellor under a Ch'i prince who was later known as King Hsiang.[95]

Hou Sheng, brother-in-law to King Hsiang, served as chancellor in his son's reign after the death of the queen (ca. 225 B.C.) until the destruction of the state by Ch'in.[96]

About Tsung Wei we know only that he was a chancellor of Ch'i and was discharged.[97]

These nine Ch'i chancellors include one prince, two members of the ruling house, one prince of a foreign state, one relative of the Ch'i ruling house, and one relative of a foreign ruling house. Only one of the nine, Tsou Chi, made his way from obscurity to the chancellorship by his own talent and effort.

The State of Ch'in

Wey Yang (also known as Shang Yang), a member of the ruling house of a small state, began as the protégé of a chancellor of Wei. After the death of his patron he traveled to Ch'in, where his ideas on political and military reform impressed the ruler, Duke Hsiao. He remained in Ch'in and in 352 B.C. attained a position equivalent to chancellor, in which he could put his ideas into effect. His reforms made the Ch'in government the most powerful, and the Ch'in people the most disciplined, of the time. Such regimentation was bitterly resented by the conservatives and the common people, and Wey Yang was executed after the death of Duke Hsiao in 338 B.C.*

---

* The *Wey* of Wey Yang should be distinguished from the *Wei* where Wey Yang spent his years before going to Ch'in. He was a member of the ruling house of Wey, a tiny principality that was once a powerful state. He worked in the house-

Kung-sun Yen was appointed chancellor in 333 B.C. He served in the same position again after 310 B.C.[98]

Chang I, a man of obscure origin, came to Ch'in from the east with ideas on strategy and diplomatic policy that were to be highly beneficial to Ch'in during the critical period of interstate struggle. He twice held the chancellorship of Ch'in (328–322 B.C. and 317–311 B.C.) and was sent several times to serve in other states in order to cement their relations with Ch'in. He was finally exiled from Ch'in and died in Wei in 310 B.C.[99]

Lo Ch'ih was chancellor in 318 B.C. under King Hui-wen during the middle part of his reign.[100] His background is unknown, although he appeared twice in other places—once as chancellor of the small state of Chung-shan,[101] and once in 312 B.C. as an escort, under the orders of King Wu-ling of Chao, for a prince of Yen on his way home to take the throne.[102] It may be inferred from these accounts that he was a career administrator, soldier, or diplomat, or a combination of all three. There is no evidence of his being related to any ruling house or noble family.

Prince Shu-li Chi, the brother of King Hui of Ch'in, began as an officer in the Ch'in army, and led his troops in several expeditions outside the state. In 309 B.C. King Wu appointed him to one of two newly established chancellorships, which he held for only a year. He was then sent to Han, where he was also given a chancellorship. During the reign of King Chao-hsiang he was again made chancellor of Ch'in. Six years later (in 300 B.C.) he died in office.[103]

Kan Mao, a native of Wei, studied under the doorkeeper-scholar Shih Chü of the town of Hsia-ts'ai. He came to Ch'in, was recommended to the king by Chang I and Shu-li Chi, and became chancellor along with Shu-li Chi in 309 B.C. in the reign of King Wu. After Chao-hsiang succeeded to the throne of Ch'in, Kan Mao was ousted from office and exiled by his opponents in the court. He served as a counsellor of high rank in Ch'u in 305 B.C., but he was never able to return to Ch'in and died in Wei. He habitually called himself "an alien subject."[104]

Hsiang Shou, who was related to a queen of Ch'in, grew up with King Chao-hsiang. He was a political opponent of Kan Mao and held the office of chancellor about 306 B.C.[105]

---

hold of the chancellor of Wei, a large and important state, apparently as a sort of page. His being related to the Wey ruling house did him no good in Wei or Ch'in, the two strongest powers of the time. That he was considered a foreigner in Ch'in may partly explain the hostility of the Ch'in people which indirectly led to his death. His biography appears in *SCHI*, 68. See also *ibid.*, 5/18, 15/18, 19, 20.

T'ien Wen served, upon invitation, as chancellor of Ch'in for a short time in 298 B.C., after which he left the state.[106]

Chin Shou, of unknown origin, is mentioned only as having succeeded T'ien Wen in 298 B.C.[107]

Lou Huan, originally a native of Chao, participated in the discussion about the reforms of King Wu-ling of Chao.[108] After the death of Shu-li Chi, he was appointed to the chancellorship of Ch'in in 297 B.C. His accession to this office was for some reason resented in Chao, and pressure from that state caused his dismissal in 295 B.C.[109]

Wei Jan, step-brother to the queen of Ch'in, in 306 B.C. helped to put the young King Chao (or King Chao-hsiang) on the throne, after which he became, as chancellor, the most influential figure in the court. Now and then he withdrew from the chancellorship, but he always resumed the office. For about forty years he remained the key figure of Ch'in politics. In 271 B.C. he was ousted from the court and sent to live on his estates.[110]

Shou Chu, after first serving as "alien minister," held the chancellorship for one year in 292 B.C. between two periods of Wei Jan's chancellorship.[111]

Fan Sui, a poor native of Wei, served as a retainer in the household of a minor official of Wei, Hsu Chia. He was flogged nearly to death by order of the Wei chancellor Wei Ch'i because he was suspected of selling information to a foreign power. Humiliated and severely injured, he was spirited into Ch'in by a Ch'in envoy, who recommended him to King Chao (ca. 272 B.C.). His warning about the great and long-term power of the chancellor Wei Jan was probably well heeded by the king. The king was also much impressed by Fan Sui's strategic ideas, which stressed maintaining good relations with distant states in order that nearer states might be forced to yield to Ch'in without fear of interference from the others. In 266 B.C. he was ennobled and named successor to Wei Jan. He held both the chancellorship and the favor of the king until 255 B.C., when he was persuaded to resign after generals he had recommended surrendered to the enemy in battle.[112]

Ts'ai Tse, a native of Yen, studied the art of persuasion of rulers, although fortune did not favor him until he went to Ch'in. There he managed to convince chancellor Fan Sui that a clever man should know when to retire, and thus preserve his prestige and the ruler's favor, before the ruler took alarm at his continued power and influence. Fan Sui (whose prestige had in fact already declined) was thus persuaded to retire and to recommend Ts'ai Tse as his successor. The latter was duly appointed chancellor in 255 B.C. but resigned after a few months, ostensibly to keep his own prestige intact.[113]

Lü Pu-wei was a prosperous businessman in the large city of Han-
tan in Chao, where he met a prince of Ch'in who was being kept as
hostage in the capital. Lü used his wealth to cause the almost forgotten prince to be named heir apparent to the Ch'in throne. Lü's protégé finally took the throne and reigned for a short time, during which
Lü was made chancellor (249 B.C.). This ruler died and a young boy,
whose custodian Lü became, was put on the throne. Lü held the real
power for a decade until the boy grew up, whereupon, in 238 B.C., the
young king had Lü removed from office. In 237 B.C., the king ordered
Lü exiled to a remote province. Two years later Lü committed suicide.[114]

Lord Ch'ang-p'ing may have been a prince of Ch'u kept in Ch'in
as hostage. He was mentioned as one of the two chancellors of Ch'in
who suppressed a disturbance in 238 B.C. in the capital.[115] In 232 B.C.
he was installed by Ch'in upon the throne of Ch'u,[116] where he caused
a rebellion with the apparent purpose of restoring Ch'u's independence. The Ch'in army was sent to put down the rebellion; Ch'ang-
p'ing's resistance, though brave, was fruitless, and he met death in
231 B.C.[117]

Though Lord Ch'ang-wen is mentioned in 238 B.C. as chancellor
together with Lord Ch'ang-p'ing, his background and even his real
name are unknown.[118]

Wang Wan was the last chancellor of the Ch'in state and the first
of the Ch'in empire. His name was first on the petition that presented
the imperial title to the first Ch'in emperor in 222 B.C. No other information concerning him is available.[119]

Among the eighteen Ch'in chancellors whose names are recorded,
only one was a prince of the ruling house and two were kinsmen of
the ruling house. Two princes of foreign states are included. Of the
rest, some definitely rose from obscurity to key positions by their own
abilities. A complication here is the foreign origin of most Ch'in chancellors, which must be attributed to the relatively low cultural level
of Ch'in.

The State of Ch'u

Wu Ch'i, a native of Lu, served in the Lu army as an officer, after
which he went to Wei, where he became the governor of a district of
strategic importance. Slander by his political opponents caused him
to leave Wei and go to Ch'u (ca. 384 B.C.), where he was appointed
ling-yin, the Ch'u equivalent of chancellor (ca. 382 B.C.). In this capacity he started a program of reforms with the support of King Tao
of Ch'u, notably measures for subjugating unruly nobles and settling

the state's waste lands. When King Tao died in 381 B.C., Wu Ch'i was slain by revengeful nobles in the very room where the dead king lay. Throughout his life Wu Ch'i was regarded as a fine strategist, tactician, administrator, and reformer. He is said to have received his education from Tseng Tzu, a disciple of Confucius, which is not unlikely since the Confucian school specialized in training such career statesmen.[120]

Chao Hsien held the chancellorship of Ch'u when Chang I was intending to be chancellor of both Ch'in and Wei (possibly in 335 B.C.). Nothing is known of his origin or background. Chao 趙 is not the name of any large Ch'u family or of any branch of the ruling house.[121]

Chang I was sent from Ch'in to serve as chancellor of Ch'u in 313 B.C.[122]

Chao Yü served as the Ch'u chancellor when Chang I went to Wei in 310 B.C.[123]

Lord Ch'un-shen, according to tradition, was not a native of Ch'u, but the scholar Ch'ien Mu is convinced that he was a Ch'u prince.[124] He was a companion of the heir apparent to the Ch'u throne when the heir was held as hostage in Ch'in. He succeeded in getting the Ch'u prince out of Ch'in and back to Ch'u, and thus won the trust of the prince, who acceded to the throne upon his return. Ch'un-shen was appointed to the office of *ling-yin*, which he held unchallenged throughout the reign of King K'ao-lieh (262–238 B.C.). He was also famed as one of the four hospitable princes. Eventually, however, he was assassinated by one of his retainers (238 B.C.).[125]

The Marquis of Chou, apparently a court favorite, was ennobled and appointed chancellor. One of his contemporaries attributes the appointment to royal favor rather than personal merit or noble birth. The ruler he served was King Ch'ing-hsiang (reigned 298–262 B.C.).[126]

Chao Tzu, chancellor under King Ch'ing-hsiang (ca. 281 B.C.), is shown by his surname to have belonged to an important branch of the Ch'u ruling house.[127]

Among the seven Ch'u chancellors whose names are recorded are one prince and two men related to an important family whose members were considered kinsmen to the ruling house. The most colorful of the chancellors, Wu Ch'i, was of both foreign birth and obscure background. On the other hand, the fact that Chao 昭 occurs twice indicates that this branch of the royal family was quite active in Ch'u during the Chan Kuo period. Ch'u was not thoroughly Sinified in the Ch'un Ch'iu period; it was still a barbarian state at odds with the Chinese states in the Yellow River valley. It adopted the Chinese lineage system relatively late, but seems to have preserved the system in its full vitality when the Chinese states in the north had evolved in another direction. Also the Ch'u royal house continued from the Ch'un Ch'iu to the Chan Kuo without suffering from the shifts in power that occurred in many northern states. These two factors may also explain the presence of royal kinsmen in powerful posts.

The State of Han

Chia Lei was called the chancellor of Han as well as the uncle of a Han ruler. His political adversary, a certain Yen Chung-tzu, hired an assassin to kill him; the various versions of what happened do not agree.[128]

Hsü I, whose name is recorded only once, was said to have been chancellor during the reign of Marquis Ai, whom he saved from assassination (ca. 371 B.C.?). The rest of his career is unknown.[129]

Shen Pu-hai was said to have been a humble subject of the erstwhile Cheng state, which suggests that he was of low or servile status. After studying government and administration, he convinced the Han ruler Marquis Chao of his capabilities for running the state. He served as chancellor for seventeen years (355–337 B.C.), the major part of the reign of Marquis Chao.[130]

Chang K'ai-ti and his son Chang P'ing are mentioned only in the biography of his grandson Chang Liang in the *Shih Chi*. He was reported to have been chancellor under three Han rulers: Marquis Chao (reigned 362–334 B.C.), King Hsüan-hui (reigned 333–312 B.C.), and King Hsiang-ai (reigned 311–296 B.C.).[131] Some scholars believed that this Chang family was a branch of the Han ruling house but had changed its name to Chang to foil a search by the first Ch'in emperor for the man we know as Chang Liang.[132] This belief is highly dubious.

Chang P'ing, the father of Chang Liang, was chancellor under two Han rulers, King Hsi (reigned 295–273 B.C.) and King Hui (reigned 272–239 B.C.).[133]

Chao Hsien's name reveals that he belonged to a branch of the Ch'u ruling house. While he was chancellor of Han, Ch'in invaded that state. The Han ruler intended to discharge him from the chancellorship, presumably to appease Ch'in by breaking off friendly relations with Ch'u. Chao Hsien informed Kung Shu, an influential figure in Han, that, to the contrary, he should be kept in office to warn Ch'in of the close ties between Han and Ch'u, and thus stop the Ch'in invasion. This indicates that his chancellorship in Han was meant to be a guaranty of interstate friendship, a not unusual diplomatic practice of the times. There is no information to determine his date.[134]

Nan Kung Chieh served as chancellor under King Hsiang and died in 308 B.C.[135]

Shu-li Chi, prince and chancellor of Ch'in, came to Han to succeed to the chancellorship in 308 B.C. after the death of Nan Kung Chieh. This is another example of the diplomatic practice that is mentioned above.[136]

Han Min once served under Kung Chung, who sent him to the state of Ch'in on a diplomatic mission. He was probably related to Kung Chung, a powerful political figure in Han, since he was later called Kung-chung Min. He became the chancellor of Han and was obviously regarded by other states as the true director of the Han government (ca. 306 B.C.).[137]

Han Ch'en became chancellor after the death of Han Min.[138]

Han Ch'i was chancellor under the last Han ruler (reigned 238–230 B.C.); his name indicates that he was related to the ruling house.[139]

Pao Ch'ien, as Han chancellor, and Pai Kuei, as chancellor of Wei (fl. ca. 344 B.C.), mutually aided each other to keep their positions.[140]

Four of the twelve Han chancellors whose names are recorded were rather closely related to the ruling house, and the two surnamed Chang may also have come from a branch of the ruling house. (It is also possible that the Chang family could trace its beginnings far back before the partition of the state of Chin, since it had existed in Chin and had already contributed a few minor officials to the Chin government.)[141] Those who served temporarily in Han because of recommendation by a foreign power were Chao Hsien and Shu-li Chi. The most important of all the Han chancellors was Shen Pu-hai, who was definitely of humble origin.

The State of Wei

Chi Ch'eng-tzu, also known as Kung Chi Ch'eng, was the brother of Marquis Wen of Wei. He was one of the ruler's two choices for the office of chancellor (between 406 and 397 B.C.). He was chosen not only because of his relationship to the ruler but also because of his practice of keeping worthy persons as his retainers and recommending them to be officials in the government.[142]

Li Kuei, one of the best-known deputies of the Wei ruler Marquis Wen (reigned 446–397 B.C.), is said to have been chancellor under this ruler (ca. 405 B.C.).[143]

Chai Huang, a chancellor (fl. ca. 405 B.C.) under Marquis Wen of Wei, was not respected by his ruler.[144]

Shang Wen, although his origin and background are unknown, seems to have been a most reliable, trustworthy minister (fl. ca. 384 B.C.). The ruler he served was Marquis Wu (reigned 396–371 B.C.).[145] Kung Shu, the husband of a Wei princess, succeeded Shang Wen as chancellor (ca. 384 B.C.).[146] He recommended to King Hui (reigned 370–319 B.C.) that his protégé, Wey Yang, succeed him as chancellor (before 361 B.C.). He died while still serving as chancellor under King Hui.[147]

Pai Kuei, while chancellor of Wei, suggested to Pao Ch'ien, then chancellor of Han, that they support each other in keeping their positions.[148] During the reign of King Hui a man named Tan was ennobled (ca. 344 B.C.); this Tan may have been Pai Kuei, whose other name was Tan.[149]

Lord Chung-shan was probably a vassal lord of the small state of Chung-shan, which had been conquered by Wei during the reign of Marquis Wen.[150] The first Wei lord of this state was recalled to accede to the Wei throne in 396 B.C. and was known as Marquis Wu.[151] The man known as Lord Chung-shan here was appointed chancellor in 342 B.C. under King Hui, the son of Marquis Wu. His name is unknown, although he was certainly a prince of Wei or a descendant of one.[152]

Hui Shih was a scholar who wrote a code of law for the state of Wei and held the office of chancellor during the reign of King Hui (ca. 334 B.C.).[153]

T'ien Hsü served as chancellor of Wei contemporaneously with Kung-sun Yen, then a general of its army. It is reported that these two key figures were hostile toward one another.[154] Kung-sun Yen wished to oust T'ien Hsü, but the Wei ruler was convinced that T'ien Hsü was loyal and should be retained to act as a check on Kung-sun Yen, who was suspected of having connections with a foreign power. T'ien Hsü himself was probably of Wei origin.[155] He died in office in 310 B.C.[156]

The crown prince of Wei was appointed to the Wei chancellorship after the death of T'ien Hsü in order to forestall pressure from foreign states to appoint a chancellor of their choosing.[157]

Chang I left the chancellorship of Ch'in and came to Wei to assume its chancellorship in the latter part of the reign of King Hui. Later he changed office twice more between the chancellorships of the two states. He died in 310 B.C. in Wei after serving one year under King Hsiang.[158] Chang I's primary concern seems to have been for the advancement of Ch'in interests, and his policies apparently aimed at very close relations between Wei and Ch'in.

Kung-sun Yen was appointed in Wei as *hsi shou,* the highest military office. He then managed to oust Chang I and replaced him as the chancellor (ca. 320 B.C.).[159]

Chai Ch'iang was mentioned in a dispute after his death over who would succeed him in office (ca. 306 B.C.). His background and life are unknown.[160]

T'ien Wen, known as Lord Meng-ch'ang of Ch'i, was exiled by his own ruler (ca. 286 B.C.) and became the chancellor of Wei under King Ch'ao. He allied Wei with other states to invade Ch'i when Yen initiated a war of retaliation with that state (284 B.C.).[161] Thus T'ien Wen seems to have been appointed chancellor for his ability rather than as an emissary sent from Ch'i to help cement friendship between Ch'i and Wei.

Wei Ch'i, a prince of the Wei ruling house and chancellor under King Chao, was forced to leave Wei under pressure from Ch'in (ca. 266 B.C.), whose Wei-born chancellor, Fan Sui, sought to avenge his mistreatment at Wei Ch'i's hands many years earlier (see p. 44).[162] After living in exile in Chao for two years he committed suicide (264 B.C.).[163]

Fan Tso was the contemporary of Lord Hsin-ling (fl. 276, d. 243 B.C.). For unknown reasons, Chao asked Wei to put him to death after he had been dismissed from the chancellorship of Wei.[164]

Lord Hsin-an's given name is said to have been Wei Hsin, indicating that he might have been a prince of the Wei ruling house. He was referred to as chancellor in an invitation from Ch'in to visit that state. His date is uncertain.[165]

The Marquis of Ch'ang-hsin was chancellor of Wei at a time when the state was defeated in battle by Ch'in. The battle was probably the one of 273 B.C.[166]

Among these eighteen chancellors there are princes of Wei as well as foreign princes, and native-born career administrators as well as persons recommended and sent by other states. Because of Wei's strategic position, foreign powers often tried to influence its policies in their favor by causing men friendly to themselves to be placed in the Wei chancellorship. The Wei crown prince was once named to this position because of his government's fear of foreign influence. However, nine of the chancellors of Wei were of obscure origin.

The State of Yen

Tzu Chih, a man of unknown origin, was chancellor under the Yen king K'uai, who, being persuaded by the friends of Tzu Chih to imitate the ancient emperors Yao and Shun, gave up his throne and made Tzu Chih ruler (316 B.C.). The consequences were dire; the heir apparent objected violently and the resulting internecine disturbance invited invasion by foreign states. King K'uai, Tzu Chih, and the crown prince were all slain in the ensuing disorder (314 B.C.).[167]

Li Fu, the chancellor of the last Yen king, advised the invasion of Chao immediately after that state had been disastrously defeated by Ch'in, and led the invading force himself. His army was defeated and he was killed (251 B.C.).[168]

Chiang Ch'ü, a contemporary of Li Fu, pointed out the shortsightedness of Li Fu's plan to invade Chao. After the Yen troops were defeated, Chao demanded that he be appointed chancellor of Yen as a condition of truce negotiations. He was duly made chancellor and settled the Yen-Chao quarrel.[169]

Chang T'ang was a Ch'in courtier sent to Yen to be the chancellor of the state (ca. 236 B.C.). His was apparently not a normal appointment, since he was sent on the very eve of the unification of China by Ch'in. He may have been sent to Yen as a commissioner to a subjugated state.[170]

These four chancellors of Yen are the only ones whose names are known. They have no clearly known histories by which to classify their origins and backgrounds. It seems almost impossible that any of the first three mentioned had royal blood; the last definitely had no relation to the Yen ruling house.

A Comparison Between Ch'un Ch'iu and Chan Kuo Chancellorships

A few significant phenomena are revealed by the foregoing data on Chan Kuo chancellors. First, the terms of office of chancellors were neither for a definite period nor for life. During the Ch'un Ch'iu period every man who held the office of chancellor or its equivalent kept his position for life, except for those who were banished while still in office. The frequent replacement of chancellors in the Chan Kuo period would seem to indicate the growing power of rulers and the decreasing authority of chancellors.

Second, the Chan Kuo chancellors were people of widely varied origins. Some were princes of states other than those they served as chancellor; some were career statesmen who were employed by several governments. Men of both classes may have been chosen by their rulers or recommended by influential foreign states. Such men could not have felt any deep-seated ties with the states they served, especially when they shifted allegiance rather often. Thus they really belonged to no community and did not constitute a hereditary class.

Third, with very few exceptions—notably the Chang family of Ch'u —the chancellorships in all seven major states were given either to the closest relatives of the ruling house or to persons who did not belong to any big family. The powerful families that supplied most of the important officials of the states in the Ch'un Ch'iu period seem to have disappeared in the Chan Kuo.

An interesting comparison along these lines comes from the state of Chin. *Chung chün* was at first the title of the commander of the armed forces of Chin, and later came to mean prime minister. From the legalization of this practice in 587 B.C.[171] to the extinction of the Chih family in 453 B.C., there were eleven *chung-chün* almost evenly distributed among six leading Chin families: one of the Luan family, two of Han, three of Hsün (Chih), two of Fan, two of Chao, and one of Wei, in the planned succession.[172] One of them, even while still young and in captivity, knew in advance that in his turn he would be in charge of state affairs.[173] Unlike the Chan Kuo chancellors, none of the chancellors of the Ch'un Ch'iu were wandering statesmen (except those who were in exile and could have no chance of going home), and all came from a group of a very few families.

The difference between the two periods is evident, but it did not occur suddenly. As we have seen, some changes in social stratification had already taken place in the Ch'un Ch'iu. Sons of rulers at first occupied key positions but later gave way to the expanding influence of the large noble families, some of which eventually deposed their rulers and usurped both title and power in establishing a new type of monarchy. In time, bitter strife among the great families reduced their number, and a new group, the *shih*, came to the fore.

In our study of the Chan Kuo period very few of the old Ch'un Ch'iu families could be identified. These old families were not simply replaced by new families of comparable power and wealth, as might have happened if the general social structure had remained unchanged. It follows that there was not merely individual social mobility within an enduring structure; there was an essential change in the social structure itself. Such a change would not occur without corresponding important changes in other aspects of the society, notably political and economic institutions and ideologies. Succeeding chapters will discuss those aspects.

Chapter 3 Wars and Warriors

The Ch'un Ch'iu and Chan Kuo periods differ in many ways, but they share one point of similarity: a high frequency of wars. These periods were two stages of an epoch of transition from feudalism to a unified empire. In the Ch'un Ch'iu period the old order broke down; in the Chan Kuo period a new order began to emerge. The people living in the interval between the breakdown of the old and the establishment of the new were bewildered by the lack of standards for settling disputes and maintaining harmonious relationships. Continuous struggle was the only proven means of survival, and was therefore held to be justified. Group fought with group, and state assaulted state; the war drums echoed for five centuries. It is not that the people of this time were unusually militant, but that they lived in a period of instability.

After centuries of bloody strife, only a handful of states, and finally just one, survived; all the others had been exterminated. Most of the old institutions having been uprooted, many members of the erstwhile upper classes were relegated to lower positions in the social scale. Persons of ability rose in status when specific situations demanded their talents and training, and when former hindrances to their ascent were removed. A sharp increase in social mobility accompanied the profound changes in social stratification.

Familial Ties in Interstate Relationships

In the early Chou feudal society, familial relationships dominated the entire social structure. Among the 71 states created by the Chou king, royal kinsmen ruled 53, and many rulers with other surnames were linked to the Chou clan by repeated intermarriages.[1] The long Mao Kung Ting bronze inscription, which is a charge from a king to one of his dukes, has as its first injunction "to defend my state and my family," and enjoins further that the duke must rule his family, avoid alcoholic drink, and be kind to his friends.[2] An agreement recorded in *Mencius* was signed by the rulers of several states at a meeting called by Duke Huan of Ch'i, the first *Pa* ("overlord") of the Ch'un Ch'iu period:

1. Slay the unfilial; change not the son who has been appointed heir; exalt not a concubine to be the wife.

2. Honor the worthy and maintain the talented to give distinction to the virtuous.

3. Respect the old, and be kind to the young. Be not forgetful of strangers and travelers.

4. Let not offices be hereditary, nor let officers simultaneously hold more than one office. In the selection of officers let the object be to get the proper men. Let not a ruler take it on himself to put to death a great officer.

5. Make no crooked embankments. Impose no restrictions on the sale of grain. Let no boundary markers be set without announcement.[3]

Of these five clauses, at least the first and the third, which deal with familial affairs, would seem to lie beyond the normal concerns of an interstate agreement. Since the agreement did include these sections, it may be inferred that in the Ch'un Ch'iu period political behavior was closely linked with familial relationships.

The Chou kings habitually addressed dukes as uncles, either paternal or maternal, according to whether or not the addressee possessed the royal surname. Other feudal lords of the royal surname were usually called "brother" by the kings. "Now you brothers of my house come and meet seasonally." On one occasion, the Chou king informed a Chin envoy that the feast prepared for his visit was a homely one, of a sort used to entertain visiting brothers, such as those from Chin. The envoy privately wondered why he, the representative of such a great power as Chin, was not treated more formally.[4]

Since heads of states treated each other as kinsmen, many familial behavior patterns came to be used in interstate relationships. Family members should help each other in times of need; so also should the states give mutual aid. Thus Chin, suffering from famine, asked Ch'in, a potential enemy, to send grain, and Ch'in complied.[5] An army from Chin was sent to invade Ch'i, but its commanding general ordered a withdrawal when he heard of the death of the Ch'i ruler (554 B.C.).[6]

An uncle may as a matter of course temporarily shelter a nephew who has run away from home to escape punishment. Nobles of the Ch'un Ch'iu period acted similarly toward one another. For instance, a minister of Cheng, having committed a misdemeanor, fled to Chin. The chancellor of Chin asked the Cheng chancellor what should be done about the minister in exile. He was told that the fugitive minister, an officer of the second degree who had been in charge of the Cheng stables, should, according to tradition, be demoted one degree in rank. Thus the exiled noble took up life in Chin with a rank one degree lower than his former one.[7] Another good example is a dialogue between the ruler of a triumphant state and a messenger from his defeated adversary. After Duke Hsiao of Ch'i invaded and defeated Lu, a messenger was sent from Lu with food and wine for the Ch'i troops. Duke Hsiao asked him, "Are the people of Lu afraid?" The messenger replied, "The commoners are, but the nobles are not." The duke said, "Nothing left in the houses, not even any green grass left in the fields—what grounds have you for confidence?" "We rely on what has been assigned to our forefathers," answered the messenger:

"King Ch'eng of Chou charged the founder of Lu, Duke Wen, and the Grand Duke of Ch'i, saying, 'Both of you, having assisted the royal house of Chou and having helped my royal father, shall be enfeoffed with lands and given the sacrificial animal that you shall use in the oath ceremony. You and your descendants, generation after generation, shall not injure each other.' Now, Your Excellency has come to punish us for our faults, but you must listen to our appeal and excuse us. You must not destroy our state deities. If you ignore the old decree merely because you desire territory, then how can you keep the other states in line? We rely on this point and are therefore not afraid."

The duke of Ch'i was convinced by this reasoning and a truce was arranged.[8]

Deference to persons of superior rank by their inferiors, even those of other states, was derived from familial rules of precedence. Several times during a decisive battle between Chin and Ch'u (575 B.C.), a Chin noble encountered the chariot of the ruler of Ch'u. Each time, the noble doffed his helmet to show respect for the Ch'u ruler. In the same battle, the ruler of Cheng, then an ally of Ch'u, escaped capture and possible death twice when pursuing Chin nobles gave up the chase in deference to his rank.[9]

It would seem clear from these examples that familial considerations to some extent reduced the brutality of war. These considerations probably survived from the Chou feudal system, which depended upon the family system and the sense of fellowship among nobles. Even when the familial system was no longer capable of keeping order among the states, the family-oriented mentality remained a powerful force for stability in a period of general disorder.

Frequent Conflicts among Ch'un Ch'iu States

A statistical evaluation of the frequency of wars in the Ch'un Ch'iu period is given in Table 5. Different numbers and sizes of states were involved in the various conflicts; campaigns have been assigned quan-

TABLE 5

The Frequency of Wars in the Ch'un Ch'iu Period

Years B.C.	War score in each year of decade[a]										Total war score	Peaceful years
	1	2	3	4	5	6	7	8	9	10		
722–713	4.5	4	0	11	11.5	4	1.5	0	1.5	13	51	2
712–703	7.5	0	2.5	1	2.5	4.5	3	4	4	5	34	1
702–693	4	1.5	4.5	8.5	6	5	6	5.5	2	0	43	1
692–683	1.5	4	1.5	6	3	0	2.5	2	10.5	2	33	1
682–673	2.5	1.5	6	5	6	0	2.5	7.5	1.5	2	34.5	1
672–663	0		1.5	0	6.5	0	8.5	1.5	1.5	0	19.5	5
662–653	1	4	4	8.5	4.5	3	22	3.5	15	2	67.5	0
652–643	1.5	2	3.5	5.5	1.5	2.5	1.5	17	3.5	4	41.5	0
642–633	10	6	3	10.5	9	4	4	7	12.5	7	61	0
632–623	18.5	0	5.5	1.5	1.5	3.5	7	7	11	5	69	1
622–613	3.5	3	4.5	2	9.5	3.5	4.5	3.5	1.5	3	35.5	1
612–603	6	6	8	0	16.5	9	7	5	4	4.5	63	1
602–593	4	3	13.5	9	6.5	7.5	5	4	3.5	2	61	1
592–583	0	6	1	10	11.5	1.5	0	10	12.5	7	58.5	1
582–573	7.5	3	1	1.5	9	3.5	3	14	22	7	74.5	0
572–563	16	9	3.5	5.5	12.5	2.5	2	4.5	14	17.5	85.5	0
562–553	21	4.5	2	14.5	3.5	12	6.5	4	4	1.5	71.5	0
552–543	1	0	4.5	21.5	8.5	7	0	0	0	0	41	5
542–533	0	3	0	0	11	11	2.5	0	2	2	31.5	4
532–523	1.5	2	5.5	3	0	2	1.5	3.5	1	4.5	24.5	1
522–513	0	5	3	9	3.5	0	2	2	5.5	0	24.5	4
512–503	1.5	1	1.5	0	2.5	1.5	21.5	5	7.5	4	44	1
502–493	10	2	2	8.5	2	5	6	3.5	3	1.5	39.5	1
492–483	5.5	2.5	4	0	8.5	8.5	6	11	7.5	2	50.5	0
482–473	7.5	2	10	0	10.5	1.5	3	1.5	0	1.5	37.5	2
472–464	2	4.5	0	3.5	3	0	0	0	2		15	4
259-year total											1,211.5	38

[a] The "war score" is calculated as follows: In any single campaign each of the thirteen major powers involved is computed as one point, while each small state involved is computed as one-half point. The yearly score is the total points of all the campaigns in that year. The thirteen major powers are Ch'i, Ch'in, Chin, Ch'u, Ch'en, Cheng, Lu, Sung, Ts'ai, Ts'ao, Wey, Wu, and Yen.

titative values in an effort to reflect these differences. Among the 172
states, there were twelve that Ssu-ma Ch'ien considered major powers.
These are Ch'i, Chin, Ch'in, Ch'u, Cheng, Lu, Ts'ao, Sung, Ts'ai,
Ch'en, Yen, and Wey. The state of Wu should also be included after
the year 584 B.C., when it appeared as a factor in Chinese affairs with a
military campaign against a neighboring state.[10] Each involvement of
one of these thirteen states in a war has been assigned one point in a
yearly score; a single participation of any of the remaining small states
is worth half a point. For example, in 645 B.C., Ch'u invaded Hsü;
and Lu, Ch'en, Wey, Cheng, Ts'ao, Ch'i, and Hsu formed an alliance
to help Hsü.* Including Ch'u, nine states were involved, seven major
and two minor. The score for this campaign is thus 8.[11] The yearly
score is the sum of the scores of all wars that the *Tso Chuan* records
for that year.

Table 5 shows the yearly scores in groups of ten years, covering the
historical period of the *Tso Chuan*. In the next-to-last column, total
scores are given for thirty-year periods corresponding to the nine
"stages" of the previous chapter. Note that the average total score for
the first two stages (107.5) is far below the average for all stages (140.4);
also that the number of peaceful years in the second stage is significantly higher than the average number (4.4) of peaceful years for all
stages. The steep fall in the score for the seventh stage, which had over
twice the average number of peaceful years, can probably be credited
to an interstate meeting in 546 B.C. that established a general truce.[12]
But by that time there were only two or three large powers capable of
launching a war. Even though the frequency of wars went up again
after the state leaders who participated in the truce conference were
replaced by a new generation, the score in the eighth stage is still below the average of 140.4. Only 15 years of the last stage are discussed
in the *Tso Chuan,* but doubling the 15-year total yields a far lower
30-year score than the average.†

The period with the highest frequency of wars lies between the
seventh and seventeenth decades of the Ch'un Ch'iu period. This century coincides roughly with the period in which the minister class
achieved its greatest power. Although it is unfair to place all the
blame for the incessant warfare on the ministers, the most ambitious
ministers probably stood to benefit from wars. The story is familiar:
under pressures of war a ruler loses control of his army to a minister-

---

* Two states were named Hsü. Here 徐 is romanized without the umlaut.

† Four of the years included in the last stage in Table 5 are simply passed over by
the annals. Since we have no information about them, we cannot assume they were
peaceful.

general, who then has the means to usurp control of the state itself. During the power shift from ruler to minister in Ch'un Ch'iu China, it seems that rulers came more and more to delegate military and diplomatic leadership to ministers. For instance, an interstate conference of 570 B.C. was attended only by ministers.[13] At least two major wars were conducted by ministers: a campaign against Ch'i in 589 B.C. was both initiated and conducted by the ministers of Chin, Lu, and Wey; and the invasion of Ch'in in 559 B.C. by an 18-state force, though nominally led by the duke of Chin, was in reality commanded by his ministers.[14] The truce agreement of 546 B.C. was signed by ministers of major powers instead of the sovereigns, whereas formerly rulers met personally; for example, an interstate conference of 651 B.C. was attended by the rulers of Ch'i, Lu, Sung, Wey, Cheng, Hsü, and Ts'ao.[15]

Successful ministers were also rewarded generously for victorious military campaigns. For example, the duke of Chin gave 1,000 families of captives as slaves to a minister who had conducted a highly successful incursion against a group of barbarian tribes in 594 B.C., and a second minister, on whose recommendation the first had been appointed, was given a piece of territory equal in size to a small state.[16] In 563 B.C. an alliance of several states attacked a small independent feudatory with the intention of presenting the entire state to Hsiang Shu, a minister of Sung.[17] Many ministers were enfeoffed with territory from conquered states. The ancient principality of Wei, conquered by Chin in 661 B.C., was given to an important Chin minister; his descendants took the surname Wei and made an important power of their domain by the Chan Kuo period.[18] The rich rewards of land and slaves increased the power of ministers relative to rulers, and helped to break up the feudal system in China.

Of the 75 vanquished states whose exact dates of conquest are known, 37 were conquered between the seventh and seventeenth decades of the Ch'un Ch'iu period, when, as stated above, the power of the minister class was at or near its zenith. The advantages this class obtained by military conquest may help explain this fact.*

Although familial relationships played an important part in the behavior patterns of the Ch'un Ch'iu people, many rulers had their

---

* Ku Tung-kao listed 172 Ch'un Ch'iu states in *CCTS*, 5, in which he recorded the locations of states, the surnames and ranks of their rulers, and the dates of conquest. Some of the states were conquered before or after the Ch'un Ch'iu period, but a majority of at least 110 came to an end during it. There are 75 states whose exact years of extinction have been recorded; 10 ended in the first 60 years of the Ch'un Ch'iu, and 21 in the last 80 years, but 44, more than half of them, saw their last days during 662–543 B.C.

territories annexed by their kinsmen of stronger states. The conquest of the small state of Yü by Chin in 655 B.C. is an example. The states of Yü, Kuo, and Chin were ruled at that time by dukes possessing the royal surname, who were regarded as descendants of Chou rulers and therefore kinsmen. The duke of Chin asked the duke of Yü to let the Chin army pass through Yü en route to an assault on Kuo. A minister of Yü warned his ruler against a possible Chin plot to invest Yü upon the army's return from Kuo. The duke of Yü was confident of the good intentions of Chin, notwithstanding the minister's argument that the duke of Kuo was no less a kinsman of Chin, and gave the desired permission. Kuo was easily taken by Chin, and Yü was, in fact, sacked by the returning Chin army.[19]

The state of Teng was defeated by Ch'u in 688 B.C. in much the same way. The ruler of Ch'u, on his way to attack the state of Shen, visited Teng, a small principality ruled by his maternal uncle, who was happy to extend his hospitality to his nephew. Three other nephews of the duke of Teng, who were in the duke's service, suspected the Ch'u ruler of treachery and recommended that he be put to death. The duke vetoed this proposal as inhumane. Subsequently, the ruler of Ch'u assaulted Teng on his way back from Shen, and ten years later Teng was annexed by Ch'u.[20]

From the two stories it may be inferred that some sovereigns, placing too much faith in feelings of kinship, were destroyed by unscrupulous relatives bent on their own aggrandizement. Despite the survival of some familial feeling and chivalrous spirit in interstate affairs, no fewer than 110 states were extinguished and annexed during the Ch'un Ch'iu period, leaving 22 that survived the struggle for existence.[21]

The Fate of the Defeated

What became of the aristocrats of the subjugated states? In general, the extant records give no answer, although some bits of information have been more or less accidentally included. In Ch'un Ch'iu times a defeated ruler usually did not know whether his conqueror would spare his life; a coffin was carried by the vanquished ruler in making his surrender to the victor. This ritual is mentioned twice in the *Tso Chuan*, when Ch'u defeated Hsü in 654 B.C. and Lai in 538 B.C. In both cases the lives of the conquered rulers were spared.[22] Other unfortunate rulers were sometimes put to death as sacrificial victims. The *Tso Chuan* records the sacrifice of the ruler of the small state of Tseng by the duke of Sung in 641 B.C., and the immolation of the crown prince of Ts'ai by the ruler of Ch'u in 531 B.C.[23]

Usually, however, a defeated ruler could expect better treatment, as can be inferred from the following excerpt from the *Tso Chuan*. In 597 B.C. Ch'u breached the last remaining defensive wall of Cheng and invested the capital. The duke of Cheng had no alternative but to surrender, and went to the Ch'u camp to make formal submission. He first confessed his fault in not having been a faithful subordinate of Ch'u, then said:

If you carry us away to the south of the Chiang [the Yellow River] to occupy the seashore lands, that will have to be. If you take the state and give it to some other to whom we shall be servants, that will have to be. If you regard the former friendly relations between our states with affection and wish to obtain blessings from the kings Li and Hsüan and the dukes Huan and Wu, then do not extinguish our altars, but let me change my course so that I may serve your lordship equally with the governors of the nine new districts that you have established. This will be your kindness, and it is my desire, but what I do not dare to hope for. I have presumed to disclose all my heart to you. Your lordship will take your measures accordingly.[24]

The plea of the duke of Cheng was heeded by the ruler of Ch'u, and Cheng was allowed to remain intact. Thus a defeated state might be treated in one of three ways. First, the state might be allowed to retain its identity, but only as a satellite of the conqueror. Second, the residents of the state might be given to other states as slaves. Third, the population of the conquered state might be resettled in territory belonging to the victorious state. The *Tso Chuan* states all three possibilities.

Only the first method allows the social order of the defeated state to remain basically unchanged. The states of Ch'en, Ts'ai, and Hsü were restored to a measure of independence after having been conquered.[25] Sometimes only the ruler and government officials of a conquered state were deported while the commoners were allowed to remain in their homes; in some cases the ruler alone was taken away. In 520 B.C. the barbarian state of Ku was defeated by Chin and its ruler was carried off to Chin. The Chin commander ordered that the Ku ruler could be accompanied only by his immediate household, and that all other citizens of Ku must remain behind and accept the authority of a governor appointed by the Chin ruler. A former courtier of Ku, despite the order, followed his lord to Chin, where he was told by the Chin ruler, "There is a lord in Ku. Go back and serve your new lord. I will settle your rank and salary."*

---

* *KY*, 15/2. Even though some ministers of a conquered government might be kept on to help the new masters govern the state, a rearrangement of personnel was sometimes made. Ministers of the ruling group were quite often not used in their former offices by the conquerors and so suffered a loss of position and social status.

The ritual for surrendering prisoners after a state's defeat is recorded in the *Tso Chuan* in some detail. In 548 B.C. Cheng occupied the capital of Ch'en. The Ch'en ruler came to surrender holding the sacred tablet of the Ch'en earth deity, and ordered that men be separated from women and the two groups be bound to await the conquerors. One Cheng commander grasped the end of the line that fettered the Ch'en captives, and another Cheng officer counted them.[26] In this case the Ch'en people were treated mercifully and none were deported to Cheng, although on other occasions captives were presented to the royal house of Chou or to other states in order to proclaim a victory. A passage in the *Tso Chuan* relates that Ch'i "reported victory" to Lu by sending captives; this act was criticized on the ground that only the royal capital, and no mere state, was the proper recipient of this form of tribute.[27]

The *Tso Chuan* records several other instances of the presentation of captives after a victory. In 706 B.C. the heir apparent of Cheng led an army to aid Ch'i in repelling an invasion by barbarians. The barbarians were soundly defeated, and the Cheng commander presented two captive generals and three hundred warriors to the ruler of Ch'i.[28] In 655 B.C., after Chin conquered Kuo and Yü, the duke of Yü and his minister Ching Po were presented to Ch'in as part of the dowry of a Chin princess married to the duke of Ch'in. This is a clear example of the degradation of a ruler and a minister to slave status.[29] In 632 B.C. Chin defeated Ch'u in a decisive battle at Ch'eng-pu. The duke of Chin reported the victory to the Chou king, sending one thousand captured Ch'u soldiers and 100 chariots, each with four horses.[30] In 593–592 B.C. Chin annexed a cluster of supposedly barbarian states and twice presented captives from these states to the royal capital.[31] When Ch'u invaded Cheng in 584 B.C., a Ch'u governor was captured and sent as a gift to Chin.[32] In the summer of 504 B.C. the chancellor of Lu went to Chin to present captives taken in a battle earlier that year with Cheng.[33]

Besides those given away as presents, large numbers of captives taken in battle or as spoils of victory were sometimes retained by the conquering state. Some were probably given to generals as rewards. In 594 B.C. a Chin general was rewarded with one thousand families of the defeated barbarians for having added new territory to the state.[34] The small state of Wey was defeated in 500 B.C. by troops commanded by a powerful Chin minister who later appropriated for himself five hundred Wey families allegedly given as tribute to Chin. He resettled them on his estates and kept them as his own serfs.[35] According to a legend-like story (dating from the Chan Kuo period but referring to Ch'un Ch'iu times), after the state of Kuo was conquered by Chin, one of its ministers was sold into slavery and finally became a herder of cattle in Ch'in. A Ch'in official who recognized the ability of the Kuo captive bought him for five sheepskins and recommended that the Ch'in ruler employ him.[36] Yen Tzu, a minister of Ch'i, while traveling in Chin happened on a man carrying a bundle of hay on a fur piece spread across his shoulders. Seeing the fur, Yen Tzu suspected that the man was not really a peasant and upon inquiry found out that he was a captive from his own state. Yen Tzu immediately unhitched one of his three chariot horses and used it to purchase the freedom of his compatriot.[37]

These few examples tell us something of the fate of war captives in the Ch'un Ch'iu period. It is safe to assume that many captives lost all prior social status and lived out their lives in strange lands, in a degraded status, and without hope of repatriation. It follows that every defeat or conquest of a state caused the social degradation of some former citizens of the defeated state; a downward social mobility took place. The number of people who thus lost status is not even approximately known, but since several hundred battles took place and one-hundred-odd states were extinguished during the Ch'un Ch'iu period, the number must have been quite large.

Wars in the Chan Kuo Period

The number of people socially degraded as a result of wars and conquests in the Chan Kuo period must have been less than in the Ch'un Ch'iu, since only sixteen states were extinguished by the seven great powers of the time, and six of these were in turn conquered by Ch'in. Despite the smaller number of states involved, however, the frequency of conflicts in the Chan Kuo period was not much less than in the Ch'un Ch'iu era, and Chan Kuo wars were in general longer and on a larger scale.

The frequency of conflicts in the Chan Kuo can be computed with the help of a chronological chart of the major events of the period given in the *Shih Chi*. The chart begins with the first year of the reign of King Yuan of Chou (475 B.C.) and ends with the overthrow of Ch'in (207 B.C.).[38] The events occurring in the seven major states and in the royal domain of Chou are set forth concurrently in the chart. A statistical evaluation of the Chan Kuo conflicts recorded in the *Shih Chi* chart appears in Table 6. The method of scoring the wars is the same as for Table 5: each involvement in a battle of any of the seven great powers—Chao, Ch'i, Ch'in, Ch'u, Han, Wei, and Yen—in a battle is assigned 1 point in a yearly score, and each participation of a small state in a conflict has a value of half a point.

The first year of the chart in Table 6 is 463 B.C., the next year after the end of the Ch'un Ch'iu period. The last year considered is 222 B.C., the year before the beginning of the Ch'in dynasty, when Ch'in Shih Huang Ti completed the conquest and unification of China, rather than 207 B.C. Thus the statistical chart in Table 6 covers a 242-year period, roughly as long as the 259-year period of the Ch'un Ch'iu chart.

It is surprising to note that the total war score of the Chan Kuo era, the so-called Warring States period, is only 468.5, with 89 peaceful years. These statistics show a period of less military struggle, even taking into account the larger scale of individual battles in Chan Kuo times, than the Ch'un Ch'iu period with its war score of 1,211.5 and only 38 years of peace. Three factors may explain the large difference in the figures for the two periods. First, the chronological chart in the *Shih Chi* is not as complete or detailed as the records in the *Tso Chuan*. The *Shih Chi* chart mentions only major campaigns and leaves out many small-scale skirmishes and raids. Second, minor disputes between states in the Chan Kuo period were less likely to develop into armed clashes, since the Chan Kuo governments wielded tighter control over their domains than Ch'un Ch'iu rulers, who lacked firm authority over their many semi-independent feudal lords.[39] Third, mathematical probability shows that, all other factors being constant, the probability of conflicts between many states is greater than that of conflict between few states. There were twelve or thirteen major states in the Ch'un Ch'iu period, plus seven or eight score small ones; seven large states held firm control of China in Chan Kuo times. The mathematics need not concern us here, but the difference between the probabilities of conflict for the two periods is considerably greater than the ratio 13/7 would imply.

The war score of the Chan Kuo period is not alone sufficient to measure the extent of interstate disturbances or their effects. The duration and larger scale of Chan Kuo wars must be taken into account. Usually a war of the Ch'un Ch'iu period consisted of a single battle, after which either the defeated troops fled or the parties negotiated a truce. Only when fortified cities were besieged did wars take longer. The battle of Ch'eng-p'u in 632 B.C. is an example of such a siege.

In the winter of 633 B.C. Ch'u besieged the capital of Sung, then an ally of Chin, and Chin sent a large force to aid Sung by attacking Ts'ao, an ally of Ch'u. Neither campaign was very intensive; no major

TABLE 6

The Frequency of Wars in the Chan Kuo Period[a]

Years B.C.	War score in each year of decade										Total war score		Peaceful years	
	1	2	3	4	5	6	7	8	9	10				
463–454	0	0	0	0	0	3	0	1.5	2.5	3.5	9		7	
453–444	0	0	0	0	0	1.5	0	1.5	1.5	0	4.5	14.5	7	23
443–434	0	1	0	0	0	0	0	0	0	0	1		9	
433–424	0	1.5	1.5	0	0	0	0	0	0	1.5	4.5		7	
423–414	0	0	0	0	2	0	0	0	0	8	10	31	8	20
413–404	4	1.5	0	2	1.5	3	0	0	3.5	3.5	16.5		5	
403–394	0	2	5.5	0	1.5	1.5	0	1.5	0	3.5	17.5		4	
393–384	0	0	5	1.5	0	3	2	4.5	0	2	18.5	60	3	10
383–374	3.5	0	6	1.5	5.5	1.5	3.5	1.5	0	7.5	24		3	
373–364	5	2	4	4	4	0	3	1.5	4	0	26		2	
363–354	2	2	0	0	2	3.5	0	1.5	4	5.5	23.5	57.5	3	11
353–344	2	2	5	0	0	0	0	0	2	0	8		6	
343–334	3	2	2	4	1.5	0	0	2	0	4	18.5		4	
333–324	2	1.5	4	4	0	1.5	0	4	0	2	20	66.5	2	8
323–314	3	1.5	2	0	6	7	3.5	2	3.5	2	28		2	
313–304	8	1.5	1.5	2	2	0	2	0	0	4	21		3	
303–294	0	10	2	2	6	2	4	5.5	2	3	34.5	85	2	6
293–284	0	2	4	4	2	2	5.5	2	8	2	29.5		1	
283–274	2	2	6	4	2	2	3	3	2	4	30		0	
273–264	4	2	4	2	2	0	2	4	2	0	24	76	1	5
263–254	4	2	2	0	0	4	7	3	0	2	22		4	
253–244	0	2	0	5	0	10	2	0	2	2	25		3	
243–234	2	8	2	0	2	0	2	3	2	2	23	68	2	6
233–224	2	2	2	2	2	0	4	2	2	2	20		1	
223–222	6	4									10			
242-year total											468.5		89	

[a] The "war score" is calculated as follows: In any single campaign, each of the seven major powers involved is computed as one point, while each small state is computed as one half-point. The yearly score is the total points of all campaigns in that year. The seven major powers are Ch'i, Ch'in, Ch'u, Chao, Han, Wei, and Yen.

battles are recorded for the siege of Sung, although the invaders of Ts'ao suffered some casualties. Chin defeated Ts'ao within a month, but the Ch'u army surrounding the Sung capital still had not taken it. On the twenty-fourth day after the fall of Ts'ao, the armies of Chin and Ch'u and their allies met in battle at Ch'eng-p'u. The fighting lasted only one day; the Ch'u forces were defeated and fled, and three days later the Chin army marched homeward. Thus, although the siege of the two cities had begun some months before, the full-scale armed conflict lasted only one day.[40]

As the Ch'un Ch'iu period drew to a close, wars tended to be of longer duration. In 506 B.C. Wu invaded Ch'u and five major battles were fought before Wu invested the capital of Ch'u. The campaign up to that time had involved troop movements of several hundred miles. After another battle Ch'u temporarily stopped the advance of Wu. Not long after, Ch'in sent troops to the aid of Ch'u, and in the summer of 505 B.C. Wu was defeated several times. After seven battles the Wu forces were driven out of Ch'u. Thus the war between Wu and Ch'u lasted more than half a year and involved at least thirteen battles.[41]

Wars of the Chan Kuo period were, in general, longer still; the siege of a city usually took several months. For instance, the Ch'u forces took five months to besiege the Han city of Yung-shih.[42] Major battles sometimes lasted ten days.[43] Reinforcements sent from Ch'in to aid the Han city of Hua-yang took eight days to defeat an army of Chao and Wei troops that had besieged the city.[44] In 314 B.C. Ch'i took advantage of internal disorders in Yen to attack that state, and invested it after a campaign of some fifty days. Although Yen put up almost no resistance, the ruler of Ch'i boasted that a miracle must have enabled him to conquer a state in "only fifty days."[45] Thirty years later Yen revenged herself by invading Ch'i, capturing the Ch'i ruler, and overrunning half of his territory. Ch'i continued to resist, however, and after five years of struggle the Yen army was finally driven out.[46]

The Size of Ch'un Ch'iu and Chan Kuo Armies

Chan Kuo wars not only lasted longer but took place on a much larger scale than Ch'un Ch'iu conflicts. Armies of the Ch'un Ch'iu period were usually measured in numbers of chariots; the following examples are taken from the *Tso Chuan*.

In 722 B.C. Cheng used a force of two hundred chariots to put down a rebellion.[47] The Wey forces surviving after being defeated by the barbarians in 660 B.C. consisted of only thirty chariots; several years later the Wey army had regained a strength of three hundred chariots.[48] In 548 B.C. Cheng invaded Ch'en with an army of seven hundred chariots.[49] The entire army of Lu, a second-rate power, at an inspection in 534 B.C. was one thousand chariots strong, and in 529 B.C. Chin, the strongest state at that time, possessed an army of four thousand chariots.[50] The small state of Chu possessed six hundred chariots at the close of the Ch'un Ch'iu period.[51]

Although we know that several hundred chariots sometimes took part in a single battle, it is difficult to calculate the actual numerical size of an army, since the number of foot soldiers per chariot is not recorded. The chariot itself carried a driver and two warriors. A tradition exists that 72 soldiers were assigned to each chariot,[52] but there is reason to believe this figure is too high. In 660 B.C. Ch'i sent three hundred chariots and three thousand men to Wey, and in 632 B.C. Chin presented one hundred chariots and one thousand Ch'u captives to the Chou capital.[53] Both examples imply a ratio of 10 men per chariot. Another possible ratio is 30 men per chariot; a couplet in one of the Lu verses of the *Shih Ching* says that the duke of Lu had 1,000 chariots and 30,000 foot soldiers.[54] The squad of five seems to be the smallest unit of infantrymen accompanying the chariot, as in the Cheng army in 707 B.C.[55]

In any case the number of foot soldiers per chariot does not seem to have been large. In 541 B.C. Chin forces opposed barbarian foot soldiers in a mountainous area. The Chin commander decided not to use his chariots, and reorganized the chariot soldiers into five-man squads. If the Chin commander had had plenty of foot soldiers accompanying the chariots, he would not have needed to use his chariot personnel to augment his unmounted troops.[56]

The evidence seems to indicate that the number of infantrymen per chariot was not large and was probably a multiple of five. If we assume it to be ten, in addition to three warriors on each chariot, then the biggest army on record for the Ch'un Ch'iu period is that of Chin in the battle between Ch'i and Chin in 589 B.C. This army, with eight hundred war chariots, may be estimated to have totaled about ten thousand men: twenty-four hundred chariot soldiers and about eight thousand foot soldiers.[57] The *Tso Chuan* also mentions the use of infantrymen in fighting units separate from the chariots. In 570 B.C. a general of Ch'u invaded Wu with an army of three hundred armored soldiers and three thousand light armored troops.[58] In a battle between Lu and Ch'i of 556 B.C., three hundred Lu warriors broke through a Ch'i encirclement in order to send a messenger for help.[59] In 484 B.C. Lu mobilized seven thousand armored soldiers to repel an invasion of Ch'i.[60] A noble of Wu led five thousand infantrymen to attack an army of Yüeh in 482 B.C.[61] The figures just given, combined with the previously stated figures for infantrymen assigned to war chariots, indicate that Ch'un Ch'iu armies had troops numbering in the thousands but rarely exceeding ten thousand.

TABLE 7

War Casualties in Chan Kuo Battles

Year B.C.	Number of casualties	Defeated state
364	60,000	Alliance of Han, Chao, and Wei
354	7,000	Wei
317	80,000	Alliance of Han and Chao
312	80,000	Ch'u
307	60,000	Han
300	30,000	Ch'u
293	240,000	Alliance of Han and Wei
280	20,000	Chao
274	40,000	Wei
273	150,000	Alliance of Chao, Han, and Wei
260	450,000	Chao

SOURCE: "Liu Kuo Nien Piao" in *Shih Chi*, 15.

The size of Chan Kuo armies, on the other hand, was much larger. Table 7 shows numbers of casualties reported to have been inflicted by Ch'in in several Chan Kuo battles. The reliability of these huge totals is open to question. The historical records of Ch'in, the main source of information used by the *Shih Chi* for the Chan Kuo period, may have greatly exaggerated these figures, especially since they concern battles in which Ch'in was the victor.[62] The total for the battle of 260 B.C., however, is not necessarily incredible, since the entire Chao army of the Ch'in frontier was apparently massacred after its surrender. Also, Ch'in had to mobilize its entire manpower for this battle, including youths down to 15 years of age.[63] After this battle Chao had only 130,000 men to resist an invasion by a Yen army of 600,000.[64]

To judge from the size of armies, the scale of war in the Chan Kuo period was ten times that of the Ch'un Ch'iu.* In the Ch'un Ch'iu period of many states, an army of 30,000 men was considered large; in the Chan Kuo period of seven great states, hundreds of thousands of men were required to seize large cities, and wars often dragged on for several years.[65] Although Chan Kuo wars were less frequent, their generally longer duration and greater scale caused interstate disturbances at least as profound as those of the Ch'un Ch'iu conflicts. Larger areas were despoiled during the Chan Kuo period, forcing many people to flee their ancestral homes and destroying their social status. Bigger wars caused greater numbers of prisoners to be captured and either massacred or enslaved. Although no statistics are available, the number of people who were deprived of social status by the Chan Kuo conflicts must have been tremendous.†

The Appearance of Cavalry and Infantry

If war spelled disaster to the defeated nobility of the weaker states, it spelled opportunity to an emerging class of career military men, both warriors and tacticians, many of them from classes not previously eligible for service. Both the negative and the positive social effects of war became more apparent as the Chan Kuo period progressed.

During and before the Ch'un Ch'iu period, fighting was the profession of the aristocracy alone. Driving a war chariot, a light, bouncing vehicle drawn by four galloping horses, required a long training period, as did accurate bow shooting from a lurching chariot. Driving

---

* Derk Bodde believes that ancient China's population was too small, its weapons too primitive, and its supply and command techniques too crude to make such huge armies credible (see Bodde, *China's First Unifier,* p. 5). However, since the state of Wei had some hundred *hsien* or districts, each with 10,000 households, its population alone must have been about five million (see *ibid.,* p. 137, and *CKT,* 20/1, 24/2). Wei could thus have raised an army of three to five hundred thousand fairly easily, and such states as Ch'i, Ch'in, and Ch'u were even more populous. A census of A.D. 2 gave the Han empire's population as 59,594,978 (see *CHSP,* 28b/49, and *KSTK,* 1956, I, 155); the Chan Kuo population may have been almost as large. The main body of the Ch'in army was once given as 600,000 men (see *SCHI,* 73/6). As for the number of casualties, even though deserting soldiers of a routed army were usually counted as casualties, military tactics that use fire and flood, sword and spear, and the deadly crossbow (which is anything but a primitive weapon) are quite adequate for perpetrating such massive slaughter. The logistics of such huge armies were not beyond ancient peoples; witness the building of the pyramids of Egypt and of the Great Wall. Although I agree with Bodde that the Ch'in official records are probably exaggerated, I think the figures in Table 7 are closer to the facts than Bodde believes.
† After the unification by Ch'in, the elite of the six conquered states lost their social status and were downgraded in rank. This phenomenon will not be discussed, however, since it took place in a period beyond the scope of this study.

and archery were listed among the six arts that were supposed to constitute the basic knowledge of a nobleman.[66] Thus the military profession was limited to those familiar with these special techniques. Commoners served in battle only as auxiliary foot soldiers supposedly accompanying the chariots; they must have had difficulty in keeping up with vehicles drawn by four energetic horses. All accounts of early Ch'un Ch'iu wars describe only the charges of war chariots; until 570 B.C. we do not hear of the use of infantry as the only force on the battlefield.[67]

The art of battle became so refined that even in fiercest combat chivalrous manners were required of the nobility. Strict procedures for driver and aide were followed in the delivery of challenges.[68] Upon encountering an enemy of superior rank, a warrior had to take care not to offend him, especially if his foe happened to be a ruler.[69] Polite words were exchanged even between a pursued charioteer and his pursuer. Courtesy in battle was the mark of a gentleman; a Chin warrior once took the trouble to shoot a deer and present it to his foe.[70] A Ch'u general, challenging the Chin ruler in 632 B.C., said, with more than a mere turn of a phrase, "Will Your Excellency permit our knights and yours to play a game?"[71] For these aristocrats, a war was also a game. Granet observed that it was much more than a clash of arms; it was a duel of moral values, a trial of honor.[72]

Toward the end of the Ch'un Ch'iu period, the role of infantry gradually became more significant. Wu and Yüeh, the two giant states of the south, favored the use of foot soldiers, since the many lakes, rivers, and swamps of their territory limited the use of chariots. The king of Wu brought 10,000 foot soldiers with him on his trip north to the meeting of Huang-ch'ih in 482 B.C.[73] In the battle between Ch'i and Lu in 484 B.C., the Lu army consisted of 7,000 armored soldiers. The commanding general, a disciple of Confucius, led a troop of three hundred foot soldiers, presumably all commoners, in a charge with long spears instead of the usual bows and arrows.[74]

The reasons for replacing chariots by infantry are not clear, although two causes may be suggested. The first is that chariots were quite expensive; the second, that they were inefficient. They were counted as units of wealth; a state would be said to possess about a thousand chariots while a noble family might own a hundred. A favorite of the chancellor of Ch'u was once envied for being rich enough to own horses for several chariots.[75] Thus the expansion of an army consisting mostly of chariots could be prohibitively expensive to a state. A solution to the cost problem was the increase of foot soldier units in an army, which lessened the importance of the war chariots. The usual description of the military strength of a Chan Kuo state was "one thousand chariots, ten thousands of cavalry, and several hundred thousand armored soldiers."[76] The number of chariots remained about the same as in the Ch'un Ch'iu period, while other units of the army were greatly augmented or newly added.

Cavalry first made its appearance in China during the Chan Kuo period. The northern states apparently adopted the idea of cavalry warfare from nomadic tribes. King Wu-ling of Chao adopted the dress of the nomads as well as their horse tactics.[77] Cavalry was probably a good substitute for war chariots, especially when high speed was required, as in charging and flanking movements. Nevertheless, when compared with the tenfold greater masses of infantry in Chan Kuo armies, as reported in documents concerning the military strength of the states, cavalry represented a very small part of the whole.[78] The foot soldier has played the principal role in warfare throughout later Chinese history.

The second reason for the replacement of chariots by infantry concerns the innate disadvantages of chariot warfare. As early as the beginning of the Ch'un Ch'iu period, a Cheng general, in a campaign of 714 B.C. against the barbarian Jung, worried over the danger of a raid on his chariots by the light infantry of the enemy.[79] In swampy areas chariots were very easily trapped; Duke Hui of Chin was captured by Ch'in troops when his chariot stuck fast in the mud.[80] Chariots were also of little use in mountainous terrain with poor roads or no roads at all. In 541 B.C. the state of Chin fought several mountain tribes in the north. The Chin commander, realizing the uselessness of his chariots, reorganized his soldiers into infantry squads and was then able to defeat the enemy.[81] Throughout the Ch'un Ch'iu period, states in the nuclear area of China, the middle and lower valleys of the Yellow River, were constantly at war with the non-Chinese tribes of the mountainous regions within or on their borders. The formerly non-Chinese states in the Yangtze valley also underwent a steady Sinification by frequent involvement with Chinese states. In the circumstances, it is natural that military tactics suitable to mountainous and swampy terrains should be favored.[82] Thus there seems to have been sufficient reason for the supplanting of expensive and inefficient war chariots by cavalry and foot soldiers.[83]

The aristocratic warfare of chariots and archery finally gave way to infantry tactics using masses of foot soldiers advancing on foot with spears or swords in hand. Such tactics required less individual skill but many more soldiers; hence the Chan Kuo army differed radically from its Ch'un Ch'iu counterpart. Chivalry and gentlemanly conduct disappeared from combat; masses of tough foot soldiers, mostly hardworking peasants inured to hardship and toil, replaced the gallant, chariot-riding noblemen.

Both the increase in the size of armies and the changes in their character made the conscription of commoners necessary. Conscription was known in Ch'un Ch'iu times, but it is not clear how it was organized. Although recruits were assigned to military units under the command of ministers, the emphasis seems to have been on the distribution of tribute among nobles rather than on military organization. For instance, the people of Lu were divided among three armies led by the three most powerful nobles of the state, who were normally supported by tribute paid by the people under their command.[84] By Chan Kuo times, military conscription systems were commonplace. Shang Yang of Ch'in imposed on the Ch'in people a militaristic system of five- and ten-family units; the draft age seems to have been 15 years.[85] In the state of Ch'u, all males under the age of 60 and 5 ch'ih or more in height were obliged to serve in the army.[86] Sometimes the people of a certain area were required to defend their territory against a specified enemy, usually the state bordering on their area. For instance, the people of western Ch'i were to be drafted only in the event of invasion by Chao, those of northern Ch'i only if Ch'i were attacked by Yen. Different areas of a state were apparently supposed to supply troops for particular units of the army. King Wu-ling of Chao charged a single district of Chao to produce only cavalrymen.[87]

Using the common people as a source of manpower, Han and Wei, the smallest states, each maintained an army of about 300,000 men,[88] while Ch'in and Ch'u, the largest states, were able to support armies of about 1,000,000 men;[89] these were mostly seasonal armies of peasant draftees. A large city such as Lin-tzu could have provided 210,000 men for military service from the population of 70,000 families.[90]

Although we know very little about the common soldier and his deeds, it seems probable that many simple peasants found army life attractive and became career military men. This transformation is itself a type of large-scale social mobility when it involves great numbers of people. Changes of this kind have occurred frequently through history; but they are particularly important in a period such as the Chan Kuo, in which many wars are fought by great masses of common people.

The Role of Career Military Men

The humiliation, degradation, or enslavement of vanquished people after their defeat or capture in battle has been discussed. We must also consider the upgrading of others who distinguished themselves in warfare. During periods of strife, a ruler is usually anxious to retain the services of those who have demonstrated skill in war and generous in rewarding them for further victories. In the Chan Kuo period, two types of military personnel were particularly needed: the fierce warrior and the cunning tactician.

The class of professional warriors had already emerged in the late Ch'un Ch'iu period, even while chivalry still survived among the aristocracy. In 552 B.C. the duke of Ch'i set up a system of conferring honorific titles on the valorous in battle and considered two of his fiercest warriors as candidates for the honor. A warrior of Chin known for his bravery asked to be given such a title when he sought sanctuary with the duke of Ch'i after the downfall of his former master. This seems to be the first instance in Chinese history of a title bestowed solely as a reward for valor in battle.[91] Two years later, when Ch'i sent a force to attack Wey, the commanders of the vanguard, the rear echelon, and both flanks, their aides, and the driver and aide to the duke himself were all renowned warriors who were seemingly unrelated to the Ch'i noble families. This state of affairs elicited harsh criticism from a Ch'i noble.[92]

During the Chan Kuo period, even common soldiers had to maintain their physical strength. A Wei soldier had to be strong enough to carry armor, to pull a heavy crossbow, and to march 100 *li* in half a day carrying a full set of armor, weapons, and supplies. Those who met this standard were exempted from taxation and labor services. In the army of Ch'i, skill at boxing was much encouraged, and rewards were given for the killing of even one enemy in combat.[93]

Able strategists and tacticians were also much in demand in Chan Kuo times. Sometimes both diplomatic talent and military ability were possessed by one person, as for example by Chang I and Kung-sun Yen. Both were clever in winning allies for their states and in isolating their enemies, and both were competent generals in the field.[94] Although such persons were respected by most of their contemporaries, Mencius took a dim view of their activities.[95] A professional tactician known as Sun Tzu or Sun Pin (Sun the Cripple) was so celebrated that he almost became a legend.[96] The *Han Fei Tzu* mentions that many an ambitious man, wishing to become a competent tactician, studied books attributed to Sun Tzu and to Wu Ch'i, another famous statesman-strategist.[97]

The way upward in the military hierarchy had already opened by the end of the Ch'un Ch'iu period; meritorious accomplishments on the battlefield were to be duly rewarded. In 550 B.C., during a feud between the Fan and Luan families of Chin, a slave of Fan asked to be freed if he slew a certain fearsome warrior of Luan. He succeeded and was promptly given his freedom.[98] In 493 B.C. a war broke out between Cheng and Chin. The Chin commander announced that persons who performed well in battle were to be rewarded according to their status. Officials were to be enfeoffed; *shih* were to be given 100,-000 *mou* of land; commoners, artisans, and merchants were to be given official positions; and slaves or serfs were to be freed.[99] Thus there is no doubt that many people rose in social status at this time.

Military prowess continued to be rewarded in the Chan Kuo period. A Ch'in soldier who distinguished himself in war was awarded the services of five families.[100] Shang Yang, moreover, ruled that only those who excelled in war could enjoy a life of luxury.[101] The twenty honorific noble ranks of Ch'in were graded virtually by degree of military accomplishment.[102] This seems to be the first system of nobility in Chinese history in which military merit counted for everything and noble birth or kinship for nothing. Possibly this practice was not confined to Ch'in, though we have no direct evidence of its existence elsewhere.

In the Chan Kuo period all or almost all of the seven states produced men who rose from obscurity to generalship. We shall next consider some well-known Chan Kuo generals whose biographies were included in the *Shih Chi*.

Sun Tzu was of obscure origin. He was known as Sun Pin (Sun the Cripple), having suffered the humiliating punishment of having his feet cut off, after which he was spirited out of his native Wei by a Ch'i envoy. His knowledge of tactics so impressed the Ch'i ruler that he was made chief of staff. His advice contributed to two major victories for Ch'i in 343 B.C.[103]

Wu Ch'i was from a rich family but lost his fortune after several unsuccessful attempts at making his way in the world. He finally obtained an office in Lu and commanded troops in a victorious battle with Ch'i forces. Unpopular in Lu, he went to Wei, where he became first a field commander, then the military governor of a district of strategic importance. Later he went to Ch'u, where he was appointed chancellor in 382 B.C. In this capacity he instituted fiscal reforms—

abolishing unnecessary offices, stopping allowances for relatives of the ruling house—in an effort to marshal all possible resources for his task of building up Ch'u's military strength.[104]

Chang I was of obscure origin; he was quite poor, and was even suspected of having committed theft. His strategy in interstate conflicts won him the confidence of the Ch'in ruler in 328 B.C. He twice commanded armies and several times acted as ambassador to foreign states. At different times he was chancellor of Ch'in, Wei, and Ch'u.[105]

Shu-li Chi, a prince of Ch'in, served the Ch'in ruler as commanding general and as chancellor (309 B.C.).[106]

Kan Mao was not of noble birth. When he first arrived in Ch'in he served under a Ch'in general in a campaign in the west. Later, during the absence of this general, Kan Mao succeeded in putting down a rebellion in a state on Ch'in's western border. In 309 B.C. he was appointed to one of Ch'in's two chancellorships. In this capacity he commanded a large army in the siege of a strategically important city of Han in 307 B.C. Subsequently he led at least one military operation against Wei, after which he fell out of favor in Ch'in and was obliged to flee to Ch'i.[107]

Wei Jan, who was related to a Ch'in queen, held the chancellorship of Ch'in for a number of years after 295 B.C. Occasionally he commanded armed forces in Ch'in campaigns.[108]

Pai Ch'i, a career soldier of obscure origin, was recommended for promotion by Wei Jan. He rose from field officer to commander-in-chief, and was finally ennobled because of his distinguished record of victories. His most famous exploit was the defeat of a Chao army of 450,000 men at Ch'ang-ping. At that time he had been in the military service of Ch'in for 35 years, 294–260 B.C. Two years later he was demoted to common soldier for refusing to command an invasion that he said would fail. He was put to death one year after his demotion.[109]

Wang Chien, of unknown origin, was a general under Ch'in Shih Huang Ti before unification. He demanded in advance his reward for the conquest of Ch'u, stating that he expected never to be ennobled and therefore wanted to be sure of a suitable material reward, in the form of houses and lands. The conquest of Ch'u in 223 B.C. was his last and greatest military accomplishment. His son and grandson also became generals, and the Wang family bred a long succession of career military men.[110]

T'ien Ying, a brother of the Ch'i ruler, commanded Ch'i troops occasionally (343 B.C.).[111]

Lord Hsin-ling, a brother of the ruler of Wei, took command of a Wei troop by force and went to the aid of the besieged state of Chao in 257 B.C. He stayed in Chao for ten years, after which he was named commander-in-chief of the Wei army in 247 B.C. He then led an allied force of troops from five states in a punitive expedition against Ch'in. Some of his advisers and assistants compiled a book on military tactics.[112]

Lord Ch'un-shen, the son of the Ch'u ruler, was chancellor of Ch'u for many years. In 258 B.C. he led a large army to the aid of Chao.[113]

Lo I was the descendant of Lo Yang, a famous general who served under a Wei ruler at the beginning of the Chan Kuo period. Lo I was renowned for his knowledge of military affairs. At first he held office in Chao, but when Chao suffered from internal disturbances in 295 B.C. he went to Yen. The newly enthroned Yen ruler, anxious to rebuild the military strength of Yen in order to avenge an invasion by Ch'i, welcomed able refugees with great generosity and made Lo I deputy chancellor. Lo I advised that an alliance be made with friendly states to strengthen the proposed expedition of revenge. He then attacked Ch'i at the head of a five-state army and occupied more than half of its territory in 284 B.C., for which he was given noble rank. When the crown prince took the throne after the death of Lo I's former patron, the new ruler's hostility caused Lo I to flee to Chao, where he was given a noble title by the Chao ruler. His son and one of his relatives became generals of Chao.[114]

Lien P'o, a career soldier of Chao, was famous for his fierceness. He was commander-in-chief of the Chao army for a long period, and later was ennobled and given a titular chancellorship.[115]

Chao She was at first a tax collector; his competence impressed a Chao prince, who recommended him to the Chao ruler. After the invasion of Chao in 270 B.C., Lien P'o and the son of Lo I both tried unsuccessfully to rescue the besieged capital. Chao She was finally picked to lead a reinforcing army, succeeded in smashing the invader, and was ennobled as a reward. His son Chao K'uo became a general after Chao She's death, but though he was skilled in military tactics, he lacked experience and was defeated and killed at Ch'ang-ping in 260 B.C.[116] Chao She, famed for his knowledge of tactics, is named as the author of a discussion of military theory in a passage in the *Chan Kuo Ts'e*.[117]

Li Mu, a career soldier of Chao, was of unknown origin. His assigned post was the northern frontier, where his mission was to observe the barbarian tribes, although he later fought in battles between Chao and other states. He was ennobled and appointed commander-in-chief of the Chao army in 234 B.C.[118]

T'ien Tan, though a remote relative of the Ch'i ruling house, was at first merely a municipal clerk in the Ch'i capital. After the defeat of Ch'i by Yen in 284 B.C., he collected the remnants of the scattered Ch'i troops, rebuilt them into an army, and recovered all the lost territory. He enthroned the crown prince of Ch'i and was given noble rank and the chancellorship.[119]

Meng Ao, born in Ch'i, became a career officer of Ch'in. From 249 B.C. on, he served three Ch'in rulers and secured much territory for the state. His son became an officer under Wang Chien and participated in the last invasion of Ch'u in 223 B.C. Meng Ao's grandson, also a general of Ch'in, commanded 300,000 men in the construction of the Great Wall.[120]

Of the above twenty-four generals, only four—T'ien Ying, Shu-li Chi, Lord Hsin-ling, and Lord Ch'un-shen—were princes. One of the four, Lord Hsin-ling, took command of a Wei troop without a legal appointment. One other general was a relative of his ruler. Six generals were descendants of generals in the four families of Wang, Lo, Chao, and Meng. All the others, including the four first-generation generals of these four families, were of either obscure or alien origin. Broadly speaking, obscure origin and alien origin amounted to the same thing in the Chan Kuo period. If a man of noble family emigrated to another state, his rank in the new state depended strictly on his own character and ability.

There is definite information concerning the origins of some of the twenty-four generals. Chao She and T'ien Tan were non-military officials of low rank; Wu Ch'i, Shang Yang, Chang I, and Kan Mao, all of early Chan Kuo times, were statesmen-generals who were important both in politics and in military affairs. Except for the four princes and the one royal relative, all attained high military positions, or even high civil offices such as the chancellorship, solely by their own brilliance as field officers or as staff strategists.

In contrast, during the entire Ch'un Ch'iu period very few generals came from other than noble families. In the state of Chin, only noblemen held the high office of *chung chün* or commander-in-chief of the army (and later, *de facto,* chancellor). In fact, all the commanders of the three Chin armies came from a small group of noble families.[121] Command of the armies by the hereditary nobility was fairly common in all the states of the Ch'un Ch'iu period, although Ch'in, then a peripheral state about which there is little information, may be an exception.

A comparison of the Ch'un Ch'iu aristocratic generals with the career military men of Chan Kuo times seems to indicate that hereditary generalship of the nobility did not survive the Ch'un Ch'iu period. The deadly serious warfare of the Chan Kuo period required the services of a new group, the professional strategists, tacticians, organizers, and warriors who possessed a specialized practical knowledge of war. Brave soldiers, able officers, talented generals, and even skilled diplomats all used the same path upward: excellence in warfare.

Summary

The familial solidarity of nobles within a state, and the class solidarity of nobility among the states, gradually broke down in the Ch'un Ch'iu period. Ministers grew stronger, rulers weaker, strong states more unscrupulous, and military ability more highly prized. Wars were harder fought and more frequent, and their consequences more serious. The leading citizens of a conquered state and the officers of a defeated army lost all social status; and since at least 110 states were conquered during the Ch'un Ch'iu period, it is clear that large numbers of people were forced to undergo this humiliation. In the Chan Kuo period wars were even longer and larger. Necessity bred a new type of fighting force, the infantry, to supplant the war chariots of Ch'un Ch'iu times, with the result that commoners became systematically involved for the first time in the whirlpool of interstate conflicts. Ultimately, able commoners were promoted into the ruling group as generals, staff members, and officials—in a word, as military and diplomatic experts entrusted with their states' survival or expansion in a period of brutal interstate warfare.

In a whirlpool, objects tend to change position much faster and more suddenly than in still water; waterweed may be drawn to the surface while flotsam is pulled to the bottom. So it was in the society of the Ch'un Ch'iu and Chan Kuo periods.

In the ancient Chinese feudal society, relationships inside the states were dominated by the same familialistic code of conduct that informed interstate relationships. A Ch'un Ch'iu state was not a purely political institution. The state resembled an enlarged household; the ruler reigned but did not rule. Ministers were not important because they held their offices; they were important and received offices because they were kin to the ruler or because they were heads of prominent families. In the state of Lu, for example, each of the three most important houses, Chi-sun, Shu-sun, and Meng-sun, was entitled to fill one of three ministerial offices. The *Tso Chuan* mentions their official titles only once. It seems unlikely that any one of the ministers could have exercised any authority over the affairs of the other ministers' clans.

In a familialistic government, it is logical that the closest relative of the ruler should have played the most important political role. Usually a ruler's closest kinsman was his brother, who should thus have been the most natural candidate for the chancellorship. Again using Lu as an example, we find that in the early part of the Ch'un Ch'iu period the governmental power was given over to a new sovereign by the brother of the deceased predecessor. The accompanying genealogy shows the line of descent of six Lu rulers and their brothers (the first ruler of this group was the fourteenth duke of Lu). Duke Yin was murdered with the sanction of the brother who succeeded him as Duke Huan. During the reign of Duke Huan, his brother Shih Fu appeared once at a reception of a state visitor to Lu.[1] Duke Chuang's three brothers began to take part in political activity; Ch'ing-fu was the first ruler's brother to lead an army in an assault on a neighboring state.[2] After the death of Duke Chuang, his brother Ya plotted to enthrone Ch'ing-fu and had Tzu Pan, the heir apparent, and Duke Min murdered, but the other brother, Yu, stepped in and enthroned Duke Hsi. Both Ch'ing-fu and Ya were punished later.[3] While on the throne of Lu, Duke Hsi shared the governmental power

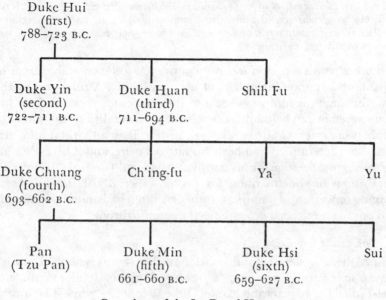

Genealogy of the Lu Ducal House[4]

with his brother Sui. Their uncle Yu was the most important political figure of the time because of his part in enthroning the duke. He held the chancellorship and was enfeoffed with a city, Pi, in the first year of the duke's reign. When Yu died in the sixteenth year of Duke Hsi, Sui succeeded to the chancellorship and apparently held it for the rest of his life.

The office of chancellor was clearly not hereditary; brothers of new rulers were able to gain the position. Since the monarchy was always hereditary, rulers could maintain some control within the ruling house and obviate dissension. But a factor that was inherent in the familial relationships and that led to the breakdown of this feudal system was that the sovereignty of rulers was not at all absolute. The respect accorded to the head of a family is personal, not institutional. Nobles, brothers, and other close relatives were far from being ruled by the ruler's command, since they actually shared his power. A new ruler's giving the chancellorship to his brother is just such a sharing of power. Thus it was said in the *Tso Chuan* that

therefore the Son of Heaven has his dukes; princes of states have their high ministers; ministers have [the heads of] their collateral families; great officers have the members of the secondary branches of their families; inferior officers have their friends; and the common people, mechanics, merchants, police runners, shepherds, and grooms, all have their relatives and acquaintances to aid and assist them.[5]

In other words a person was not considered to be separable from his assistants, who were members of his own family. A ruler was unable to discharge his ministers because they were not appointed by him but were born to help him rule. Under such conditions the ruler had at best imperfect control over his ministers. If an ambitious minister's son were determined to inherit his father's office, and if his father had gained great prestige for his family, a ruler could do little to check the ambitious one in his quest for power, especially if the ruler were young or weak, and ambitious ministers often had ample opportunity to put inexperienced or weak persons on the throne.

Intrastate Conflicts

Since the most detailed information in the records is about Lu, I will use it to begin my discussion of the second stage of development. Duke Hsi ruled for 33 years and his son Duke Wen for 18 years. The brother of Duke Wen is never mentioned in the *Tso Chuan,* which indicates that Sui, the son of Duke Chuang, held the actual power throughout the reigns of two dukes. After the death of Duke Wen, Sui killed the two legal successors and enthroned his favorite, Duke Hsüan.[6] According to the analysis of Professor Li Tsung-t'ung, Sui attended interstate meetings alone or led the army into battle eight times in the reign of Duke Wen, while the sons of Ch'ing-fu, Ya, and Yu performed these functions 19 times. Sui was accompanied once by Shu-sun Te-ch'en, the son of Ya. Sui, while retaining his dominance, shared some of his power with the three families.[7] In the reign of Duke Hsüan, however, Sui and his son Kung-sun Kuei-fu had almost complete control of the government. Of 14 diplomatic missions, 10 were carried out either by Sui or by his son; members of the other three families that descended from Duke Huan conducted only the remaining four.[8] Toward the end of Duke Hsüan's reign, Kung-sun Kuei-fu plotted with Chin to destroy the three Huan families; the plot won the approval of the duke.[9] The struggle that ensued between the three older families and Sui's family, the Tung-meng lineage, ended in the destruction of the Tung-mengs; Kung-sun Kuei-fu was banished after the death of Duke Hsüan in 591 B.C. This event ended the custom that let governmental power pass from the brother of a ruler to the brother of his successor in Lu. From that time on, few brothers of Lu rulers were ever given important positions, and few new ministerial families were founded in Lu. The three Huan families, led by the Chi-sun (i.e., the Chi clan), occupied the top positions in the Lu government while a few older families such as Tsang held the minor positions. Ministers of the Chi clan eventually eclipsed even the Lu dukes; they took over not only political power but also many of the religious prerogatives that were normally held only by sovereigns in the Ch'un Ch'iu period.[10] In 566 B.C. Chi-sun Su built a wall around the capital city of his fief in order to strengthen his position.[11] Eight years later the three Huan families jointly fortified the capital of the Meng domain.[12] In later times they enlarged their domain more than once by force.[13] In 562 B.C. they reclassified the people of Lu into three corps, each led by one of the three families.* By 537 B.C. the Chi family controlled over half of the Lu people, while the other two families shared power over the other half. The duke of Lu had lost all authority over his subjects and his domain, and had only whatever tribute the three families chose to give him.[14] The dukes of Lu were naturally anxious to change this situation. An opportunity came in 530 B.C., when an official under the Chi family, Nan K'uai, the magistrate of the capital of the Chi fief, offered to support a son of a Lu duke in extinguishing the Chi clan. If the *coup* succeeded, the duke's son was to take over the ministerial powers held by the Chi clan, Nan K'uai was to be promoted to an office in the ducal court, and the duke himself would regain authority over the state and subjects of Lu. But Nan K'uai started an ill-timed rebellion during the absence of the duke, the *coup d'état* failed, and all concerned were banished.[15]

A second attempt was made in 517 B.C., when Duke Chao, urged on by his son Kung Wei, rallied several noble families, including Tsang and Hou, to attack the Chi clan. The soldiers of the duke gained entrance to the Chi house and almost captured Chi-sun I-jü, but were repulsed by retainers of the Shu-sun family. Soldiers of the Meng household also slew Hou Chao-po of the house of Hou. The three

---

* *TCCI*, 31/8 (Hsiang 11). Taxation in the Ch'un Ch'iu period usually took the form of labor service for such military expenditures as the maintenance of war chariots. People assigned to a certain army organization were in fact under the direct control of the commander of the unit. An army thus could be considered an economic entity as well as a military organization. Miyazaki, Eberhard, and Utsunomiya interpret this incident as the elevation of the common people, who were not of the Chou ruling group, to a military status which was formerly a privilege reserved for the aristocrats. Eberhard goes further to say that this is a measure by which feudal lords managed to raise a "popular army" against the ruler. Cf. Miyazaki, "Taxation," p. 12; Eberhard, *Conquerors and Rulers*, p. 12; Utsunomiya, pp. 20–22.

Huan families then mounted an allied assault against the forces of the duke. Duke Chao was defeated and fled abroad with several of his followers; he died in exile eight years later.[16] From that time until the end of the Ch'un Ch'iu period the three Huan families held firm control over the state, with puppet dukes on the throne and no further protests from other nobles. At the beginning of the Chan Kuo period, Lu reappeared in history as a very small, weak state, and the three families of Huan had disappeared. The domain of the Chi family was occupied by Pi, a new, small state that may have been established some time between the Ch'un Ch'iu and Chan Kuo periods by the Pi clan. In the *Mencius* Pi is treated as an independent dukedom.[17]

The state of Chin can illustrate an intrastate conflict that involved ministers who did not belong to the ducal house. At the beginning of the Ch'un Ch'iu period there had been a quarrel between the duke of Chin and his powerful brother, whose fief occupied a strategic position. In 734 B.C. several noble families that had been assigned by the Chou king to accompany the founder of Chin became involved in the succession to the throne when they invited the branch established by the brother to take the place of the ducal house.[18] During the reign of Duke Hsien the families established by his uncles and granduncles became so powerful that they constituted a threat to the throne. In 671 B.C. the duke plotted to extinguish these families; two years later he massacred all his relatives in these clans. Quarrels about the succession among the sons of Duke Hsien inspired the Chin custom of sending abroad all rulers' sons other than the heirs apparent.[19] This custom also eliminated any conflicts between sons of different generations of dukes such as happened in Lu. However, the followers who had accompanied Duke Wen in his exile occupied all the key government posts of Chin during and after his reign. Their descendants formed several hereditary noble houses, whose members in turn held the important offices. The most influential families were Luan, Hsi, Hsü, Yüan, Hu, Hsü (another family), Ch'ing, Po, Yang-she, Chih, Ch'i, Fan, Chung-hang, Han, Chao, and Wei.

Relations among these Chin families were far from peaceful. In 621 B.C. Hu She-ku was banished because of pressure from the Chao family and their allies, and a relative of the Hu family, Hsü Chien-po, was killed. The Hu family does not appear in the records after this time.[20] In 607 B.C. a minister, Chao Tun, murdered his ruler and enthroned a ducal heir who had been in exile. The sons of ministers were then given titles, *Kung tsu, Kung hang,* etc., that had originally been those of ducal house members, and it was ruled that genuine ducal scions could not be so entitled.[21] In 574 B.C. Duke Li planned to replace three ministers of the Hsi family with three of his own favorites. The three Hsi ministers were slain, but the Luan and Chung-hang families killed the duke and enthroned a ducal heir who had been living abroad.[22] In 552 B.C., when Fan Hsüan-tzu initiated the banishment of the Luan family from Chin, Luan Ying went to Ch'i. Two years later he returned with an armed troop from Ch'i and led the men of his fief in an attack on the Chin capital. The Wei family was ready to aid the Luan forces, while Han, Chao, Chung-hang, and Chih all took the side of Fan Hsüan-tzu. Fan seized the duke and Wei Hsien-tzu as hostages, and the Luan army was defeated. Luan Ying withdrew to his fief, which was soon captured by his enemies, and he was executed.[23] After the Ch'i and Yang-she families were extinguished in 514 B.C., their territory was divided into ten districts, four of which were governed by scions of the families Han, Chao, Wei, and Chih as district magistrates. In effect these four families shared the spoils of the ruin of the Ch'i and Yang-she houses. The land formerly owned by defeated noble families was no longer given to new nobles as fiefs. Instead, administrators were dispatched by the victorious families to run the new territories. No doubt this heralded the future institution of local administration through *hsien* and *chun*.[24]

A serious feud broke out in 497 B.C. between the Chao family and the Fan and Chung-hang families. Both sides fortified their cities and fought sporadically for six years. With the aid of the duke, Chao Yang finally overcame Fan and Chung-hang, even though they were assisted by troops from the states of Ch'i and Wey. Both families then disappeared from Chin politics.[25]

In 454 B.C. Chih Hsiang-tzu forced the Han and Wei families to join him in besieging the capital of the Chao family, but Han and Wei soon joined with Chao and succeeded in destroying the Chih family. The land and subjects of Chih were divided among the three. The heads of the three families were invested with the title of marquis in 403 B.C. and formed three independent states from the former territory of Chin.[26]

The oldest ministerial families of Ch'i were Kao and Kuo, both of which were active until 449 B.C., when the ministers of the two families were banished from Ch'i.[27] Ministers were also often chosen from the families Pao and Yen; the Yen clan was banished with Kao and Kuo in 449 B.C. The Ts'ui family once killed the duke of Ch'i and ruled the entire state with the aid of the Ch'ing family, but was extinguished in 546 B.C.; the following year Ch'ing was also banished.

TABLE 8

The Fate of the Noble Families of Sung

Family	Year B.C.	Fate	Reference in *TCCI*
Hua	520	banished to Ch'u.	50/6
Huang	520	banished to Ch'u, later restored, survived until Chan Kuo period.	50/6
Lao	573, 576	unknown.	28/19, 27/12–13
Chung	500	voluntary exile to Ch'en.	56/4
Yü	576	voluntary exile to Ch'u.	27/12–13
Tang	611	a Tang minister killed.	20/3
Ling	576	voluntary exile to Ch'u.	27/12–13
Hsiang	481	Hsiang ministers banished to Lu, Wey, and Ch'i.	59/10
Lin	469	one appearance, no later information.	60/12
Families descending from Dukes Mu and Wu	609	collectively banished.	20/11
Lo		only important family known to survive into the Chan Kuo period.	

Luan and another family named Kao were both offshoots of the clan of Duke Hui; in 532 B.C. two ministers of Luan and Kao exiled themselves by going to Lu.[28] The family that eventually replaced the ducal house of Chiang in Ch'i was the Ch'en clan, which was founded by a duke's son from Ch'en who had sought shelter in Ch'i after a political disturbance in his home state.[29] Ch'en and Pao often worked together to destroy other ministerial families; they divided the lands of Luan and Kao between themselves and expelled the ministers of the Kuo, Yen, and Kao families. With the support of Pao, Ch'en placed another son of the ruler on the Ch'i throne when the legal successor was murdered.[30] Eventually the Ch'en family became the dominant force in Ch'i. In 481 B.C. Ch'en Ch'eng-tzu killed the duke of Ch'i; his grandson later usurped control of the entire state.[31]

In the state of Sung all the noble ministerial families were branches of the ducal house. Hua, Lo, Huang, and Lao were descended from Duke Tai; Chung from Duke Chuang; Yü, Lin, Tang, and Hsiang

from Duke Huan; and Ling from Duke Wen. There were also families whose names are not known that descended from the dukes Wu
and Mu. Brothers of dukes were given important positions on several
occasions. Since it would take up too much space to describe the complicated relations and conflicts of these families, the final fate of each
family is given in Table 8.

The Lo family remained powerful until the very end of the Ch'un
Ch'iu period; it may still have been in existence when the *Tso Chuan*
was written.[32] The ruling house of Sung during the Chan Kuo period
may actually have been the Lo family, which could have usurped control of the state.[33]

The most important ministerial houses in Cheng were families that
had been established by eleven sons of Duke Mu; seven of the families
were of paramount importance. Table 9 gives dates of and information about the last appearances of these families.

The situation in Ch'u was rather different. Chancellors, military
ministers, and other important officials were recruited from a few
noble families that were all branches of the ruling house. However,
no position was the monopoly of one family; Ch'u rulers apparently

TABLE 9

The Fate of the Noble Families of Cheng

Family	Year B.C.	Fate	Reference in *TCCI*
Han, Ssu, and Feng		possibly remained in power until the close of the Ch'un Ch'iu period.*	47/11, 55/10, 56/11
Yu	500	last appearance.	56/1
Kuo	510	last appearance.	53/13
Liang	543	Liang minister killed.	40/4
	535	son of Liang minister restored the house.	44/6
Yin	526	last appearance.	47/11
K'ung	526	last appearance.	47/8–9
Yü	543	Yü minister banished to Chin.	40/5
Families of Tzu-ko and Tzu-liang	554	banished to Chu together.	34/4

* Han seems to have been the only powerful family in the state of Cheng in the
Chan Kuo period.

had much more real authority than their counterparts in the northern states. For instance, a Ch'u ruler had the power to execute his chief minister for serious faults or crimes.[34] Yet there were conflicts between the ruler and the noble families. The first subjugation of a noble family was recorded in 605 B.C., when the chancellor Tzu-yüeh Chiao became overly ambitious and his family, which was descended from an earlier Ch'u ruler, waxed too prosperous for the ruler's peace of mind. A battle was fought between the Tzu-yüeh clan and the ruler's troops, who barely succeeded in overcoming the rebels.[35] In 530 B.C. another noble family was extinguished for the sole reason that it was also descended from the same ruler as the ancestor of the Tzu-yüeh clan.[36] The chancellor Tzu-nan was executed in 551 B.C. because he used illegal means to enrich a protégé.[37] There are at least two instances of conflicts between nobles. In 584 B.C. several noble families divided up the property of three noble clans they had destroyed; the three clans were related to an exiled minister.[38] In 515 B.C. a noble family that had been slandered was massacred; every member of the slanderers' families was also slain.[39]

Consequences of the Conflicts

The oligarchies of the several states shared some points of similarity. One significant common feature was that most of the families that gained hereditary ministerial power were established about the middle of the Ch'un Ch'iu period.* The three Huan families of Lu were founded by sons of Duke Huan (reigned 711–694 B.C.), the second Lu ruler of the Ch'un Ch'iu period. The important families of Chin were established by followers of Duke Wen (reigned 635–628 B.C.), the sixth Ch'un Ch'iu ruler of that state. The seven Mu families of Cheng were descended from sons of Duke Mu (reigned 627–606 B.C.). As for Ch'i, the families Kao, Kuo, and Ts'ui allegedly descended from rulers who reigned before the beginning of the Ch'un Ch'iu period, but the first appearances of members of these three families as officeholders occur in the *Tso Chuan* in 632, 685, and 632 B.C., respectively.[40] The Ching family of Ch'i was founded by Duke Huan (reigned 685–643 B.C.) but does not appear in the *Tso Chuan* until 574 B.C.[41] Luan and Kao sprang from the sons of Duke Hui (reigned 608–599 B.C.) and appear for the first time in 545 B.C.[42] The

---

* See pp. 31–34, in which the segmentation of lineages is discussed. What should be noticed about the middle Ch'un Ch'iu period is that repeated segmentation of the ducal houses had greatly reduced their strength, which perhaps weakened the position of dukes in their power struggle with their ministers.

Ch'en family was founded by the son of a Ch'en duke who came to Ch'i in 672 B.C.; the duke's grandson began to play an important part in the Ch'i government in 550 B.C.[43] Five important families of Sung were allegedly founded by Duke Tai, who reigned before the Ch'un Ch'iu period. The earliest appearance of any of their members in the records is in 711 B.C., when a high official named Hua Fu-tu is mentioned.[44] The Hua family does not appear in the records again until 620 B.C.[45] Of the other four families, Lo first appeared in 620 B.C., Huang in 564 B.C., Lao in 576 B.C., and Tai in 534 B.C. The first appearance of the Chung family, founded by the son of Duke Chuang (reigned 709–693 B.C.), was in 609 B.C. Of the families descended from Duke Huan (reigned 681–651 B.C.), Yü appeared in 651 B.C., Ling in 620 B.C., Tang in 620 B.C., and Hsiang in 576 B.C.[46] These dates show that the families that would become important did not gain any power before a time well into the Ch'un Ch'iu period.

The second common point is that once they had established themselves in their own states, the great families became so essential a part of the ruling group that sovereigns found it hard to get rid of them. In a previous passage about the struggle between the Lu ruler and the Chi family, we have seen that the Shu-sun clan aided the Chi family at a decisive moment. The steward of the Shu-sun family insisted that the continued existence of each family was guaranteed by the survival of the other.[47] In 575 B.C. a Lu envoy to Chin, then the leader of the states, was asked whether the Chi family might be destroyed. The Lu noble answered that Chi and Meng were integral to Lu, that the end of those two families would mean the end of Lu. Another noble compared Chi and Meng to the Luan and Fan families of Chin, which he called the very source of the sovereign authority.[48] A minister of the Shu-sun family was once seized by Chin at an interstate meeting; the meeting had been convened because the Chi chancellor of Lu had invaded a neighboring state and thus had violated the Chin edict of nonaggression. After the Shu-sun minister had somehow gained his freedom and returned to Lu, he was visited by the Chi chancellor. Although he still deeply resented his experience in Chin, he held his temper and received his visitor graciously, saying that he knew the Chi family had always been a pillar of the state.[49]

The third common point was that although rulers and nobles realized the importance of the noble families, they did little to halt the chronic conflicts among them. The dates of the struggles and disappearances of the great families indicate that most of them did not survive the close of the Ch'un Ch'iu period. The family that remained in power did so by extinguishing other noble families. The Lo family of Sun, the T'ien (alternate name for Ch'en) family of Ch'i, and the Han, Wei, and Chao families of Chin were clans that survived the deadly struggles with their contemporaries.

The later development of these oligarchies had manifold effects on social mobility. In the first place, since noble families acquired *de facto* regency of a state, the rulers possessed only nominal sovereignty; some rulers, such as Duke Chao of Lu, even suffered exile from their own states. The class of rulers was degraded in function although its social status was not changed. The final step in this process was the removal of the nominal ruler from the throne and his replacement by the ruler-in-fact. Members of the former ruling house were then degraded to a position from which they could hardly expect to ever attain noble rank again.

A second effect was the downward mobility forced on sons of dukes. In earlier times the son of a duke could expect to occupy an important government position. But when several noble families had monopolized the power, a ruler's son was most unlikely to hold high governmental office or to establish a long-lived, important family. New families were occasionally created in Sung, but so rarely that they must be considered exceptions. Most ducal offspring were as unknown in history as their descendants. A younger son of the Chin ruling house was especially unfortunate since he was compelled to live and die in exile. These rulers' sons lived much less nobly than would heirs of ruling houses that still controlled their states. A close kinsman of a ruler rarely received social status consonant with his title and birth in the middle Ch'un Ch'iu period.

The third effect was the upward mobility of the ministerial families, which lifted themselves to the highest positions of power in the states, even eclipsing the ruling houses. Although technically still of the noble class, they had risen to its uppermost stratum at the expense of the rulers and their kin. The most serious consequence of the development of the oligarchies followed the struggles among the nobles and the ruling houses. The members of the families destroyed by those struggles were not just reduced to the status of ordinary nobles. They were forced either to till rural lands as plebeians, as the Fan and Chung-hang clans were,[50] or to become slaves, in their own country, of the victorious clans.[51] No more than seven major states and a few minor principalities remained at the beginning of the Chan Kuo period, each ruled by the single house that survived the Ch'un Ch'iu strife. Comparison of the small number of noble houses in all of Chan

Kuo China with the many powerful families when they were at their
zenith during the Ch'un Ch'iu period shows the disappearance of the
noble class itself, not merely social mobility. An enormous number of
people lost their aristocratic status; the remaining small fraction became state rulers. The noble ministers of the Ch'un Ch'iu period committed class suicide by their internecine struggles, causing not social
mobility but the reshaping of the former social stratification.

A few decades after the beginning of the Chan Kuo period, when
historical information is again available, not a single minister belonging to Ch'un Ch'iu ministerial families appears in the records. This
is the fourth and most important effect of the intrastate conflicts on
social mobility. The fifth effect was the rise of the *shih* class, which
originally consisted of stewards and warriors of noble households. The
aristocracy and the commoners overlapped in this class. A son of a
noble family, who had neither inherited his father's title and office
nor been appointed to a ministerial position, might serve in his own
or another noble household as a steward, a warrior, or both.* The records mention that a meritorious commoner might expect to be recruited to serve in a noble household and thus gain *shih* status.†
However, sons of *shih* were not allowed to inherit their fathers' offices,
a rule that was set down in an interstate covenant, although it may
not have been enforced.[52] The *shih* class, consisting of the educated
sons of the nobility and the most able and talented of the commoners,
was therefore the foundation of the feudal administration. Since they
were placed in office because of their ability instead of their heredity,
and since their numbers exceeded those of the noble minister class,
the *shih* produced some quite outstanding persons.

The noble ministers were forced by their internal conflicts to support their own stewards and warriors and to use them to govern newly
taken territory. Thus the *shih* eventually came to hold many positions
that had usually been held by noble ministers. It was quite common
for a *shih* to be appointed magistrate of an area that had formerly
been the fief of a minister.[53] The *shih* then began to take increasingly
significant roles even in state politics. In the state of Lu, magistrates
again and again rebelled against their masters. In 530 B.C. Nan K'uai,

---

* *TCCI*, 28/12 (Ch'eng 17). A scion of the Pao family of Ch'i served in the Shih
household of Lu. The head of his own family was banished from Ch'i; he was recalled, became the family head, and later became an important figure in the state.
† On the eve of battle, a commander of Chin announced that outstanding plebeians,
merchants, and artisans were to be rewarded by being allowed to enter public service, which could have meant attaining the rank of *shih*. *Ibid.*, 57/6 (Ai 2).

a magistrate of the Chi family in charge of Pi, caused a rebellion that the Chi could not put down until two years later.[54] Hou Fan, magistrate of Hou, rebelled against the Shu-sun clan in 500 B.C. One of his aides, also a *shih*, successfully plotted Hou Fan's defeat and exile after the Shu-sun had besieged Hou to no avail.[55] Two years later, Pi again revolted under another magistrate of the Chi family; the rebel forces even entered the Lu capital.[56] In 480 B.C. the magistrate Kung-sun Su revolted in the city of Ch'eng against the Meng family.[57] During the final conflict between Duke Chao of Lu and the Chi family, a steward of the Shu-sun clan had them aid the Chi and himself led the armed force that defeated the followers of the duke.[58] Tzu-lu, a disciple of Confucius and a steward of the Chi family, instigated and led troops in the destruction of the fortifications of the three Huan family capitals in 498 B.C., apparently in order to weaken the power of unruly local officials.[59]

Another of Confucius's disciples, also a steward of the Chi family, commanded the Lu army that resisted an invasion from Ch'i, and at another time dealt with a diplomatic envoy as the representative of the Chi clan.[60] The most outstanding rebel was Yang Hu, an official of the Chi household, who captured his erstwhile master in 505 B.C. He then held the *de facto* regency for four years, during which time he forcibly seized ministers, led the Lu army in battles with invaders, and even invaded a neighboring state. In 501 B.C. a steward of the Meng family defeated him and ended his dictatorship.[61] At the end of the Ch'un Ch'iu period, the *shih* had been rising in power and influence, and they were to rise still higher in the following period.

The sixth effect of intrastate conflict was the greater attention the noble ministers paid to the common people. During the struggles among the nobility, support by the people became an important asset; the power of the mob was often exploited by ambitious nobles. When Duke Chao of Lu fought with the Chi family, a minister of Lu predicted the defeat of the duke because the Chi, during their period of power, had won a great many loyal followers by their generosity to the poor.[62] In the state of Chin the duke increased the stability of his government by distributing surplus wealth among the people.[63] It is reported that the duke needed the support of the people to establish new noble families, and only the old families that were unpopular could be replaced.[64] This effect was even more marked in Ch'i, where popular aid was necessary for victory in intrastate struggles. Duke I of Ch'i gained the throne after he had exhausted all his wealth in feeding the poor and supporting his followers.[65] Two of Duke Ching's brothers made him uneasy by giving generous material aid to the people; the duke had to do the same in order to retain his throne.[66] The Ch'en family, which finally usurped the throne of Ch'i, had for generations endeavored to please the people by many means. For instance, loans from this family could be paid back at substantial discounts, and the prices charged by Ch'en-sponsored merchants were quite equitable, whereas the ducal government taxed the people heavily and imposed a harsh penal code.[67] The Ch'en family was so popular that twice when this clan fought battles with other noble families, the commoners of Ch'i took its side.[68] It was thus natural that the Ch'en family gradually overcame the other noble families and finally took control of the entire state.

Wooing the people became common and even fashionable in the various states. During a famine the Han family of Cheng fed the entire state by distributing rice to each family. The result was such popularity among the commoners that the Han family chiefs were able to make the Cheng chancellorship a hereditary Han office. The Lo family of Sung copied the Han family and issued a free loan to the people of Sung. It was prophesied that the Han and Lo families would take over their states.[69] In the state of Sung at least one ruler, Duke Wen, gained the throne by being generous to the people in time of famine.[70] In Ch'u the pretender Pai Kung Sheng planned to secure the support of the people by all possible means in order to take over that state. At first he succeeded, but after he took control he did not give the state treasury goods and stored grain to the people as he had been advised. This was done by his adversary, and Pai Kung Sheng was defeated.[71] That winners in intrastate conflicts often had to have the support of the people implies that some of the most able commoners would have been able to rise socially by aiding nobles in their struggles. Commoners were promised entrance into public service as a reward for their accomplishments during the conflict among the nobility.[72] This could mean that commoners had been recruited to fight on both sides. Rewards at such times were usually generous and lavish; not only were commoners given government positions but in some cases slaves and serfs were given their freedom.[73] It is recorded that a slave who achieved high merit in a battle between nobles was freed in 550 B.C.[74] There must have been many other such instances that were not recorded. Since we possess very little material dealing with the effects of intrastate struggle upon the common people and the slaves, we must at least temporarily be satisfied by what we can infer about those effects.

Let us sum up the direct results of the intrastate disturbances of the Ch'un Ch'iu period. First, a ruler often lost control of his state and became merely the nominal head of state; eventually some of the old ruling families were extinguished. Second, after the rise of the powerful families, sons of rulers generally lost the chance to occupy significant governmental posts. Their social status was therefore not as high as that of their predecessors who had lived before the ministerial families gained control. Third, for a while the powerful ministerial families increased in number. Fourth, a few of them became the new ruling groups of states while the majority sank to the bottom of the social scale as a result of the interfamily struggle for power. Fifth, the *shih* class rose to prominence by serving their masters in the conflict and being rewarded by promotion when those they served gained ruling powers. Sixth, occasionally commoners began to take part in the strife. The social rise of some commoners remains a mere logical deduction, since there is little clear direct evidence of its occurrence. On the other hand, the effect that intrastate conflict had on political institutions was that a new type of state appeared. This in turn created a demand for a new kind of minister, who was to place himself at the disposal of the master, that is, carry out orders instead of making or influencing policy as his counterpart had done in the oligarchical structure.

The Consolidation of the State

The intrastate struggles resulted in the consolidation of state governments. A ruler who had outlived his rivals for the throne was well aware that he could not continue to share a considerable part of his authority with local feudal lords. Domains were no longer to be divided among the relatives and sons of rulers as fiefs; by the end of the Ch'un Ch'iu period the common practice was to appoint magistrates to govern the districts of a state.* Such an administration had long been in effect in Ch'u, where several annexed states were managed by governors appointed by the Ch'u court. Although these governors possessed ducal titles, they did not inherit their offices or enjoy

---

* Max Weber makes a distinction between two kinds of state. One is that in which the administrative staff itself *owns* the administrative means; the lord rules with the aid of an autonomous "aristocracy" and hence shares his domination with it. Another is that in which the administrative staff is "separated" from these means of administration. They are merely directed by the lord. See Weber's "Politik als Beruf" in Gerth and Mills, pp. 81–82. The Ch'un Ch'iu states were of the former kind; the Chan Kuo states (and some states in the late Ch'un Ch'iu) were of the latter kind.

a vassal-lord relationship to their rulers. Vacancies in these posts were generally filled by sons of rulers or other nobles, although governors were occasionally shifted to other offices.[75] The three Huan families entrusted each of their fiefs to the management of a steward. The ministers of Chin divided the territory of defeated nobles into ten districts, each governed by a magistrate who was not an enfeoffed vassal. One of these magistrates once remanded to the state government of Chin a judicial case upon which he had been unable to pass judgment.[76] Thus the control of the central government over the local administration was clearly much tighter than the control of a lord over his vassal in early Ch'un Ch'iu times. That is to say, the state had become more consolidated than the feudal domain of the previous period.

Such a consolidated state demands that persons of the highest ability be selected as officials and be well controlled to avoid jeopardizing the position of the sovereign. In order to provide such officials, professional education became a necessity. During the Chan Kuo period the new type of state reached a high stage of development: an organized administrative staff of well-trained career experts.[77]

At the beginning of the Chan Kuo period several states underwent political reformations that destroyed the last vestiges of the feudal system and laid the foundation of a new type of state. One of the earliest of these was Wei, a part of the once great state of Chin, which had been divided up by the three most powerful families of the state after a long period of deadly struggle among the clans. The other two states were Han and Chao. Marquis Wen of Wei (reigned 446–397 B.C.) hired a group of competent men to serve in governmental positions in his state. The two candidates for the chancellorship, the brother of the marquis and a man of obscure origin, were considered on equal terms even though the marquis's kinsman was selected for the office.[78] After the death of Marquis Wen, his former aide, Wu Ch'i, became a Ch'u official. Wu Ch'i persuaded King Tao of Ch'u to lessen the influence of his relatives and even to have them cultivate waste lands to help maintain the armed forces. He gave as his reasons that the ministers and nobles were not performing good works but were intimidating their ruler and oppressing the people. The enraged nobles revenged themselves on the luckless Wu Ch'i after the death of King Tao.[79] The political and governmental activities of Shang Yang in the state of Ch'in followed a similar course. Under his administration the nobles were suppressed and a new aristocracy based on military merit was created. The people were organized into squads of five and ten, and were ruled directly by functionaries of the state.[80] Another important figure was Shen Pu-hai, chancellor of Han, who was of humble origin. According to the recent research of Dr. H. G. Creel, Shen Pu-hai should be given credit as one of the most significant shapers of the Chinese bureaucratic system. He devised a system for investigating personnel for the government, which unfortunately is not described in any extant source. However, some of his theories are preserved in a few works, of which the *Han Fei Tzu* is the most important. He stressed the role of the ruler, and the organization and operation of bureaucratic government. As quoted in the *Han Fei Tzu,* some main points of his theory were

to bestow offices according to the capacity [of the candidate], to demand actual [performance] in accordance with the title [of the office held], to hold fast the handles of [the power of] life and death, and to examine the abilities of all of his ministers; these are the things that the ruler keeps in his own hands.[81]

Like the hub of a wheel to the spokes, a ruler caused all his ministers to advance together.[82] A ruler held his ministers firmly in control by applying rigorous administrative techniques. The ruler was to determine policies; his ministers were entrusted with routine functions while the ruler evaluated their performance according to a fair standard—a process that is compared to weighing with a scale.[83]

The process that reduced the many Ch'un Ch'iu states, each ruled dividedly by several noble families, to a few states, each governed by one ruling house, increased the authoritarianism of the state and the despotism of the ruler. The ruler had acquired absolute power, for there were no longer noble families that were able to challenge his sovereignty. The feudal stratification disappeared and was replaced by a two-part system of authority: the sovereign above and his subjects below. Officials were subjects as well as functionaries; they served their lord with their competence and knowledge of statecraft but, in contrast to the nobles of the Ch'un Ch'iu period, they did not share his power. The demand for this new type of official required new means of recruiting the needed men, retaining the competent ones, and screening out the unqualified.

When government offices were the property of a few families, the ruler had virtually no voice in the selection of his aides. Only the concentration of authority in the hands of the ruler enabled him to choose his own ministers. This change in the power of rulers may have caused the situation in Chan Kuo times, as discussed in Chapter 2, in which no important family existed for very long and key positions in government almost always went either to close relatives of rulers or to unusually able persons unrelated to the ruling house. The former were probably considered trustworthy. The latter were not only useful but, being social "nobodies," much more dependent on the favor of the ruler and presumably more loyal to him than the hereditary ministers had been; thus they were preferred by authoritarian sovereigns. In addition, the ruler interested in preventing the degeneration of his own power had to forestall the growth of any new noble families; most of the ruling houses, being veterans of the struggle for power, knew well the dangers of tolerating several powerful groups inside a state at one time. Thus it was that none of the relatives of rulers in any state were able to found long-lived, prosperous families.[84] A prince of no particular merit, in office merely because he was a ruler's brother, could hardly expect to keep his position after his brother's reign had ended; when the new ruler took the throne, his career was finished.[85]

Chan Kuo rulers assiduously maintained their dignity, which is always of great significance to despots. An illustrative story tells that after the unsuccessful siege of the Chao capital, Chin-yang, the Chao ruler awarded highest honors to an official who could not be credited with merit in battle but who never once failed to show due reverence to the ruler.[86] In a feudal society of familial relationships, not much attention was paid to such reverence nor did it need to be strictly enforced. Only when the ruler alone held the supreme authority and was served by ministers who were not intimately connected to any organization such as an old and powerful clan did reverence need enforcement. The story reveals not only the despotic character of the ruler but also the instability of the entire court.

It is logical to assume that a despotic government needs a very effective system of supervision to keep the officials in line. Such a system, called "presenting report," did exist and may have been originated by Shen Pu-hai, although it was common in states other than his and is mentioned many times in different records. It worked as follows: The various departments of the central state government were required to send in detailed yearly reports. (The king of Ch'i was said to have become tired of reading these boring reports.[87]) Local magistrates had to report yearly to the governors of prefectures, who in turn reported to the sovereign; a magistrate of the K'u-ching district of Wei sent reports to his supervisor, the governor of Chung-shan prefecture. Hsimen Pao, the governor of I, and Chieh Pien, the official in charge of the eastern territory of Wei, sent the Wei ruler annual reports that included the yearly income of their areas.[88] Under such a system the officials could be regarded as functionaries subject to reward by promotion or punishment by demotion within the bureaucratic machinery. It is unimaginable that if a noble of a feudal society, born to rule his household, were to hold a ministership, he would be promoted or demoted according to his performance in office. Yet in the bureaucracy paths were opened whereby an official could gain a higher position and social status by his own competence or could be degraded for having been proved unqualified for his office. There were paths not only of movement within the bureaucracy but of social mobility.

Rewards for merit and punishments for incompetence or peculation in the Chan Kuo governments covered a wide range. A dutiful governor of Ch'i was rewarded highly whereas another who was guilty of neglect in office was given the death penalty.[89] The three local magistrates of Wei who were mentioned earlier each seem to have received some sort of promotion or punishment that, though not specified, is implied by the context. Hsi-men Pao thus eventually became a very important figure of the Wei court.*

In brief, the Chan Kuo ruler now needs a strong bureaucracy, a corps of officers that will help him steer his ship of state through the life-and-death struggles of the times.†

New Administrative Expertise

From what sources were the members of the bureaucracy recruited? We have seen that the former hereditary aristocracy had been ruined by the struggle for power, since a very few of the old noble families finally attained the rulership of a state at the expense of the rest of the noble families. With a small fraction entering the class of rulers and the majority losing all their social status, the hereditary aristocracy virtually disappeared. This process may explain the disappearance of the great family names from the list of Chan Kuo officials, as was pointed out in the second chapter. The social vacuum left by the

---

* In the *Han Fei Tzu* it is pointed out that good chancellors and generals were those who had risen from the rank and file after being several times tested for ability (*HFT*, 19/15).

† Max Weber listed the technical advantages of bureaucratic organization: precision, speed, unambiguity, knowledge of the files, continuity, discretion, strict subordination, reduction of friction and of material and personnel costs. Most of these points he named are of paramount importance from the point of view of a Chan Kuo ruler as well as from that of a modern state. See Gerth and Mills, p. 214. It should be noticed, however, that the Chan Kuo government was merely the incipient stage of the vast bureaucratic machinery in China. Compared with the bureaucratic organization of later China or of Imperial Germany, the Chan Kuo government was still inferior both in scale and in complexity.

disappearance of the aristocratic ministers had to be filled, most logically by the followers who had been stewards, knights, magistrates,
and other retainers of the noble households before their masters took
the thrones of the various states. The situation cited here probably
obtained in the states of Chao, Han, Wei, and Ch'i, while circumstances seem to have been different in Ch'in and Ch'u, where the
Ch'un Ch'iu ruling houses remained in power during the Chan Kuo
period. Note, however, that both Ch'in and Ch'u were located outside
the nucleus of Chinese culture. Information about the situation in
Ch'in is quite meager; the only seemingly certain fact is that no strong
hereditary noble family (aside from the ruling house) ever appears
in any source for Ch'in history. From the Ch'un Ch'iu beginnings to
the Chan Kuo period—from the time of Pai-li Hsi, born in an eastern
state, to the era of Shang Yang, formerly a member of the Wey ruling
house and later a retainer in Wei, another eastern state—Ch'in seems
to have welcomed people from abroad. Somewhat free social mobility
may have existed in Ch'in from an early date. During the Chan Kuo
period it is evident that, over and over again, foreigners contributed
their abilities to Ch'in to help further the unification of China.[90] It
may not have been difficult for the rulers of Ch'in to hold the changes
linked with social mobility, which occurred with great rapidity in the
eastern states, to a slower and more even pace.

Much more information is available about Ch'u, although it still
does not compare with that for Chin and Lu. Ch'u seems to have
been somewhat slower in some aspects of change; for instance, princes
of Ch'u still occasionally occupied key positions in government at a
time when princes of the central states were compelled to give way to
the dominant noble houses. Of twenty-five persons who held office as
ling-yin (chancellor) of Ch'u, eight were brothers of the ruler and the
other seventeen were men from a group of eight families. The Tou
family contributed five chancellors, three of whom were put to death
by the Ch'u ruler. The Ch'eng clan produced three *ling-yin,* one of
whom was executed; the entire family was extinguished in the fourth
generation. Four chancellors were of the Wei family; the Ch'u, Yang,
Nang, Tzu-hsi, and Shen lineages provided one chancellor each. All
these lineages were segmentary branches of the Ch'u ruling house.
These data reveal that the ruling house held the balance of power
and that the Ch'u sovereign was usually strong enough to destroy even
the most powerful of the noble families.[91] Governed by this strong
ruling house, Ch'u enjoyed comparative stability throughout the
Ch'un Ch'iu period. As a consequence the hereditary aristocracy was

kept from destroying itself through struggles for power. In fact, Ch'u was the only state that, in the Chan Kuo period, still selected most of its chancellors from noble families.

With Ch'u probably the sole exception, the destruction of the aristocracy left the way clear for the rise of the new elite; the first sign of that rise occurred in the late Ch'un Ch'iu period. On one occasion the duke of Lu tendered a state reception to a foreign envoy; the ceremonies included an archery contest. Only two pairs of competing archers could be selected from the attendants of the ducal court, and a third pair was supplied from among the retainers of the Chi family.[92] Later on, stewards of the Chi family came to command half the army of Lu.[93] One of them, Yang Hu, even occupied the supreme office of the Lu government for four years. This is an exceptional case, but it nevertheless indicates the rise of the *shih* class.[94] The next advance was the appointment of retainers of noble houses to positions in state governments. For example, when the domains of two ruined noble families of Chin were divided into ten districts, most of the new magistrates, who were appointed in the name of the duke of Chin, may have been retainers of the noble clans then in power. Even after their appointments, two of them still resided as attendants in the households of their masters. In this case two persons still with the status of family retainers had been appointed to an area managership that formerly would have been filled by a noble.[95]

The last step took place when the domain of a noble family became a state and its followers naturally became the ministers of the new court. When the Chao family was under siege in Chin-yang, only the retainers of the lord of the family stayed to help repel the attackers. When Chao later became a sovereign state after a successful counterattack against the Chi family, the Chao retainers were made ministers of the new principality. They were thus shifted from the steward class to the elite of government, an automatic and large-scale rise in social status. Unfortunately we lack information for the period between the Ch'un Ch'iu and Chan Kuo periods, at which time this transfer was presumably taking place; hence we can only speculate about it.

The techniques of personnel control possible under a despotic regime facilitated the screening of officials recruited from the *shih* class. Though formerly composed of stewards and warriors of noble households, the *shih* class was transformed during the Chan Kuo period into a virtually new group. The main difference between the old and the new *shih* groups was caused by the difference between a Ch'un Ch'iu feudal noble household and a state of the new Chan Kuo type.

If a state were several times the size of a noble fief, the complexity of governing it was not merely proportionally multiplied. For instance, a steward who was competent to collect tribute from a few farms of several square miles could have felt completely at a loss in administering a state the size of a major European country. A chariot-warrior of the early Ch'un Ch'iu period, who was used to fighting game-like battles with thousands of his fellow knightly warriors, could have felt quite confused if he were asked to lead an army ten times larger in tricky, bloody, and brutal infantry warfare. Statecraft had become so complicated and specialized that the former type of training was no longer useful. New methods of education were needed to turn personnel of many origins into officials able to meet the demands of specialized statecraft. The fact that these men were of diverse backgrounds implies that mobility in the elite group was also quite free.

In a feudal society in which occupations were generally inherited within families, the knowledge needed to engage in these occupations was also inherited within families; hence the proverb that the son of a bow-maker learns to make bamboo utensils by playing with bamboo sticks. The ministers in the feudal society learned the art of ruling a state in similar ways. Young nobles were sometimes sent to other aristocratic families as trainees or pages. Chi-sun Hsing-fu of Lu on one occasion quoted the words of Tsang Wen-chung, another Lu noble, and referred to the latter as his teacher, who apparently taught him moral principles rather than techniques of administration.[96] What may have concerned the noble ministers more than statecraft was a code of proper etiquette for various circumstances. Also it appears that people were of the opinion that a magistrate could learn the duties of his office by on-the-job training. In 542 B.C. there was a controversy in Cheng over the necessity of training an official before appointing him to office. Tzu-p'i, the Cheng chancellor, wished to appoint his protégé magistrate of a city; his deputy, Tzu-ch'an, objected, saying that the protégé was too young. Tzu-p'i answered that the young man could learn his duties by working in that position. Tzu-ch'an then objected that in his opinion this would be the same as putting a knife into the hands of an inexperienced person who would probably hurt himself or giving a piece of fine silk to a man for use in learning to make clothing.[97] There is a similar story concerning Confucius and his disciple Tzu-lu, the chief steward of the Chi family. Tzu-lu wished to appoint Tzu-kao manager of a city, and Confucius objected that such a position of responsibility might ruin so young a man. Tzu-lu answered, "There are common people and officers; there are the altars of the spirits of the land and grain. Why must one read books before one can be considered to be learned?"[98] It appears that Tzu-lu did not think that a man necessarily needed special training to run a town, whereas Confucius thought such training necessary. During the Chan Kuo period, the need for professional competence became commonly recognized. It was thought that state affairs should not be entrusted to a ruler's kin inexperienced in statecraft, which was compared to ordering an official to make a cap from a piece of cloth instead of letting a tailor perform the task.[99] This attitude presages the appearance of experts in government.[100]

Many of the scholastic works of the Chan Kuo period are concerned with the design and philosophical bases of practical or visionary governmental systems, military strategy, or administration. Examples are the dialogues that are alleged to have taken place between Mencius and the rulers of Liang and Ch'i and that disclose the ideal economic measures of Mencius.[101] Many passages in the *Chan Kuo Ts'e* contain discussions of both grand strategy and tactics, as for instance the discussions attributed to Chang I.[102] A noble page, busy learning religious ritual, techniques of war, and courtly manners, could hardly be expected to accumulate a broad and firm knowledge of government or interstate relations, which in the Chan Kuo period became so significant that a miscalculation of an enemy's strength or a wrong appraisal of one's own state could lead to disaster.[103]

Institutions for Education

To meet the demand for training the new administrative experts and strategists, a new institution emerged in late Ch'un Ch'iu times. This was a school in which a master taught his disciples his own concepts about various subjects; the disciples learned by living with, listening to, and arguing with him. It is generally believed that the first of these masters was Confucius, who established the institutional pattern for those who followed. According to his own statement, Confucius was of humble origin, once served as an accountant, and at another time had charge of some pasture land. His ancestry is not certain, although tradition alleges that he was a scion of the Sung ruling house. He devoted himself to the acquisition of what we may term a liberal education that included history, ethics, government administration, and literature. These studies seem to have been part of his preparation for his final goal, which was to serve in a state government in order to build his ideal society, an opportunity that he never attained. In the last years of his life he had obviously given up this hope and devoted himself entirely to teaching.[104] The sound moral training that Confucius impressed upon his students gave them a dependable moral character, which was no doubt highly appreciated by rulers who had reason to be uneasy about unethically ambitious subordinates. The principles and techniques of government he taught his disciples made them valuable to sovereigns, who needed such competent men to handle their more and more complicated state affairs.[105] He considered mere bookworms inferior to able diplomats. Of his disciples, perhaps the most noted diplomat was Tzu-kung, whose international reputation stemmed not from noble blood, for he was a commoner, but from his own competence.[106] Confucius must have included statecraft in his curriculum, since he was consulted more than once by rulers and by his disciples on methods of good government. His answers were usually theoretical and may therefore have sounded impractical, but they show that he understood perfectly such basic principles as the primary importance of popular confidence in a ruler and in the reliability of his rule.[107] Education and prosperity were also the proper concern of the government of a populous state.[108] Confucius also stated that two criteria of a good minister were hard work and faithful fulfillment of duty.[109] He informed his disciples who held government office that an executive should be an example to his subordinates, should tolerate minor mistakes, and should make use of worthy men.[110]

These rather fragmentary statements show that he made sure his disciples were well educated in the art of governing. Thus his instruction produced some very able and efficient administrators. At least two influential men, one of them Chi K'ang-tzu, the *de facto* ruler of Lu, sought to employ his disciples as aides.[111] No fewer than three of them, Tzu-lu, Jan Yu, and Jan Yung, became chief stewards of the Chi family (that is, chief administrators of the Lu state). According to H. G. Creel, nine of the twenty-two students mentioned in the *Analects* attained positions of some importance and a tenth refused a position that he was offered. The offices held by these men varied from the chief stewardship to the managership of a town; some were also envoys who carried out diplomatic missions, as were Tzu-kung and Kung-hsi Hua.[112] As Creel points out, training and recommendation by Confucius had resulted in high office for so many of his disciples that some came to follow the master simply with a view to securing good positions. Confucius himself once lamented the scarcity of sincere students who could complete their three years of learning without thinking of salary.[113]

That some persons were enabled to rise from obscure backgrounds to influential positions by Confucius's own training and recommendation of them is not, however, his most important accomplishment. What is most significant is that he opened a new and lasting path by which any low-born but able young man could gain high office by his own competence. The master said he had never refused anyone who had aspirations for learning.[114] The disciples of Confucius multiplied the number of educated people by transmitting what they were taught. One of his disciples, Tzu-yu, taught ritual dance and music to the people of the town he governed. Both of these activities formerly belonged exclusively to the aristocracy.[115] While we have only limited data on the dissemination of education among the common people by followers of Confucius, it was obviously significant in accelerating social mobility.

Confucius's disciples Tzu-hsia, Tzu-chang, and Tseng Tzu, and perhaps others, spread the thoughts of the master throughout China, and were themselves respected and generally looked to as counsellors by the various rulers.[116] The followers of Confucius's disciples may in turn have reached higher positions than their predecessors. The social vacuum left by the extinction of the aristocratic class had to be filled with the best men available; this provided opportunities for men from the schools of the great masters. Wu Ch'i, for example, an early reformer and an important figure in both Wei and Ch'u, was allegedly a pupil of Tseng Tzu.[117] The instruction of these schools allowed ambitious men to acquire the education necessary to implement their plans; there was thus an obvious effect on social mobility.

The example set by Confucius was followed by many other masters, the first of whom was Mo Tzu. Mo Tzu's official career was a term of service in the Sung court; he was imprisoned after a court intrigue against him.[118] He was probably given his position in the Sung court because he had once dissuaded a ruler of Ch'u from a planned invasion of Sung and had stationed his disciples in that state to help defend it.[119] Sun I-jang lists fifteen of Mo Tzu's disciples, six of whom were recommended by him to offices in various states and another two of whom presumably reached positions of importance.[120] Mo Tzu attracted young men to study under him by promising them future opportunity to enter public service. It is reported that one of his students demanded the promised chance after a year with him.[121]

Learned masters in the Chan Kuo period almost all became leaders of large numbers of disciples and followers, as did Mencius, Tien

Shen, Hsü Hsing, and others. They traveled from state to state with their students and received gifts, respectful treatment, and emoluments. Learned men, like other persons of high reputation, were invited by rulers to fill high offices, though these were sometimes merely consultative positions. Tzu-hsia, Tuan-kan Mu, and T'ien Tzu-fang all held such offices under Marquis Wen of Wei.[122] King Hsüan of Ch'i was the greatest patron of the scholars; he gave about a thousand learned men residences in the Ch'i capital and bestowed upon them the title of *tai fu,* the old feudal title of noble ministers. They lived in luxury, discussing many philosophical problems at their leisure, and were not expected to make any practical contributions to the state. Among them were such important persons as Hsün Tzu, Ch'un-yü K'un, T'ien Pien, and Shen Tao.[123] All of them gained their high social status by their literary or academic excellence, and they thought little of noble birth. Ch'un-yü K'un is even believed to have been a former household slave.[124] Sometimes learned men were more active in state affairs than these Ch'i dilettante philosophers. The earliest reported instance of such activity in the Chan Kuo period was when three scholars were invited by Marquis Su of Chao to serve as his advisers. They initiated a political reformation in Chao and thus came to exercise a considerable degree of leadership.[125]

Most of the reformers, strategists, and career diplomats studied for a long time in preparation for their careers, and many of them eventually reached the highest governmental positions of the states. Wu Ch'i studied under Tseng Tzu; Shen Pu-hai impressed the ruler of Han by his knowledge of statecraft; and Shang Yang must have made a thorough study of administration before he fled to Ch'in, impressed the ruler with his theories, and later put them into practice. Su Ch'in, Kan Mao, Yü Ch'ing, Ch'en Cheng, Kung-sun Yen, Lo I, Fan Sui, and Ts'ai Tse, whose names have already appeared in this study, were all men of obscure origin who made their way to the highest social stratum by acquiring knowledge useful to monarchs during the time of struggle for power. Su Ch'in is a semi-legendary figure whose name is linked to an attempt to organize the eastern powers against the expansion of the ambitious state of Ch'in. However, most of the events in which he is supposed to have taken part show anachronisms when their dates are examined.[126] The dramatic story of his rise from the status of a poor student of international relations and of his struggles before he achieved success can help us understand the aspirations of such students and their road to success. It is said that Su Ch'in's family lived in a crude hut in the slums of Lo-yang. After several years of study either by himself or under the tuition of the legendary scholar Kuei Ku Tzu, who was also supposed to have been the teacher of Chang I, he decided to look to his future. He visited the Ch'in court, where he tried to interest the ruler in a plan for conquering the eastern states, but the ruler was not interested in his proposals and he was not given a court position. While in Ch'in he ran out of money and had to walk back to Lo-yang, where he appeared like a vagabond, tired and weary, before his family. They turned their backs on the exhausted Su Ch'in; even his wife continued her weaving without giving so much as a warm glance to her husband when he entered the house. This cruel treatment by his family, rather than his previous failure, drove him to work even harder. Day and night for years he worked to learn about the contemporary world and to master the technique of persuasion. He was determined never again to advise a ruler unless he felt that his reward would be riches and glory. When he had built up sufficient confidence he went to Chao to explain his theory that an alliance of the eastern states would be able to resist Ch'in, and this time he succeeded. The ruler of Chao sent him as envoy with a generous salary to win the other eastern powers to his plan. When he returned to his home in Lo-yang he received a welcome so warm that he could not help lamenting over the fickleness of human nature. At this time he said that if he had had a small piece of land to till, he might not have achieved so much.[127]

This story reveals that a man might, with no aid whatsoever, improve his status by acquiring knowledge and techniques that could be valuable in government service. With few exceptions, these men did not desire to contribute anything to the world or to improve society; their motivation was strictly selfish, the desire for a materially comfortable life for themselves. Education and hard work were nothing but a path to riches and fame; these were no quixotic idealists, but practical seekers after wealth and high position.* The successful ones accomplished their goal with such apparent ease and sudden-

---

* The motivations of such men were well expressed by Ts'ai Tse and Ning Yüeh. The former declared that his ambition was to enjoy before his death the glory and material wealth of being a minister (*SCHI*, 79/12; *CKT*, 5/10). Ning Yüeh is said to have become tired of tilling the land as a common peasant, and to have asked a friend which was the easiest way to riches and fame. His friend answered that the way was education, and that to become a learned man, one had to study for thirty years. Ning Yüeh replied that he would neither rest nor sleep in order to reach the goal in fifteen years. After fifteen years his scholastic reputation secured him a post as counselor to the ruler of Chou (*LSCC*, 24/9).

ness that others were inspired to follow their example. It is noted in the *Chuang Tzu* that, for the above reason, as soon as people heard of a good teacher they flocked to him, leaving family and occupation and often traveling far to hear his instruction.[128] Reading became so popular that Han Fei claimed that books on the theories of Kuan Chung and Shang Yang were to be found everywhere.[129] There was great enthusiasm for learning, but behind the enthusiasm lurked the practical motive of a desire for a rise in social status. According to the *Han Fei Tzu*, the appointment of two scholars to official posts stimulated half the population of their native town to sell their houses and lay aside their tools in order to seek education. No doubt this account is exaggerated, yet it reflects the Chan Kuo mind.[130]

The effect of this thirst for learning was that people of many different professions jammed into the one channel leading to the higher social strata. This is emphasized in a passage in the *Lü Shih Ch'un Ch'iu,* a work written at the close of the Chan Kuo period, as follows:

Tzu-chang was from a humble family of Lu; Yen Cho-chü was a robber in Liang-fu. Both studied with Confucius. Tuan-kan Mu was a market broker in Chin; he studied with Tzu-hsia. Kao Ho and Hsien Tzu Shih were both ruffians in Ch'i and both were objects of reproach to their neighbors. They studied with Mo Tzu. So Lu Sheh, a man of the east, was a great dissembler. He studied with Ch'in Hua Li. All of these six should have been the victims of punishment and humiliation, but they escaped these hardships and even became dignitaries who enjoyed good reputations, lived out their years, and were respected by rulers, all because they changed their lives through education.[131]

Summary

During the Ch'un Ch'iu period, brothers of rulers lost their power to the rising oligarchies of noble houses. Next the oligarchical aristocracy was ruined by the interfamilial struggles of the noble houses. At the close of the Ch'un Ch'iu period the class of noble ministers had been practically destroyed, and shortly after the beginning of the Chan Kuo period, when historical data again become available, the social stratification had changed radically because of the disappearance of the large noble ministerial families. During the power struggles among the nobles, the aid of the steward-warrior class and the commoners was sought by the involved aristocrats, and thus these two classes became more important than ever before. Some members of the two groups were promoted to higher social strata as a reward for their valuable support. At the start of the Chan Kuo period a new type of state appeared—a state in which the ruler wielded despotic power and ministers could be brought into and discharged from a bureaucratic system that selected and promoted competent men and rejected the unqualified. The much greater complication of state affairs required the services of a group of experts in statecraft instead of courtly mannered gentlemen. The necessary training, either by study under a master or by self-education, took many years to acquire. There emerged a new elite class that formed a great supply of government officers and candidates for higher social grades.

Chapter 5   Economic Changes

The economic life of pre-Ch'un Ch'iu China in general resembled the manorial system of western Europe. The manor in China was the fief of a noble household. Peasants tilled its land under the supervision of a field bailiff, and their food and clothing were supplied by the lord of the manor. When not working in the fields the peasants supplied game to the kitchens of the manor, repaired houses, and gardened, among other tasks. The peasant women were kept busy rearing silkworms, weaving and dyeing cloth for the master, and tending to their regular household duties.[1] There may have been some commercial activity around the cities, but it was probably no more than small-scale barter.[2] The cities themselves were not large; the largest cities of noble fiefs were theoretically one-third the circumference of the state capital. Other noble fief cities were supposedly one-fifth or one-ninth the circumference of the capital. The cities seem to have served as military strongholds rather than as centers of commerce.[3] The manorial economic structure was compartmentalized; each small area, usually a manor, was a self-sufficient unit. It is probable that neither inter-area exchange nor professional specialization was very significant in that structure.

During the Ch'un Ch'iu and Chan Kuo periods, ownership of the land gradually shifted from the lords of the manors to independent farmers or to landowners who were not necessarily of the nobility. Commercial activities prospered, industry became specialized and grew to major size, and urbanization appeared as a new factor in Chinese economic life. All these changes resulted in more social mobility and thus inevitably transformed the social structure.

Taxation Replaces Labor Service

The first great change was in agriculture and the land system. In the manorial system the peasant was dependent on his lord, who used his labor to grow the grain that fed the entire manor. There was no such thing as private ownership of land by the tiller and consequently there was no need to tax the peasant. The well-field system as proposed or described by Mencius seems too impractical and idealized to be a functioning layout.[4] However, his suggestions seem to have been based on the practice, already in existence in the previous period, of using the labor service of dependent peasants instead of taxing them; this is called *chi*.[5] The service was presumably for the manorial lord. In fact since the state and the government were identical with the ruling household or the ruler, there was no way to distinguish state taxes from service to the lord. A ruler could obtain his income both from his own manors and from the tribute paid by his vassals, who were in turn supported by what manors and tributaries they might have. The flaw in the system was that the peasants were hardly disposed to work efficiently on manorial land unless they were supervised by bailiffs. New economic methods were needed to eliminate this weak point.

In the state of Lu the first tax based on the amount of land held was supposedly instituted in 594 B.C.[6] This reform may have led to a basic change in the manorial system. If a peasant were commanded to pay taxes in kind, he also had to be entrusted with possession of the manorial land that he had formerly tilled for his lord. Under this circumstance he could claim the total production of the fields that he worked after paying a fixed amount of taxes in kind. The taxation rate in the time of Confucius was 20 per cent of the total yield.* Since, as has been suggested, state organization was somewhat vague before the appearance of despotic governments in the Chan Kuo period, the taxes might have been collected by landlords rather than by states.

* Legge, *Analects*, 12.9. The equivalent passage in the *Tso Chuan* states that the peasant serves his seigneur "by labor," but the *Mo Tzu* has the peasant presenting a "tax" to his lord (*TCCI*, 32/2; *MOT*, 12/1). Kato interprets the three terms mentioned by Mencius, *kung*, *chu*, and *tse*, as indicating regional as well as developmental differences; he suggests that one is labor service, one is tax according to annual yield, and one is tax at a fixed rate. It seems to me, however, that this tax reformation was more a developmental phenomenon than a regional difference, since labor service involves both direct control by the landlord over the peasant and annual shifting of fields. The latter practice is necessary for any type of technologically undeveloped agriculture, such as that of the early Ch'un Ch'iu, whereas a land tax is possible only when the peasants can use their land permanently. The purpose of tax reformation is not merely to increase the burden on the tiller. As Maspero points out, one of several variables in this reformation process was the increase in reclaimed arable land that was outside the manorial system and that needed to be incorporated into the income base of the state. Miyazaki suggests that tax reformation should be interpreted as an elevation of peasants to the tribute-paying status that had been reserved for aristocrats. See Kato, pp. 555–86; Maspero, "Le Régime féodal," pp. 124, 138; Miyazaki, "Taxation"; Amano, pp. 141–44; Bodde, "Feudalism," p. 67.

Since Ch'un Ch'iu rulers were usually overshadowed by powerful nobles, it is doubtful that there was a steady flow of taxes from the nobles to the state treasuries.

Although the Chi family governed Lu in fact, they found it difficult to extend their authority to include other noble households. A passage in the *Tso Chuan* says that the three powerful families, Chi-sun, Shu-sun, and Meng-sun, treated their dependents differently.[7] In 493 B.C. in Chin a tax collector of the Fan clan was kidnapped by retainers of an adversary clan while he was gathering taxes from Fan subjects. He was released by the adversary lord because he had been performing his duties inside the Fan domain.[8] This implies that noble families had much freedom of action inside their own fiefs. Tax rates were defined by manorial lords instead of by state governments; a steward of the Chao clan once queried his lord about the amounts set as taxes.[9]

Thus the peasant was less a subject of a state than a member of a certain noble household, and the taxes he paid could be likened to rent. A manorial dependent before the tax reform, he became a kind of rent-paying tenant after the establishment of taxation in kind. However, the former obligation of the lord to feed, house, and clothe the dependent now fell upon the peasant himself. Thus the reform of the tax system brought about a major change in the social structure; the emancipation from the status of manorial dependent and upgrading to the status of tenant gave the peasant greater freedom, but at the same time it released the lords of manors from many responsibilities.

The *Han Shu* gives an account of the yearly budget of a peasant family of five persons; the account was allegedly written by Li Kuei, the aide to Marquis Wen of Wei, who reigned 446–397 B.C. It states that a peasant tilling one hundred *mou* of land could produce a crop of one hundred and fifty *shih* of grain; each *shih* was worth thirty coins.[10] Simple calculation will show that a deficit of about 450 coins or 15 *shih* of grain existed in the budget of this representative family, as follows:

Revenue	(Coins)	Expenditures	(Coins)
Crop	4,500	Food for five persons	2,700
		Clothing	1,500
		Religious activities	300
		Tax	450
		Total	4,950

It is clear that life as depicted in the *Shih Ching* no longer existed; the peasant himself, and no one else, looked to his livelihood. A pas-

sage of the *Mo Tzu* reveals also that a peasant was held fully responsible for his work and its production. Whether the peasant would be
prosperous and well-fed or would suffer from poverty and starvation
depended only on how hard he worked, whereas in the manorial system the dependent worked only for his lord and not toward his own
ends, over which he had no control.[11]

Private Ownership of Land

The next step away from tenancy is the private ownership of land,
the concept of which was somewhat ambiguous in ancient China. In
theory, the Chou king personally owned every square inch of the
empire.[12] However, a ruler could also claim ownership of the land
in his state, which he then possessed as well as ruled.[13] In wars among
the states, territory was freely ceded, annexed, and even conquered
without consulting its nominal owner, the Chou king. In the same
manner, ministers who had been enfeoffed with land hardly respected
the nominal ownership of their seigneurs or rulers. As suggested in
Chapter 4, the fiefs of defeated noble families were redistributed by
division among victorious families, a practice in many states. There
are almost no cases on record in which a noble asked a state ruler for
permission to seize land from other noble households. It is therefore
misleading to think that the ancient Chinese concept of ownership
was the same as the modern judicial idea of ownership. What seems
to have mattered in ancient China was the actual control of a given
piece of land, not the legality of its ownership. The term "possession"
is probably more apt here than "ownership."

A lengthy discussion of these terms may help us understand the
changes that made it possible to buy and sell land. If a state owned
the land in a strict sense, land could not possibly become a purchasable commodity. However, the idea of ownership was not that clear
in ancient China. If a manorial lord kept effective and direct control
of the land, he was considered its possessor. By letting tax or rent payments be substituted for the labor service that dependents had to ren-
der in the manorial system, the lord yielded his possession in part to
the tenant, who was now the direct land user.

The strife among the nobles, as discussed in Chapter 4, decimated
the hereditary aristocratic houses. Just who survived the struggles in
a given state is not important; what matters is that afterward the sur-
vivors had become the rulers of the state. The tenants of the erstwhile
noble houses of the state found themselves tenants of a single master,
the ruler of the state. For a time, before the appearance of a new type

of landowner who expanded his holdings by purchase, there were in effect the tenants of a state; the phrase "L'Etat, c'est moi" would not have been out of place in the mind of a Chan Kuo ruler. Hence the rent a tenant paid to his lord became identical with the tax paid by a subject to his state. If land then became a purchasable commodity, the holders of titles to land were not bound to it as the manorial dependents had been.

On the other hand, the reclamation of waste land was an important project all during the Ch'un Ch'iu and Chan Kuo periods. Newly reclaimed land in Ch'un Ch'iu times did not always belong to specific manors. In 563 B.C. Tzu-ssu regulated the boundaries of fields in Cheng in order to clarify the ownership of the land, a measure that enraged some nobles who were compelled to give up parts of their land.[14] The excess land in this case was probably newly reclaimed. Twenty years later, Tzu-ch'an extended this regulation to include the entire state, whereupon some complained that Tzu-ch'an had taxed their land by incorporating it into the regular administrative system of Cheng.[15] The complainers were probably independent farmers who tilled land that they themselves had reclaimed and that had for a time been exempt from taxation. Such new territory may have accounted for a great deal of the land area of China. On the border of the states of Sung and Cheng there was a piece of no-man's-land on which six towns eventually appeared. A dispute arose about which state had sovereignty over the towns, and a war was waged to settle the problem by force.[16] In order to gain strength, the Chan Kuo states paid great attention to reclaiming cultivable land from waste territory.[17] State governments even encouraged this activity by establishing offices in charge of reclamation.[18] Thus a certain number of plebeians became independent farmers working land that had never been a part of a manor. Their claims to ownership of former waste land were no doubt stronger than claims of tenants after the tax reform to land they formerly tilled as manorial dependents.[19]

A third group of landowners existed in Chan Kuo times. To encourage military valor, Chan Kuo states often rewarded distinguished soldiers with exemptions from taxes and with grants of fertile land, as was done in Wei.[20] When Wu Ch'i was governor of Hsi-ho, he announced that the first men to reach the enemy fortifications during a charge would be given public office and rewarded with good houses and land.[21] The status of persons so rewarded was no doubt quite dissimilar to that of tenants.

Therefore, with the disappearance of the hereditary manorial lords, the emergence of independent farming on reclaimed land, and the official creation of new landowners, private ownership of the land came into existence. Only after the establishment of private ownership could the land itself become a purchasable commodity. About the period 356–338 B.C. Shang Yang initiated a series of reforms in Ch'in, some of which were to encourage the development of agriculture. He is usually held responsible for the abolishment of the field paths that are believed to have been necessary as boundaries in the manorial system. State taxes on land were also instituted for the first time in Ch'in under his administration.[22] As early as the Han dynasty it was said that his measures had caused private ownership of land to develop, and had led to the concentration of land in the hands of the rich, who bought it from the poor since the latter were not protected by state ownership.[23] This, however, is an unfair accusation. As I explained in the first chapter, the ancient land system, which has been labeled the well-field system and has been stoutly defended as a system of state-owned communes by scholars from Mencius to the Marxists, was really something like a manorial system, under which the peasant was merely a manorial dependent.[24] Moreover, the evolution toward private ownership had got under way long before the reformation of Shang Yang. His changes in the land system do not seem to have been much more than an official recognition of an existing situation. However, the concentration of land ownership and the widening of the gap between the rich and the poor may indeed have been effects of private ownership, as Shang's critics alleged.

The *Tso Chuan* seems not to mention purchase of land, but it took place quite commonly in the Chan Kuo period. It was said that when two scholars were appointed to important positions in the Chao government, half the people of their district sold their land and houses to pursue learning also.[25] The story is obviously an exaggeration, yet it reveals that land was purchasable. About the end of the Chan Kuo period, a general of Chao spent a large sum of money to buy profitable houses and land.[26] The concentration of land in the hands of the rich accelerated to such a degree that the rich owned extensive lands and the poor possessed none.[27] A Chan Kuo Confucian claimed that "in ancient times" it was improper to sell land, which seems to be an idealized disapproval of the concentration of land.[28] A consequence of this process was the widening of the gap between the rich and poor classes. A peasant who lost his land holdings usually became a hired laborer, who earned a living by helping independent farmers or the new type of landowner tenants. The hired laborers might expect a

raise in wages if they worked especially hard to till and glean the fields
of their employers.[29] Laborers were hired to drain the water in
swampy areas.[30] Horticultural gardens hired men to keep the fields
watered. A prince of Ch'i was once hired to do such work after he
had fled Ch'i to avoid capture by invaders.[31] Some of the landless
peasants also became tenants, who were sometimes charged up to 50
per cent of their crop yield for rent.[32] This was a crushing burden
compared to the legal state tax of 20 per cent. However, since many
influential persons apparently had their tenants exempted from the
onerous state labor service, many peasants preferred to pay the high
rent and have the protection of tenant status under persons of consequence.[33]

Of the many reasons why the peasants lost their land, the two that
are most apparent are, first, the heavy taxation and unseasonable
labor service imposed upon the peasants by the state, and second, the
availability of surplus capital, through political or commercial-indus-
trial prosperity, to the rich. According to the *Mencius* and the *Hsün
Tzu,* a common farmer of the Chan Kuo period had to pay the state
both in grain and in cloth produced by his wife, and was subject to
labor service in addition.[34] The field tax in Lu had reached two-
tenths by the time of Confucius, and the government apparently intended to raise it.[35] The corvée was less predictable; the government
could summon people to work on public or private construction at
any time. Chan Kuo scholars, for instance Mencius, now and then
cautioned rulers that untimely calls for labor service, especially when
the farmers should be at work in the fields, would ruin the agricultural economy of their states.[36] The farmers would have been grateful if the state had in fact taxed them only one-tenth of their crops
and three days of labor service yearly, as Tung Chung-shu supposedly stated was the "ancient" practice.[37] The peasant toiled the year
round, from the first thaw of spring, when he plowed the hard soil,
through the summer with the hot sun burning his back in the fields,
to the final harvest that still could not meet his expenses.[38] In a good
year he could feed himself and his family adequately; in poor years
he was threatened by starvation.[39] If the man of a family were recruited for corvée or military service, his dependents not only suffered
the loss of his help but had to pay certain necessary expenses for him,
thus using up their last bit of money.[40]

To save himself from utter ruin the peasant had to borrow money
from any available source; usury became common and oppressive.
He realized that after paying back a usurious loan he could be even

worse off, but he had no choice. The *Kuan Tzu* describes this miserable state of affairs as follows: A farmer received his income only after the harvest, but the state tax had to be paid before the maturity of the crops. The peasant therefore had to borrow at 100 per cent interest to pay his taxes.* Sometimes when extra water was needed at once for the grain, a farmer had to hire a laborer to help him irrigate his fields and then had to borrow to pay the man's wages. The rich, taking advantage of the farmer's lack of capital, might offer to buy his grain in the fall and then would sell it at twice the price in the spring, when the peasants were short of grain. In addition to labor service and the various taxes, the peasant had to borrow money at usurious interest rates once during each season of the year. The author of the *Kuan Tzu* account concluded that under such conditions, even the harsh penal codes could not stop the farmers from leaving the countryside. They had no assets at all; even if a farmer had the best of land and could count on a good annual crop, he could save nothing. Sons were even sold into slavery to help pay off debts.[41]

In the same book another account, which is apparently fictitious, states that in Ch'i there were thirty thousand families living on money borrowed from noble houses and other rich families at usurious rates varying from 20 to 100 per cent.[42] Mencius believed that the levying of taxes without regard for whether the crops had been good or bad forced the people to rely on moneylenders to pay the taxes and thus ruined entire families "till the aged and the children are found lying in the ditches and water channels."[43] That usury was a serious social problem is indicated by the fact that, from the Ch'un Ch'iu period on, rulers considered debt-canceling to be a measure to release the people from their burdens.[44] The best-known political figure who profited from usury was T'ien Wen or Lord Meng-ch'ang of Ch'i, who inherited the fief of Hsüeh from his father, a prince of the Ch'i ruling house. T'ien Wen was renowned for his generosity to a great many retainers of varied talents, who are said to have numbered about three thousand. On one occasion he sent a retainer supposedly skilled in accounting to collect interest payments from his fief, Hsüeh. He told this man that the interest from the debts collected in Hsüeh amounted to one hundred thousand coins, which helped to finance the tremendous expenses of keeping three thousand retainers. However, the messenger did not collect the money but burned all the notes in order to

---

* The repayment period of the loan is not mentioned, but the debt presumably was to be paid after the harvest.

win the sincere loyalty of the Hsüeh people for his lord.[45] This story illustrates two facts: the existence of usury, to the advantage of the landlord, and the change in the lord-subject relationship from a familial one, in which the lord had to provide for his dependents, to a contractual one of creditor to debtor.

Another group that could have loaned to the poor was the rich merchants and entrepreneurs, although there do not seem to be any clear accounts of their usurious activities comparable with the above stories. Nevertheless, since they had accumulated much money in the Chan Kuo period, they were logically men to whom peasants might look for loans and to whom they sold their land. The rich were accused of concentrating land in their own hands at the expense of the poor. The landless were depicted as "without one square inch of soil," an expression often used in the Chan Kuo period.[46] The rich merchants and entrepreneurs could be included among the new landowners; in fact after making their fortunes they continued to invest their capital principally in land, since there were not many other attractive outlets for investment.[47]

To summarize the situation of the farmers: During the period before the breakdown of the manorial system, the hereditary nobles possessed and controlled most of the arable land. Most of the farmers were dependents who cultivated the lord's land; in return the lord had to feed the farmers and their families. When this manorial system was replaced by taxation in kind, some of these farmers were allowed to "own" the land they worked because of the greater efficiency of the taxation system. New soil was reclaimed by independent peasants who did not necessarily belong to any manor; also some persons of merit were rewarded with land. These three groups held land outright, and thus private ownership of land was established. Land, now being available for transfer from one individual to another, was therefore a purchasable commodity. If a landholder could not keep his land because of some difficulty, it was bought up by whoever could pay the price, and the process of concentration accelerated rapidly. The new class of prosperous merchants were the potential buyers of the land, since they had accumulated much wealth by their commercial and industrial activities. The free purchase of land led almost inevitably to a widening of the gap between those who had accumulated the land and those who had been deprived of it. The former were the new class who had neither been enfeoffed with nor inherited their land. The latter were landless plebeians who either lived on their wages as hired hands or lost the struggle for life. Consequently, a new social stratification appeared in the rural population. The heavy burdens of taxation, rent, and usury quickened the growth of the army of landless peasants. Many landless peasants became a disturbing force in society by joining bandit or other outlaw groups. It was those who had no "fixed livelihood," according to Mencius, who turned against the social order.[48] Also a great many formerly independent farmers became tenants of great landowners. The jobless, the tenants, and the hired laborers suffered different degrees of downward mobility in the new social structure.

Progress of Commercial Activities

During the Ch'un Ch'iu and Chan Kuo periods several factors increased the importance of commerce. First, the increasing area controlled by individual states gave the merchant more territory in which he could safely travel. Second, the frequent contacts, both peaceful and militaristic, among the states led to improvement of highways and waterways. Third, the different regions became more interdependent because of specialization of local production. Fourth, the appearance of money facilitated commercial transactions. Local trade, accompanied by the extensive specialization of occupations, also became active. A new, powerful class of merchants thus could appear in the society that emerged after the economic changes of the Ch'un Ch'iu and Chan Kuo periods.

As suggested in the first chapter, merchants were formerly retained by noble households.[49] Their function was to obtain goods not available in their localities and to sell their local products, in order to supplement the generally self-sufficient economies of small areas. During the Ch'un Ch'iu period, a state could collect tariffs at its borders or even exact tolls from travelers at the gates of cities. The rulers of Sung once bestowed upon a meritorious person the privilege of collecting tolls at a gate of the capital.[50] A minister of Lu was accused of having established six customs houses, presumably on the state border.[51]

There were probably several tollgates in Sung and more than six customs houses in Lu; moreover, there were hundreds of states in the Ch'un Ch'iu period. In a China so compartmentalized, a merchant would have found it hard to carry on any large-scale trade if each state and city insisted on having its own customs houses to stop the passing goods. The Ch'un Ch'iu states therefore had to make agreements to ensure that trade could continue, since it was essential to all of them. It was to the ruler's advantage to encourage commercial activity by at least treating merchants generously. A state could please its neighbors by lifting the tariff, as Ch'i did during the reign of Duke Huan.[52] Facilitation of travel also became a concern of interstate relations. When Chin and Ch'u, the two greatest powers of Ch'un Ch'iu times, agreed on a policy of "peaceful coexistence" in 579 B.C., one clause of the agreement guaranteed convenient travel and transportation.[53] The interstate conflicts of the Ch'un Ch'iu period reduced the hundreds of states that had existed at the beginning of the period to seven large states and a few smaller ones. The intrastate conflicts of that period consolidated the sovereignty and efficiency of the state governments. Therefore every state in the Chan Kuo period was an effectively controlled and relatively large area, in which rule by noble households with narrow spheres of influence had been replaced by unified government. A traveling merchant could thus feel secure within the territory of any single state, and the people could enjoy good social order under the rule of an effective government. For example, we are told that while Ch'in was under the administration of Shang Yang, nothing lost on the highways would be taken by anyone.[54] Ch'i also was proud of its good order during the reign of King Wei.[55] An orderly society, no matter how the order is produced, certainly provides one element of a favorable climate for the development of prosperous business.

The second factor that aided commercial development was the improvement of highways. According to the *Shih Ching*, the Chou government built highways, straight and having a solid surface, presumably for military purposes.[56] Trees were supposedly planted along the roadsides and watchmen appointed to maintain the road.[57] This road system was probably limited to begin with or allowed to deteriorate; traveling conditions in the Ch'un Ch'iu period were sometimes very poor. For instance, the highways in Ch'en became so bad that a Chou envoy complained when he got home that the road he had taken was unrecognizable.[58] If the road system had not been improved, the large-scale transport of commodities for any great distance would have been difficult and inter-regional trade would have been almost impossible. However, throughout the Ch'un Ch'iu period official contacts among the states were frequent and important; almost every year saw several interstate meetings. For example, in 722 B.C., the first year of the reign of Duke Yin of Lu, five of the eleven events recorded in the *Tso Chuan* were visits by dignitaries from other states to Lu, or meetings between the duke of Lu and other rulers.[59]

Visits to the *Pa* ("overlord" or "First Noble") by his allies were especially frequent. An alleged regulation ordered that interstate meetings were to be held both once every three years and once every five
years. In fact, after so trivial an event as the death of a concubine of
the Chin ruler, other states sent envoys to express their condolences
to him.[60] Envoys sometimes traveled together and often carried gifts
to the host ruler. The smaller states were expected to send tribute
with their missions to the leading powers, notably Chin and Ch'u.[61]
For example, when a duke of Chin died, Cheng had an ambassador
convey its condolences. The ambassador was prepared to bring along
gifts, but another minister protested that it was improper to deliver
gifts during a period of mourning. Besides, the latter stated, the gifts
would fill up one hundred chariots attended by one thousand men.[62]
If the envoys of the Ch'un Ch'iu period were accustomed to traveling
with one hundred chariots, the road system must have been fairly
good. Thus it was the duty of a state such as Chin not only to provide fine quarters for its visitors but also to keep the roads in repair.[63]

In Chan Kuo times inter-regional communications seem to have
been more convenient than in the previous period. It was unusual
for an envoy to be sent out without at least several tens of chariots,
and even private individuals traveled without much difficulty.[64] Many
persons walked from one state to another to seek employment or to
sell their ideas concerning world affairs.[65] Scholars were also among
the army of wanderers. Confucius presumably had only a few scholars
in his entourage.[66] In later times Mencius was accompanied by several
tens of chariots and hundreds of students in his peregrinations from
state to state, and the agriculturalist Hsü Hsing traveled with a group
of students.[67] The people of centrally located Wei could see great
numbers of chariots moving upon the roads both night and day.[68]

Waterways were also developed throughout the Ch'un Ch'iu and
Chan Kuo periods, especially in the southern states of Ch'u, Wu, and
Yüeh. When Wu decided to enter the struggle to dominate the north,
she built a long canal connecting the Yangtze delta to the Huai valley and later extended it to the I and Chi rivers.[69] According to the
Shih Chi, in the eastern plain (i.e., in present Shantung and Honan
provinces) there was a canal connecting the waterway systems of the
Chi, Ju, Huai, and Ssu rivers; there were also watercourses that linked
the Han River valley with the Yangtze and Huai rivers. In the Wu
territory a cluster of lakes and rivers were connected by waterways,
and a canal in Ch'i joined the Tzu and Chi rivers. All these were
used for both navigation and irrigation.[70] In Ch'in large canals were

built in what are now Shensi and Szechwan provinces. Transportation
of grain seems to have been facilitated by the use of watercourses.[71]
The Yangtze, the greatest river in China and an important navigable
way even in ancient times, was the scene of many battles between Ch'u
and Wu. In 506 B.C. an army of Wu was transported to Ch'u by water
and inflicted upon Ch'u its greatest defeat.[72] In Chan Kuo times
boats that were able to carry fifty soldiers and their supplies for three
months could sail downstream from Szechwan to Ch'u at the rate of
three hundred *li* per day, the entire journey taking less than ten
days.* Coastal navigation was also used; on one occasion a Wu general sailed north along the seacoast to attack Ch'i.[73]

The foregoing discussion indicates that, in later Ch'un Ch'iu and
in Chan Kuo times, both land and water transportation were developed to the point that hundred-chariot loads on the roads and car-
goes of fifty persons and their belongings in boats could be moved
from one region to another. Good transportation obviously helped
commerce develop.

Regional Interdependence

Another phenomenon that went with prosperous inter-regional trade
was the regional interdependence needed to obtain specialized products. The products of local areas are listed in two sources. One of these
is the *Yü Kung* chapter of the *Shu Ching,* traditionally connected
with Yü, the founder of the Hsia dynasty (?2205–?1818 B.C.), but generally considered to be a chapter written in the Chan Kuo period.[74]
The commodities mentioned in the *Yü Kung* were allegedly items
given as tribute by vassals to the emperor; they can be regarded as
local products of the different areas. From Ch'i and Lu, located in
Yen and Ch'ing, respectively, came lacquer, silk, silk from wild silkworms, hemp, linen, dyed fabrics, salt, sea food, pine timbers, lead,
and odd-looking rocks, presumably for garden decoration. From Hsü,
which included parts of Sung, Ch'i, and Wu, came pearls, fish, musical stones, colored feathers, and fine, dark silk. Yang, which consisted
of Wu, Yüeh, and part of Ch'u, produced gold, silver, copper, jade,
tin, bamboo, ivory, raw hides, feathers, grass cloth, fabrics made from
strings of seashell pieces, oranges, and grapefruit. Ching, the area
where the state of Ch'u was located, produced gold, silver, copper,
timbers of various woods, hard stone, flint, cinnabar, bamboo, two

---

* *CKT,* 14/7. One Chan Kuo *li* equaled 1800 *ch'ih* (*CKTL.,* pp. 96–97). Therefore
three hundred *li* was equal to about 124 kilometers.

kinds of grass, dark red silk, and silk strips decorated with small pearl beads. From Yü, the central plain, came lacquer, hemp, and various grades of linen. Liang, which comprised the Pa and Shu states later annexed by Ch'in, produced iron, steel, flint, hard stone, silver, and wild animals such as bears and foxes. Yung, a part of Ch'in, produced many kinds of jade.[75]

The second source is the *Chih Fang Shih* chapter of the *Chou Li*, a work traditionally ascribed to the duke of Chou but now believed to have been written in the Chan Kuo period.[76] The *Chou Li* lists of "profitable items" or natural resources of various areas agree generally with the *Yü Kung* records. Yen and Ch'ing produced fish and seaweed, and in Yang profits could be made from copper, tin, and bamboo. From Ching came cinnabar, tin, ivory, and raw hides. Timber, lacquer, silk, and hemp were from Yü. Jade and stone were the main products of Yang. Yu, the coastal region of the state of Yen, produced fish and salt. Chi and Ping, both being areas in Chao, produced pine and fir timbers, and clothing and silk, respectively.[77]

These lists are supported by other, more scattered data. The richest area during the Chan Kuo period was apparently Ch'u, with its fertile soil, mild and moist climate, and virgin woods and lakes, which were sources of valuable goods such as large timbers and wild animals, including rhinoceroses, elephants, and deer.[78] Ivory, raw hides, and feathers were exports of the state of Ch'u.[79] Gold-bearing sand beds in Ch'u were considered state property; death was the punishment for illegally panning gold.[80] Fish and other aquatic animals were plentiful in the lakes and rivers of Ch'u, and jade, pearls, and other precious stones were available.[81] Adjoining Ch'u was the territory that is now Szechwan, where cuprous carbonate and cinnabar, useful in making dyes, were mined.[82] The eastern peninsula was occupied by Ch'i, a rich state that from early times had exported silk, hemp clothing, fish, and salt to all parts of China.[83] The special products of Yen were dates and chestnuts, while Chao was renowned for its fine hunting dogs and horses.[84]

Most of the listed commodities are natural resources; even those that were manufactured, such as fabrics or dyed clothing, were made from the raw materials found only in certain areas. It can also be observed that the products traded did not change very much from Ch'un Ch'iu to Chan Kuo times. For instance, in the Ch'un Ch'iu period Ch'u was famous for the production of metals, feathers, furs, ivory, raw hides, and timber, and horses were being raised in north China at this time.[85]

Products of the regional industries seem to be mentioned very little in the *Tso Chuan* and the *Kuo Yü*. In Chan Kuo times, however, not only did each area continue to produce its own natural commodities, but certain areas developed specialized industrial products. For instance, a type of lance was named for Hu-fu, where these weapons were manufactured, and the state of Han specialized in making swords, halberds, and other iron weapons.[86] Ch'i was well known for its purple cloth, and thus apparently had a flourishing dyeing industry.[87] The *K'ao Kung Chi*, an addendum to the *Chou Li*, states that there were no professional blacksmiths making agricultural implements in Yüeh, no armor smiths in Yen, no spear shaft makers in Ch'in, and no bow makers or chariot builders among the nomadic peoples because every man in these states or tribes knew how to make these items himself. Apparently these items were the specialized products of these areas.[88] Sabers from Cheng, axes from Sung, blades from Lu, and swords from Wu and Yüeh were considered far superior to similar weapons from other regions.[89] The story of Ching K'o's at-

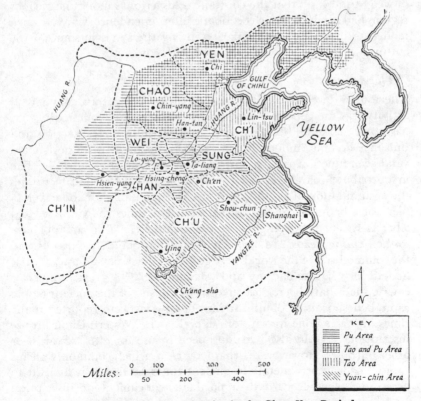

MAP 2. Distribution of Coins in the Chan Kuo Period

tempt to assassinate the Ch'in ruler mentions that the best daggers were made in Chao.[90]

The specialization of industry in some areas probably created a demand for better trade facilities among the different regions. It is also probable that new convenience in exchanging goods could have stimulated that specialization. In any case, the development of inter-regional trade seems to have been aided by such specialization, which Hsün Tzu had already noticed.[91] A jar of metal money from practically every state of the Chan Kuo period was discovered recently at a site in Jui-ch'eng, Shansi province. This discovery indicates fluid circulation of commodities and wealth between different regions. The changing frequency of various types of money also shows changes in economic influence (see the accompanying map): thus the prevalence of Ch'i knife money in Chao and Yen late in the Chan Kuo period coincided with the expansion of Ch'i economic influence over these areas. Furthermore, the wide distribution of a standardized unit of weight indicates that the constant transactions among the various regions had produced much economic interdependence, which in turn tended to produce more similarity among the states in some of the cultural traits most closely associated with commerce.[92]

The Appearance of Coinage

The fourth development that accompanied prosperous commercial activity was the general use of bronze money. Any commodity that has great marketability may serve as a medium of transaction and thus may become "money." Yet only metallic money with designated values can function as a measure of value and as a store of value. The first attribute guarantees fair transactions and the second facilitates the accumulation of capital. Both are indispensable for the development of a booming trade.[93] In very ancient times the Chinese used a barter system of exchange.[94] A passage in the *Hsi Tz'u,* an appendix to the *I Ching,* reads: "Market time was set at noon. The people and the commodities of the world were gathered. Each person traded what he had for what he had not and was satisfied."[95] A great number of cowrie shells have been excavated from the site of the ancient Shang capital. Bestowals of double strings of cowries were reported many times in oracle bone inscriptions as well as in Western Chou bronze inscriptions.[96] Gold also had long been in use for gifts, rewards, or other purposes. However, the character *chin,* which commonly means "gold," had meant "metal" in ancient times, so that it is difficult to determine whether *chin* in a particular document or inscription means gold, silver, or copper, the three valuable metals. It is certain that these metals were used as money in standardized units of weight, but the actual weight of the unit is uncertain. Yang believes that the *yüan* or *lieh* unit weighed about 3/100 of a catty, but other scholars are of different opinions.[97] Two bronze inscriptions mentioned that metal was to be used for payment.[98]

Cloth was also used as a medium of exchange. A discussion of cloth money presents two difficulties. First, the character *pu* 布 refers both to a certain type of spade-shaped money and to hemp cloth, and it is sometimes hard to tell from the context which is meant. Second, it is difficult to decide whether the cloth money was regulated as to weight, length, and value, or whether it was merely a commodity of exchange with no fixed units. Cloth seems to have been used in both ways, although there is evidence that bundles of cloth, silk in particular, had definite length and weight, and therefore definite value.[99]

Both hemp cloth and silk were sometimes used as commodities for barter transactions. An inscription on a bronze tripod records that five male slaves were once traded for a horse and a bundle of silk.[100] The *Tso Chuan* describes more than one instance of the use of hemp cloth or silk for bribery, as when a messenger of Lu bribed an important Ch'i courtier with a piece of cloth eight *chang* long, which was nevertheless so fine that it could be rolled into a bundle no thicker than an earring.[101] Such unusually fine material seems not to have been regular cloth money, but an article of barter.

The mention of *pu* in the *Mang* verse of the *Shih Ching* has been considered evidence for the existence of spade money in Ch'un Ch'iu times. However, the poem in question says that the *pu* here was carried in the arms of a girl, implying that it was really cloth instead of spade money, which was small enough that one did not have to carry it in one's arms.* Other items in use in Ch'un Ch'iu times as exchange commodities were grain, chariots, horses, and raw hides. On one occasion, a captured general of Sung was ransomed by a payment from his state to Cheng of four hundred horses and one hundred chariots.[102] A Lu envoy promised a minister of Ch'i five thousand measures of grain if Ch'i would not interfere with the exile of

* Legge, *She King*, 1.5.4. Wang Yü-chüan insists that this *pu* should be spade money, which, he thinks, was bound in a bundle so that the phrase "carried in arms" is still meaningful. His argument, however, does not seem convincing, since the heroine in this poem is going to the market to purchase some silk. It is rather doubtful that she would carry such a large amount of metal coins, which would be much more valuable than silk. See *CKHP*, p. 32.

the duke of Lu.[103] A captive from a conquered state was bought by a
Ch'in minister for five sheepskins.[104]

Commodities were also used generally for payments in the Chan
Kuo period. Many instances are given in literature of the payment
of officials' salaries in grain; for example, a disciple of Mo Tzu was
offered a salary of five hundred vessels of grain to serve in the government of Wey.[105] The brother of Ch'en Chung-tzu received a salary
of ten thousand *chung* or cups of grain.[106] Silk and other cloth were
still used as valuable presents in the Chan Kuo period. The ruler of
Wey, fearing an invasion from neighboring states, sent an envoy with
three hundred bundles of heavy fabrics and three hundred *i* of gold
to Ch'u to appeal for aid.[107]

However, even though commodities continued to be used for payments throughout the Ch'un Ch'iu and Chan Kuo periods, metallic
currency of fixed value was introduced in the fourth and third centuries B.C., according to Yang Lien-sheng.[108] In the twenty-first year
of the reign of King Ching of Chou (524 B.C.), the issue of heavy coins
is said to have been discussed. As reported in the *Kuo Yü*, the discussion went into much detail about the weight relationship between
the heavy coins and the light coins. As Yang suggests, this passage may
have been written in the Chan Kuo period, when coins differing in
denomination, size, and weight were in circulation.[109] The discussion
about weight relationship under the date 524 B.C. might have been
inserted by the author of this passage in the *Kuo Yü*, but this sug-
gestion can hardly be proved. The appearance of money in 524 B.C.,
however, is not impossible, since many varieties and denominations
of money had appeared by Chan Kuo times.[110]

In any case, the use of money in the Chan Kuo period was quite
common; this conclusion is amply supported by both documentary
and archeological evidence. (See Fig. 1.) Metallic currency generally appeared as spade money (*pu*), knife money (*tao*), round coins
(*ch'ien*), and checker pieces (*yüan*). The *Mo Tzu*, which contains
much early Chan Kuo material, mentions money several times.[111] In
later works, such as the *Hsün Tzu* and the *Han Fei Tzu,* the references to the use of money are still more definite and conspicuous.[112]
As for archeological evidence, many different denominations of
money have been excavated. Each of the seven large states and the
tiny Chou domain issued its own money of whatever shape, designation, weight, and value it chose, each coin stamped with the name of
the place where it was minted. Typical inscriptions read "Legal
money of Ch'i" or "Legal money of Chi-mo" (Chi-mo was a city in

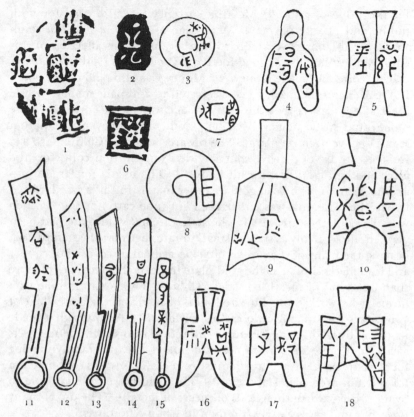

Fig. 1. Varieties of Bronze Coins: after *KKCC*, Fig. 24.
1. Chen Lei; 2. T'ung Pei; 3. Li Shih; 4. An-yang; 5. Hsiang-ping; 6. Yin Lei;
7. I Huo; 8. Huan; 9. Pu (hollow head); 10. Chin-yang Erh Chin; 11. Ch'i Fa
Huo; 12. Huo (pointed head); 13. Ming Tao; 14. Han Tan; 15. Chin-yang
Hsin Huo; 16. Li Shih; 17. Ch'ang-tzu; 18. Yin-chin I Chin.

Ch'i). Generally speaking, spade money was from the central plain
states, Han, Chao, Wei, Sung, Cheng, Yen, and Chou. Knife money
originally appeared exclusively in Ch'i, yet one variety of it invaded
Chao and Yen. Round money was the money of Ch'in until the unification, when it became the only denomination of all China. Checker
pieces occupied the Yangtze valley territory of Ch'u. (See the map on
p. 121.) Money was often discovered several hundred miles away from
its place of origin, mixed with money from other places.[113]

In the Chan Kuo period money had many functions. In the *Mo
Tzu* it is written that the king-knife, or *wang-tao,* served as a standard

for the value of grain.[114] Metallic currency was also used for both
public and private payments. A passage of the *Han Fei Tzu* states
that a hired laborer worked hard not because of his affection for his
employer but because of good food and good wages paid in what was
called "coins and spade money."[115] Money was also paid out as taxes;
in the *Mencius* the market tax is referred to as "spade money," while
the *Hsün Tzu* says that the military tax was in the form of "knife
money and spade money."[116] The amount of money in circulation
seems to have been very large. The reward posted by Ch'in in 238 B.C.
for the capture of a rebel courtier was "one million coins for him
alive and half a million for his body."[117] The media for large transactions seem to have been gold or other metals in units standardized
by weight. The unit was either the *chin* (one catty) or the *i*, which
varied in different areas.[118] In the state of Ch'u gold plate had been
marked into as many as sixteen small squares per plate by stamps each
bearing the name of the capital city. Occasional discoveries of copper
and lead pieces similar to the gold plate indicate that currency of more
than one kind of metal existed in Ch'u.[119] The yearly income of a
farmer who worked one hundred *mou* of land was the equivalent of
two pieces (presumably two catties) of metal.[120] A family that made
its living by washing and beating silk refuse into small, useful sheets
earned not more than a few pieces of metal, but this family's recipe
for a medicine to protect the hands from chilblains was sold by them
for one hundred pieces of metal.[121] The rich, however, were able to
own property worth thousands of pieces of metal.[122] The use of many
types of money was clearly common in Chan Kuo times.

With relatively stable political situations inside the large states,
good highways and watercourses to facilitate transportation, and the
convenience of metallic money, a merchant could make a good living
from the special products of the different areas. Thus prosperous inter-regional commerce was made possible.

Types of Professions

Occupational specialization and efficient trading systems promoted
prosperous commerce in local areas. Both factors may have been both
cause and effect of each other and of the prosperity. The *Shih Ching*
depicts the economy of a manor as quite self-sufficient. The farmer
hunted for meat and fur, repaired his own house, and even made his
own rope. His family raised silkworms, and wove and dyed silk and
other cloth; vegetables were grown in gardens to supply the manor,
and sheep were raised in pastures.[123] By Mencius's time, however, the

life of an independent farmer was far from self-sufficient. The *Mencius* says that a farmer could not supply his own cloth, cooking pots, or implements, but depended for them upon people in other occupations, whom he in turn supplied with grain.[124] Thus by Chan Kuo times the specialization of occupations had caused the persons in these occupations to become interdependent.

Other documents also point to specialized occupations. The *Chuang Tzu* tells of a destitute man who made his living by tailoring and doing laundry.[125] The business of washing silk refuse has already been mentioned, as well as the special recipe for medicine to protect the workers' hands from chilblains.[126] The blacksmith and the carpenter were specialized artisans.[127] There were weavers of reed curtains.[128] Plantation-keeping was referred to as a specialized occupation.[129] Bow-making also demanded knowledge of a very specialized technique.[130] In the state of Sung there was a shoemaker's shop recorded as having been in business for three generations.[131] Manufacturing a chariot required the services of several distinct types of artisans; the complexity of professional differentiation is evident.[132] The *K'ao Kung Chi* also mentions many different occupations.[133]

The existence of occupational specialization is further supported by archeological evidence. Eight thousand stone pieces, including finished and semi-finished stone obelisks and jade objects, were excavated from the Chan Kuo strata at the site of the ancient city of Loyang, from what is believed to be the site of a sculptor's workshop that specialized in ritual burial objects.[134] In the remains of a Chan Kuo smithy, excavated at Hsing-lung in Jehol, eighty-seven pieces of molds for tools and implements were found.[135]

A bronze foundry that was excavated at Hou-ma (Shansi province) in 1959 reportedly yielded tens of thousands of crucibles and molds of varying shapes and sizes, most of them for casting spades, chisels, and spade money. Great quantities of molds for making belt hooks and bronze chariot parts were excavated from a neighboring site. Three workshops for making decorative objects from bone and deer horn existed in the same area; the raw materials and semi-finished products found here seem to show highly refined techniques of cutting and engraving. Remains of pottery kilns containing unbaked clay vessels and unshaped clay balls were found in a half-kilometer circle in the area.[136] These excavations disclose that certain Chan Kuo industries carried on large-scale production of one line of goods such as iron implements, bronze vessels, or pottery; this in turn shows a high degree of specialization.

This specialization implies a demand for a specialization in the storage and distribution of the products. Otherwise, as Mencius stated, the farmer's surplus grain and cloth would be wasted instead of traded for other needed materials.[137] Towns in the Chan Kuo period seem to have had markets that opened for business in the mornings.[138] There were apparently brokers who made their profits in these markets by storing low-priced goods and selling high-priced goods, and who therefore had to be familiar with everything that went on in the market. Such brokers were said by Mencius to "look out for a conspicuous mound" and get up on it in order to spot immediately any possibility of profit.[139] Inter-regional and local trade thus prospered by exchanging specialized products among different areas or among people of different occupations. The people who carried on this trade constituted a new class, whose members did not have to toil in the fields but who nevertheless possessed more wealth and even more grain than the hard-working farmers.[140] The merchants seemed odd to the ruling groups because they held no offices and were of no political consequence, yet they could live as luxuriously, even spend as much money, as state rulers.[141] Indeed, persons of the merchant class possessed as much material wealth and importance as rulers and ministers, but still had the social status of subjects and commoners.

There may have been many successful merchants, but information about them seldom found its way into the historical records. Ssu-ma Ch'ien was the first and indeed the only conventional historian to devote a chapter to these prosperous businessmen. Three of them, Tzu-kung, T'ao Chu Kung, and Pai Kuei, lived during the transition from the Ch'un Ch'iu period to the Chan Kuo. A passage of the *Analects* seems to imply that Tzu-kung, said to be the richest of Confucius's disciples, gained his wealth in commerce.[142] T'ao Chu Kung was said by Ssu-ma Ch'ien to have been Fan Li, a minister under the ruler of Yüeh; this identification is doubtful, however. In any case T'ao Chu Kung happened to move to the city of T'ao, a center of inter-regional transport, where he amassed tremendous wealth. His theories of commercial enterprise included such concepts as the relationship between money circulation and the effective use of capital, and the axiom that one must not fail to grasp opportunities.[143] Pai Kuei was a minister of Wei. One of his theories was the very modern idea, "buy cheap and sell dear." His servants apparently aided him in his commercial enterprises.[144] Besides the above three, the same chapter of the *Shih Chi* mentions a salt manufacturer, an iron producer, a rancher, and a widow who owned a cinnabar mine. The last two were highly esteemed by the Ch'in ruler, who gave the rancher a high-ranking seat among the nobles at court and built a terrace for the widow.[145] Lü Pu-wei, who started out as a merchant in the Chao capital, should also be listed among the rich and successful. He realized that to "sell" a king could be infinitely more profitable than to sell pearls and jade, which could return only a limited profit. He spent a large amount of money to install his friend, a son of the Ch'in heir apparent, on the throne of that state and was duly rewarded with the chancellorship. His may have been a unique case, but it indicates a great change from the time when merchants were little better than dependents of noble households.[146]

Another rich man (there is no proof that he was a merchant) was appointed because of his wealth to the governorship of a Han prefecture. His money—about ten thousand pieces of metal—was considered a source of support for the state of Han.[147] This was not an unusual case; Han Fei said that the custom by which courtiers recommended a person for office was a system of selling the offices, since only rich men could afford the necessary bribes. He stated that since the office could be sold, a businessman need not remain in a humble position. He expressed concern that this easy channel to high position might lure the farmers from their fields, which demanded more work and afforded little opportunity for social ascent.[148] Others also worried about the farmer's leaving his toilsome occupation. The *Kuan Tzu* says that an artisan or merchant could earn five days' expenses by working one day, whereas a farmer could toil the year round and still not be able to feed himself. Thus the people were leaving their farms and taking up other occupations.[149]

In summarizing the discussion about the development of commerce, we find that several correlated factors aided the prosperity of commerce and industry. The appearance of the class of rich businessmen probably affected social mobility in many ways. These men won their social standing neither by owning land nor by the hereditary prestige of nobility but by their wealth alone. However, both land and high office now become available to the rich merchant if he were willing to spend large amounts of money to obtain them.* Lü Pu-wei was evidently quite successful in gaining both. Most of the rich merchants may have eventually become large landowners, since they had surplus capital to buy up the land that farmers were forced by high taxes, usury, and other causes to sell. On the other hand, the ease and

---

* Even in Ch'in, the state where the only channel to a noble title was supposed to be military merit, during one famine anyone who could present one thousand *shih* of grain to the government was to be granted one degree of noble rank (*SCHI*, 6/2).

comfort of the merchant's life attracted farmers, who left their land to seek the pot of gold at the end of the rainbow of commerce and industry. Some of them were probably successful in entering the class of *nouveaux riches,* but perhaps most of them ended up joining the army of vagabonds, bandits, and proletarians. It is possible, even if speculative, that conditions for this latter class were much the same as for the landless peasants who were not tenant farmers yet could not find employment as hired hands on the farms of others.

The Effects of Technological Progress

In this section we will consider economic developments that increased agricultural production, such as the use of iron implements, fertilizer, and irrigation; we will also consider urbanization, which was primarily a consequence of commercial and industrial development. The two phenomena are related in that increased farm production may lead to a labor surplus in the countryside that urbanization can absorb. Thus there may have been horizontal mobility from the countryside to the towns, which might have been accompanied by a rise or fall in social status.

As for iron implements, Chang Hung-chao believed that their use in China began some time between the Ch'un Ch'iu and Chan Kuo periods.[150] Archeological excavations support this theory, since iron tools and implements were found only in Chan Kuo and in later strata.[151] There is also documentary evidence: for instance, a mention in *Mencius* of farmers' using iron implements.[152] The adoption of iron implements can be regarded as a revolutionary advance in agriculture.[153] However, it must be noted that the Chan Kuo iron tools were not yet widely adopted and were so poor that they might not have been much more useful than bronze tools. In fact, the Chan Kuo iron implements in many instances were found buried side by side with bronze, stone, and even seashell tools. (See Fig. 2.)[154] The Chan Kuo iron tools all seem to be made of cast iron and are uniform in shape everywhere in China. Wooden implements tipped with iron blades were found in quantity; the iron tools were usually small, thin, and fragile. The efficiency of such primitive forms is doubtful. Plow blades, for example, were set at too wide an angle to dig deep furrows. (See Fig. 3.) As Huang suggested, Chan Kuo agriculture was still at a low level in learning to use iron implements.[155] Iron tips on wooden implements are no doubt advantageous, but their importance is hard to evaluate.

A hypothesis that satisfactorily relates improvements in production

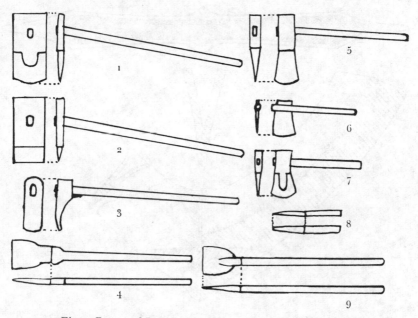

Fig. 2. Restored Iron Implements; after *HHPK*, Fig. 100.
1, 2, and 3—hoes; 4—spade; 5, 6, and 7—adzes; 8—chisel; 9—spade.

to changes in social institutions has yet to be propounded and accepted; the importance of the use of iron, although it does bear on this question, cannot be determined for the Chan Kuo period until more evidence is available. Cheng Te-kun rightfully points out that the new society demanded the introduction of iron and the improvement of technology, but that in return they accelerated the shaping of a unified China. Any statement that goes further than this seems at present to be mere exaggeration of the importance of iron implements, to which the dynamics of social change in the Chan Kuo period have often been attributed.[156]

Many irrigation systems were also built; in the early Chan Kuo period, the formerly useless soil of Yeh was made fertile by an irrigation system built by the governor that drew water for the territory from the Chang River.[157] Another great engineering work is the world-renowned Tu-chiang Dam in Szechwan, built in the third century B.C. and still in use today.[158] The "Rivers and Canals" chapter of the *Shih Chi* contains a good, brief description of irrigation systems. The effect of irrigation on agricultural production is shown by a canal three hundred *li* long that watered an area of forty thousand *ch'ing*

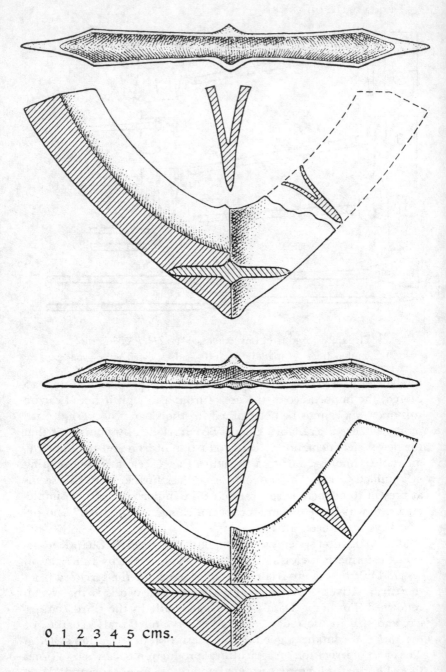

0 1 2 3 4 5 cms.

Fig. 3. Iron Plow: after *HHPK*, Fig. 108.

in what is now Shensi. Each *mou* of land produced a crop of one *chung,* five times the pre-irrigation yield.* The well-sweep or *chieh k'ao* seems to have been common, even though it was newly introduced; its design and efficiency are mentioned in the *Chuang Tzu.* It is praised for making it possible to raise much more water than could have been raised by hand.[159] Fertilizer was also in use in Chan Kuo times; it was mentioned by Mencius and in a *Chou Li* passage that indicates that different kinds of fertilizer were used on different soils.[160] The last chapters of the *Lü Shih Ch'un Ch'iu* and the *Yü Kung* chapter of the *Shang Shu* contain detailed discussions about various means for improving soil conditions.[161]

Despite these techniques and devices, Chan Kuo agriculture, though somewhat superior to that of previous periods, still remained more or less crude. A statement attributed to Li Kuei (ca. 460–400 B.C.) reveals that in the best years the crop yield could be as much as four times the average, while in the worst years it was sometimes one-fifth the average yield. Li Kuei also said that the most diligent farmer could add one-fifth to the yield and the laziest would reduce it by one-fifth.[162] Nature apparently had far more influence on the crops than man did; this ratio between natural and human factors is a fairly good measure of how highly developed an agricultural system is. Thus a Chan Kuo farmer, though he might enjoy most of the remarkable innovations we have discussed, still had to pin most of his hopes for a good harvest on nature. The rural areas were probably affected not only by iron implements and other technological advancements, but also by the changes in the taxation system, in the ownership of land, and in the other social institutions that were discussed in the first part of this chapter. A population shift from the countryside to the city could be just as well attributed to heavy taxes, high rent, and usury, as to the smaller demand for labor and the surplus population on farms that would be caused by technological progress.

---

* *SCHI,* 29/2–3. One *ch'ing* equaled one hundred *mou.* The *Kuan Tzu* says the average crop was twenty *chung* per *mou* (*KT,* 23/15). A study of Chan Kuo irrigation engineering was written by a geologist and hydraulic engineer, Weng Wen-hao; see *KTKK.* The effects of irrigation and hydraulic engineering are very much overstated by some scholars, notably by K. A. Wittfogel, who claims to have derived his concepts of "Oriental Society" and "Oriental Despotism" from Karl Marx and the Marxists; see Wittfogel, *Oriental Despotism,* and his recent paper, "The Marxist View of China"; cf. Meisner. For a brief description of such theories, see Fairbank, pp. 47ff. For critical discussion of them, see Eberhard, *Conquerors,* pp. 20–21, 23–26, 34ff, and Bodde, "Feudalism," p. 80. At least in this case, we can see that all the public works were constructed and probably managed by local officials, not by the central government as Eberhard clearly stated.

The Emergence of Cities

The ancient cities were more or less the fortresses of nobles who controlled the surrounding areas from them and made them places of refuge for their subjects in times of war. These cities were usually small; it was said that a large city should be small enough to be surrounded by a wall no more than 4,600 meters long so that it would be one-third the size of the capital and would not overshadow it. A medium-sized city was supposed to be one-fifth the size of the capital, and a small one, one-ninth.[163] One Wey minister was enfeoffed with sixty to one hundred towns. Wey was not a large state and the towns may have been quite small.[164] In fact, some towns were said to have populations of only ten families.[165] The new Wey capital was established after invading barbarians had destroyed the old one; at that time it had a population of about five thousand. The population of the old capital must have been greater; however, the new capital equaled in population two smaller cities, which could not have been very large.*

A city in the domain of a Ch'un Ch'iu noble was of military rather than economic importance. The fall of a city meant the fall of the noble household that ruled it, as was shown, for instance, by the assignment of a steward to run the capital of the Meng-sun estate.[166] By the end of the Ch'un Ch'iu period, a city could serve either as a fortress or merely as a source of revenue for its ruler. When one Chao subordinate was sent to govern a town, he asked his superiors which of the two functions they expected him to carry out.[167] Here, perhaps, is a hint of the fusion of fortress and market that Max Weber theorized about.[168]

A passage of the *Chan Kuo Ts'e* records that a large city of the previous period did not exceed three hundred *chang*, which presumably refers to the length of one side of its wall, and that its population would be no more than three thousand families. The passage says fur-

---

* TCCI, 11/5–6 (Min 2). Japanese scholars do not agree about the nature of cities in ancient China. Some of them, such as Miyazaki Ichisada and Kaisuka Shigeki, try to put Chinese cities into the Greek mode by borrowing the term "city-state" and suggesting the existence of "citizens" in these ancient cities. Others, such as Utsunomiya Kiyoyoshi and Matsumoto Mitsuo, suggest that under the feudal system, each city should fit into a hierarchy. I tend to agree with the latter school, though later development saw the hierarchical system collapse. I strongly doubt the existence of "citizens" in the Greco-Roman sense in ancient Chinese cities. See Miyazaki, "The Age of City-States"; Utsunomiya, pp. 16–17; Oshima, pp. 40, 53; Amano, p. 90; Kaizuka, pp. 43–62. The Chan Kuo states were all territorial states with cities serving many functions, particularly as centers of commerce and of administration. See Amano, p. 156, and Miyazaki, "Towns and Cities," pp. 342ff.

ther that in Chan Kuo times settlements of ten thousand families and one thousand *chang* on a side were located within sight of one another. This section, allegedly a conversation between two strategists, concludes that it would be difficult to besiege a settlement of such a size with only thirty thousand men, since this number could barely hold one corner of it.[169] A typical Chan Kuo city was supposed to have an outer wall of seven *li* in circumference and an inner settlement three *li* in circumference; these specifications appear frequently in Chan Kuo writings. An excavation of the site of Han-tan, the capital of Chao, revealed that the main castle, which served primarily as a palace for ruler and staff, occupied a square with 1,400-meter sides.

Recent archeological discoveries confirm the accounts in ancient documents of the structure and general size of Ch'un Ch'iu and Chan Kuo cities. The largest site is Yen Hsia-tu of Hopei province, excavated in wartime, which covers an area of 6,500 meters from east to west and 5,000 meters from north to south. A city at Loyang, Honan, dug up by the Communists in 1958, covers an area of 8,000,000 square meters. Han-tan, also excavated during the war, consists of two walled sections with eight gates in the walls. Earth mounds dotted inside the walled areas of both Yen Hsia-tu and Han-tan have been interpreted as sites of platform buildings that probably housed part of the ruling group. The ruins of a city with three concentric walls at Yen-ch'eng village in the lower Yangtze valley were found at the top of a small hill. There are several small ruins that range from a few hundred meters on each side to several thousand meters. Some of these are in fact the sites of inner cities. The following tabulation shows the sizes of some sites in terms of the size of Han-tan. (See Fig. 4.)

Yen Hsia-tu	11.42 times Han-tan area
a Ch'i city	5.26 times Han-tan area
Hsüeh	3.42 times Han-tan area
a Lu city	2.11 times Han-tan area
T'eng	0.47 times Han-tan area

All the sites vary in both size and nature; some were probably state capitals and others were presumably provincial towns. It is difficult to determine their general features from the generally accepted data. However, some constants have been noted by Chang Kwang-chih. They were all surrounded by stamped earth walls that were arranged to be fairly square or rectangular, though in some cases they were irregular. The orientation of the city enclosure and of the ceremonial and palace structures was consistently guided by the cardinal directions. Earthen mounds were the foundations for political or cere-

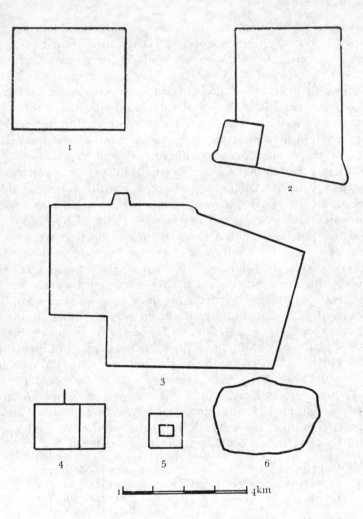

Fig. 4. Chan Kuo City Sites: after *KKCC*, Fig. 26.
1. Hsüeh; 2. a Ch'i city; 3. Yen Hsia-tu; 4. Han-tan; 5. T'eng; 6. a Lu city.

monial structures. Most significantly, a city always consisted of sections that were specialized, though not self-sufficient, for carrying out
economic, political, and religious functions.

A change of great significance in city layout that occurred toward
the end of the Ch'un Ch'iu period was the construction of new outer
walls to embrace large industrial, residential, and commercial quarters. In the Yen-ch'eng case, we can even see the three circles. The
existence of this process that brought within the walls sections other
than the original core, which later became the center of administration and of aristocratic residences, was suggested by Miyazaki and
has been confirmed by archeological evidences. The process was one
consequence of the change in the function of cities from that of mere
fortified strongholds to that of industrial-commercial centers.[170]

Chan Kuo cities developed even further in this direction. Chan Kuo
city sites are normally quite large. Such sites as Lo-yang, Lin-tzu, and
Yen Hsia-tu seem to have housed a considerable population of remarkable density. Even more important was the increasing specialization in handicrafts. All kinds of business and all walks of life were
jammed into the commercial streets.[171] Lin-tzu, a first-class city, was
described as follows: It had a population of seventy thousand families.
The streets were packed with people, the roads jammed with traffic.
There were even all sorts of games to amuse the populace. Yen-ying,
the capital of Ch'u, seems to have been quite as prosperous as Lin-
tzu.* There were market areas or business zones in the cities. Shop-
keepers were obliged to pay a special tax, which was sometimes high.
The market tax near the northern frontier of Chao was earmarked
for the support of the garrison troops and was therefore collected by
a military officer.[172] In the market place there were all kinds of shops,
from butcher shops to wine houses; persons of all trades, from divin-
ers to brokers, plied their callings.[173] According to the *Yen T'ieh Lun*,
eleven cities were of first-rate importance and prosperity.[174] The importance of the big cities was discussed by Ssu-ma Ch'ien, who saw
that their greatest significance, and the reason why they were commercial centers, was that they were located at the junctions of main
trade routes.[175] The people of Lin-tzu, one of the big cities, were of

* For information on Lin-tzu, see *CKT*, 8/8, and *SCHI*, 69/10. The population of
Lin-tzu is a moot question. It is said that each of the seventy thousand households
could provide three males for military service. Though the number of households
does appear possible, the statement that three soldiers could be drawn from each
household seems highly suspect. Cf. Miyazaki, "Towns and Cities," pp. 345–46;
Sekino, *Chinese Archaeology*, pp. 279–80. For information on Yen-ying and Han-
tan, see *TPYL*, 776/3.

all professions and origins, and were depicted as generous, witty, argumentative, shrewd, and courageous in private fighting but cowardly in the face of enemies of their state.[176] This seems to be a good description of a big, noisy, insecure metropolis not unlike Chicago.

In modern industrial society, metropolitan areas have fluid social mobility because occupational specialization opens up more opportunities, because most positions require some sort of training, because new positions are created by economic growth and population expansion, and because the cities have a lower birth rate than the rural areas. The city of Chan Kuo China was hardly comparable with the twentieth-century industrial city, yet in contrast to the rural community or the "fortress" administrative center of the preceding period, it does show remarkable similarity to its modern counterpart.[177]

Unfortunately we lack records of the activities of the bourgeois and proletarian urbanites. But, as has been suggested previously, many people who fled their miserable and arduous existence in the country were lured to the city by its comfortable and easy life and, after gaining employment, joined the already crowded urban population. It is not unreasonable to suppose that there was more social mobility in the big cities than in the countryside. There may have been a great many people exerting themselves to the utmost to win wealth, but very few succeeded. Of the few successful ones, only T'ao Chu Kung, Tzu-kung, Pai Kuei, and Lü Pu-wei were recorded by historians. The rest, successful or unsuccessful, triumphant or despondent, rich or poor, have all been forgotten. In the state capitals there were usually many people who had trained themselves for government service, but of these only Mo Tzu, Mencius, Hsün Tzu, and a very few others were entered in the historical records. One can imagine that some of them, upon meeting with disillusionment, either returned to their home villages, like Su Ch'in after he had spent his fortune in the Ch'in capital, or stayed in the city and sought a career in some other field. These milled about in the urban society, ascending or descending in status as chance and their abilities dictated.

Summary

Because of great changes in agriculture, commerce, and industry in the Ch'un Ch'iu and Chan Kuo periods, the self-sufficient local economy of the manors broke down. Private ownership (or at least possession) of land emerged because of changes in the tax system. Land became concentrated in the hands of fewer people because of heavy taxation, high rent, and usury, which caused farmers in desperate financial straits to sell their land to whoever could buy it. Manorial dependents became tenants, as did some of the independent farmers who reclaimed waste lands. Some of the farmers held on to their land and became independent landowners; others lost it and became hired laborers, bandits, or proletarians. Some traveled to the strange and bewildering cities, and sought careers as scholars, public servants, artisans, or merchants.

The political unification of large areas, the relative security of travel, the specialization and differentiation in occupations and in production of commodities in different areas, and the appearance of metallic money, all heralded the emergence of prosperous commerce. People appeared who owed their social status to their wealth instead of to noble birth or to merit in military or civil service. The surplus capital of this class accelerated the concentration of land. Some of them even became involved in politics, aided by their accumulated wealth, as did Lü Pu-wei. The great commercial development led to the growth of commercial cities whose inhabitants led an urban life radically different from life in the fortress or manor. Thus new channels of social mobility were formed and a new structure of society emerged.

Chapter 6 Changes in Ideas

The social changes discussed in the preceding chapter were both reflected and supported by changes in concepts and attitudes. New values modified or replaced the old, and the traditional terms acquired radically different meanings.

The ruler-minister relationship shifted from a familial to a contractual basis; the ruler ceased being a semi-divine paternalistic figure and became the head of a secular government. Pious groups such as the Mohists believed that heaven was concerned equally with all mankind, that all men were created equal, that therefore no one man had any heavenly mandate to rule, and that moreover the members of the ruling group had no grounds for claiming heavenly backing for their high social positions. Meanwhile in statecraft the idea was developed that government offices should be filled by persons qualified either in virtue as advocated by the Confucianists or in competence and merit as emphasized by the *Fa Chia*, "Administrative School," to meet the demands of the new pattern of government.[1] Both schools argued that birth should not be a criterion for appointment to government office or for social status. The skeptical philosophers, usually called the Taoists, denounced both the established moral concepts and the worldly vanity of seeking high position, since they thought inner tranquility was the only worthwhile goal. This school, in opposition to the Confucianists and the Administrative school, did not encourage people to seek higher status, but the Mohists, like the other two groups, justified the ascent of competent persons from the lower classes to positions of higher status and hence favored social mobility. However, the denunciation of established moral concepts by the Taoists helped bring about social change, since it undermined the values that justified the established social structure. Thus all these philosophical schools either positively or negatively helped provide the ideological background for the appearance of active social mobility in Chan Kuo society and for the rise of the new moral values that are exemplified by the changing connotations of the term *chün-tzu*.

Heredity Versus Qualification

The concepts of charismatic endowment of nobles, of the state as a family, and of respect for the past were subject to radical revision in the late Ch'un Ch'iu period and in the Chan Kuo. Rulers and ruling groups were still usually considered to have sacred ancestry during these periods, but a few bold men ventured to ask which should be considered more important, the ancestry or the personal competence of a minister or sovereign. In other words, this was the turning point when a status formerly reserved for a closed group became open to competition, when, to use the useful dichotomy coined by Ralph Linton, "ascribed status" was replaced by "achieved status."[2] In a passage of the *Analects,* Confucius praised one of his disciples by saying, "He might occupy the place of a prince."[3] H. G. Creel says it is remarkable that a man of obscure origin had been so mentioned.[4] That Confucius's praise had meaning shows that the concept that the criteria for rulers and ministers should be virtue and capability rather than noble birth was already in circulation. This idea is completely alien to a society which would label the following six situations "transgression": a person of mean status standing in the way of a noble, the young presuming to oppose their elders, those distant cutting out those who are near, new acquaintances alienating old friends, the small attacking the great, and lewdness in preference to righteousness.[5] A new society had emerged when Chan Kuo scholars such as Mo Tzu could say that rulers and officials should be worthy persons qualified both in virtue and in ability. A passage in the works of Mo Tzu reads:

Therefore in administering the government, the ancient sage-kings ranked the morally excellent high and exalted the virtuous. If capable, even a farmer or an artisan would be employed—commissioned with high ranks, remunerated with liberal emoluments, trusted with important charges, and empowered to issue final orders. . . . When emoluments are distributed in proportion to achievements, officials cannot be in constant honor and people in eternal humility. If a person is capable, promote him; if incapable, lower his rank. . . . Here, then, is the principle.[6]

Mo Tzu also stated that social position should depend on capability and virtue:

The ancient sage-kings greatly emphasized the exaltation of the virtuous and the employment of the capable. Without special consideration for relatives, for the rich and honored, or for the good-looking, they exalted and promoted the virtuous, enriched and honored them, and made them governors and leaders. The vicious they kept back and banished, dispossessed or degraded, and made laborers and servants.[7]

Whether the "ancient sage-kings" actually did these things is another question; what is important is that Mo Tzu had these ideas that he attributed to the ancient rulers. He also would not allow discrimination because all men were equal under heaven:

And the ancient sage-kings in exalting the virtuous and employing the capable in government were following the ways of Heaven. Even Heaven does not discriminate among the poor and the rich, the honorable and the humble, the distant and the near, and the related and the unrelated [to those in power]. The virtuous were promoted and exalted; the vicious were kept back and banished.[8]

A little after Mo Tzu, Mencius, while lamenting the decline of the old families, yet realized the necessity for employing the capable and virtuous. Thus he told King Hsüan of Ch'i, "When men speak of 'an ancient kingdom,' it is not meant thereby that it has lofty trees in it, but that it has ministers from families which have been important for generations. Your Majesty has not even an intimate minister. Those whom you advanced yesterday are gone today and you do not know it." The king then said, "How shall I know that they have no ability and so avoid employing them at all?" Mencius's reply was, "The ruler of a state advances to office men of talents and virtues only as a matter of necessity. Since he will thereby cause the low to overstep the honorable, and distant [relatives] to overstep his near relatives, he ought to do so but with caution."[9]

Thus both ministers and rulers should be men of talent and virtue. A wicked and vicious ruler was not to be called a sovereign; Mencius said of the death of the infamous King Chou of Shang, "He who outrages the benevolence proper to his nature is called a robber; he who outrages righteousness is called a ruffian. The robber and ruffian we call a mere fellow. I have heard of the cutting of the fellow Chou, but I have not heard of the putting of a sovereign to death."[10] But Mencius seems to have suspected that there were no born rulers. He attributed the dignified manner of a sovereign to his environment. Once Mencius saw the son of the Ch'i ruler at a distance and was apparently impressed by the young prince, for he sighed, "One's position alters one's air, just as the nurture affects the body. Great is the influence of position! Are we not all men's sons in this respect?" Then he added:

The residence, the carriages and horses, and the dress of the king's son are mostly the same as those of other men. That he looks so is occasioned by his position. How much more should a peculiar air distinguish him whose position is in the wide house of the world! When the prince of Lu went to Sung, he called out at the T'ieh-tse gate, and the keeper said, "This is not our prince. How is it that his voice is so like that of our prince?" This was occasioned by nothing but the correspondence of their positions.[11]

Mencius here was trying to prove that one could distinguish oneself by taking a position in "the wide house of the world" that emphasizes personal integrity.[12] However, he casually revealed his idea as to why aristocrats had such an impressive air. Those who believed that a ruler was born a sovereign would think his dignified demeanor was an integral part of his nature. Mencius seems to have held that a ruler is dignified because of his position and not because of his divine nature or superior heredity. Thus Mencius was able to tell his disciples that "Yao and Shun were just the same as other men," and that "all men may be Yao and Shun."[13] He also said that a number of great men rose from obscure origins to high positions; he said, listing them, "Shun rose from among the chaneled fields. Fu Yüeh was called to office from the midst of his building frames, Chiao Ko from his fish and salt, Kuan I-wu [from the] seashore, and Pai-li Hsi from the market-place."[14] It is not important whether these men really originated thus. Such stories had become popular in Chan Kuo times; the *Mo Tzu* says:

So, in days of old, Yao brought forward Shun from Fu-tse and entrusted him with the government and the world had peace. Yü brought forward I from Yin-fang and entrusted him with the government and the nine districts became organized. T'ang brought forward I Yin from the kitchen and entrusted him with the government and his plans were successful. King Wen brought forward Hung Yao and T'ai Tien from their rabbit nets and entrusted them with the government and the western land showed respect.[15]

The appearance of such stories implies that at the time it was necessary and moreover possible to recruit qualified persons of varied origins to fill high political and social positions. Besides Mo Tzu and Mencius, Hsün Tzu more straightforwardly advocated the same new ideas:

Yet although a man is the descendant of a king, duke, prefect, or officer, if he does not observe the rules of conduct [*li*] and justice [*i*] he must be relegated to the common ranks; although he is the descendant of a commoner, if he has acquired learning, developed a good character, and is able to observe the rules of proper conduct [*li*] and justice [*i*], then elevate him to be minister, prime minister, officer, or prefect.[16]

He emphasized this principle even further:

Hence the uppermost of the worthy persons should be given the empire as emolument. Those next to these worthy ones should be given states as emolument. Those of the lowest class [among the worthy persons] should be given fields and cities as emolument. Honest and upright people [should] have plenty of clothing and food.[17]

Apparently the worth, or capability and virtue, of a person was Hsün Tzu's only criterion for high position. He also held that all men, the sages and the depraved alike, are born biologically equal, saying:

Everyone has characteristics in common with others. When hungry he desires to eat; when cold he desires to be warm; when toiling he desires to rest; he wants what is beneficial and hates what is injurious—with these attitudes man is born; he has them without waiting to learn them; in these respects Yao and Chieh were alike. The eye distinguishes white and black, beautiful and ugly; the ear distinguishes clear and confused tones and sounds; the mouth distinguishes sour and salt, sweet and bitter; the nose distinguishes perfume and fragrance, strong-smelling and rank odours; the bones, the body, the skin, and the wrinkles distinguish cold and hot, sickness and itching. Man is born with these senses too; he has them without waiting to learn them; in these respects Yao and Chieh were alike. A person can become a Yao or a Yü; he can become a Chieh or a Chih; he can become a day laborer or an artisan; he can become a farmer or a merchant; it depends on what training he has accumulated from his ways of looking at things and his habits. . . . Yao and Yü were not born great [lit. "wholly as they were"—translator's note]; but they began in trouble and completed their development by artificial cultivation; they had to wait and strain all their resources and then only could they be perfect.[18]

Hsün Tzu seems to have believed that a person achieved his social position by acquiring and developing characteristics that were shaped by his surroundings. Such a theory provides social mobility with an ideological background.

The so-called *Fa Chia* included persons who developed and taught the art of government. Though they differed in many points, those termed "Administrators" agreed on at least one point: that the state should be ruled by a new type of monarch with the aid of a competent group of carefully selected officials. None of the Administrators, however, even so much as touched upon the question of sovereignty itself. It seems that no one on the throne at the time cared to see the issue discussed. In any case, techniques for selecting able persons, recruiting them for public office, and checking and controlling them were widely studied.

Shen Pu-hai, a *Fa Chia* scholar whose theories have long been ignored, will be discussed first. His principle for selecting personnel has been preserved in the writings of a later *Fa Chia* scholar, Han Fei Tzu, who said of two of his predecessors:

Now Shen Pu-hai speaks of *shu* [method] while Kung-sun Yang practices *fa* [law]. What is called *shu* is to bestow office according to the capacity [of the candidate]; to demand actual [performance] in accordance with the title [of the office held]; to hold fast the handles of [the power of] life and death; and to examine into the abilities of all his ministers; these are the things that the ruler keeps in his own hands.[19]

Shen Pu-hai was chancellor of the state of Han and had the opportunity to put his principles into practice. His ruler, Marquis Chao,
was an enlightened monarch, who seems to have followed faithfully
the teachings of Shen. A passage in the *Han Fei Tzu* contains the following anecdote about the two:

Marquis Chao of Han once said to Shen Tzu, "Method is not easy to practice." "What is called method," said Shen Pu-hai, "is to examine achievement [as a basis for] giving rewards, and to use ability as the basis upon
which to bestow office. Now Your Highness establishes method and yet grants
his attendants' requests. This is the cause of the difficulty in practicing method." "From now on," said Marquis Chao, "I will know how to practice method. I will not grant requests." One day Shen Tzu asked the Marquis to appoint his elder cousin to an official post. Marquis Chao said, "This is not
what I learned from you. If I grant your request, I nullify your teaching.
It would be better not to allow your request." Shen Tzu withdrew to his
residence for his fault.[20]

According to this philosophy, competent persons were to be given
free access to the channels that lead to government posts and to higher
status, since the ruler would use ability alone as a criterion for can-
didacy. Thus the feudal familial state changed into a domain run by
an administrative staff carefully chosen without regard for whether
its members were related to the ruler. This situation increased social
mobility by providing members of the lower strata with an upward
channel into officialdom.

Shang Yang did not stress the establishment of a benevolent bureaucracy but, according to the *Han Fei Tzu,* seems to have over-
emphasized military merit. Critics of his position argued that a good
soldier was not necessarily a good administrator, that it would be as
bad to appoint a meritorious soldier to an administrative post as to
make him a physician or an engineer.[21] The criteria adopted by Shang
Yang for the selection and promotion of officials were obviously far
from perfect. There is little chance that a very effective and smooth-
running government could be produced by meritorious military men
who have been given control of a bureaucracy that requires knowledge beyond their training in tactics and strategy. However, the effec-
tiveness of the Ch'in government under Shang Yang need not concern
us here. What should be noted is that through the peculiar channel of
military merit (which may have been but one of many channels)
Shang Yang recruited a group of persons from widely varying origins
to man the posts and participate in the honors of government, while
royal kinsmen were deprived of their privileges.[22] In this manner
Shang Yang, like Shen Pu-hai, gave the people of the lower strata the
means to rise in social status.

The last and probably the greatest *Fa Chia* scholar of the Chan Kuo period was Han Fei Tzu, who developed the theories of his predecessors and discussed them in great detail. In the *Han Fei Tzu* one can find hundreds of passages that advocate choosing persons of ability, not the favorites or relatives of the ruler, to run the state. The following passage from this work discusses the differences betwen good rulers and vicious ones.

Sage-kings and enlightened rulers . . . when selecting men for office avoided neither relatives nor enemies. Whoever was right they found and the excellent were advanced; the vicious and wicked were dismissed. . . . Suppose we look at the personages [the five good rulers*] appointed to office. They were found in the midst of mountains, forests, jungles, swamps, rocks, and caves, or in jails, chains, and bonds, or in the status of cooks, cattle breeders, or cowherds. Nevertheless, the intelligent sovereigns, not ashamed of their low and humble origin, considered them able to glorify the law, benefit the state, and profit the people, and accordingly appointed them to office. In consequence they gained personal security and honorable reputations.[23]

The authenticity of the backgrounds of these ministers is questionable, but in any case the appearance of such stories in Chan Kuo literature indicates the prevalence of the belief that important figures could rise from obscure origins. Han Fei Tzu apparently used these stories to support his theory that a person's ability and character are his most important qualities, not his birth. It is safe to assume that genuine ascents from humble origin to high position were even more numerous than the frequently quoted and possibly fabricated stories about such ascents.

The idea of such ascent became popular partly because it was advocated by scholars and partly because it frequently happened. By the end of the Chan Kuo period, people no longer thought it unusual for a man to ascend from lower-class status to the top of the ladder. Upward mobility was taken for granted; one had to grasp the opportunity when it appeared—the opportunity that could change a humble person into a minister or even an emperor.[24] Nothing was socially impossible or improper anymore; the bonds of *li* had been loosened and the old regulated social order had broken down. Anyone with the necessary ability could now seek for and expect to gain a higher social status no matter what his origin and birth. Greater social mobility was based on the idea that a man's brains and character were more important than his heredity.

* The "good" referred to in this quotation are ministers who are devoted to their rulers as well as to their offices. Previously in the same passage the author discusses several groups of ancient people who he thought behaved otherwise. One group among them he praises as being "good."

The Position of the Ruler

When a ruler reigned because he had the mandate of heaven or some other holy trusteeship, he was considered more important than anything else, including his subjects. During the Chan Kuo period, however, the attitude toward rulers seems to have been quite different. This change can be shown by a passage in the *Chan Kuo Ts'e* that recounts a conversation between Queen Wei of Chao and an envoy from the king of Ch'i to the Chao court. Before reading the message from Ch'i, the queen asked the envoy, "Is the year good? Are the people well? Is your king well?" The envoy, disliking the order of the questions, replied, "Your servant was entrusted with the errand of carrying a message to Your Majesty. Now Your Majesty, instead of asking after the health of our king, asked about the year and the people. How can it be that the humble is made prior to the noble?" The queen answered, "No. If there is no crop, there are no people. If there are no people, there is no ruler. How can I first ask about the result [of the state] while ignoring the origin of the state?"[25] Mencius expressed essentially the same ideas in a different order:

> The people are the most important element in a nation; the spirits of the land and grain are the next; the sovereign is the lightest. Therefore to gain the peasantry is the way to become sovereign; to gain the sovereignty is the way to become a prince of a State; to gain the prince of a State is the way to become a great officer. When a prince endangers the altars of the spirits of the land and grain, he is changed, and another appointed in his place. When the sacrificial victims have been perfect, the millet in its vessels all pure, and the sacrifices offered at their proper seasons, if yet there ensues drought, or the waters overflow, the spirits of the land and grain are changed, and others appointed in their place.[26]

Mencius apparently implies here that a state would not be a state if it had no people, which may be why he considered the people to be the most important element.

An unqualified ruler was to be denied the sovereignty; Mencius told King Hsüan of Ch'i that the execution of the vicious King Chou of Shang by Wu of Chou should not be termed regicide, since the Shang ruler had been nothing but a "mere fellow" who had outraged benevolence and righteousness.[27] A person jeopardized his noble status whenever his virtue failed to meet the standards of his high position. Mencius said:

> There is a nobility of Heaven and there is a nobility of man. Benevolence, righteousness, self-consecration, and fidelity, with unwearied joy in these virtues—these constitute the nobility of Heaven. To be a *kung* [duke], a *ch'ing* [minister], or a *tai-fu* [great officer]—this constitutes the nobility of man. The men of antiquity cultivated their nobility of Heaven, and the nobility of

man came to them in its train. The men of the present day cultivate their nobility of Heaven in order to seek for the nobility of man, and when they have obtained that, they throw away the other; their delusion is extreme. The issue is simply this, that they must lose that nobility of men as well.[28]

Hsün Tzu, another Confucian scholar, spoke more bluntly about the position of the ruler than Mencius did. A passage among his sayings collected by his disciples reads:

Heaven does not create people for the sake of the sovereign. Heaven made the sovereign for the sake of the people. Therefore in antiquity states were not enfeoffed in order to ennoble the rulers; offices were not established and emoluments and ranks were not differentiated in order to honor the officials. The duty of the ruler is to know the people; the duty of the subjects is to take care of their affairs.[29]

According to the *Fa Chia* scholars, the ruler is but one part, the functional head, of the government, who cooperates with the other parts. A saying attributed to Shen Pu-hai reads, "An enlightened ruler is like a body; his ministers are like his hands. The ruler is like the sound; the ministers are like the echo."[30] The reason for having a ruler is that some arbiter must keep order. A passage attributed to another *Fa Chia* scholar, Shen Tao, is:

In antiquity, the emperor was not enthroned and honored in order to benefit him. [It was because] order could not be maintained if there was no honored person in the world. Order is maintained for the sake of the world. A ruler is set up for the sake of the state; it is not that a state is set up for the sake of the ruler. Officials are appointed for the sake of the offices; it is not that offices are set up for the sake of the officials.[31]

Therefore the function of the ruler is to avert the chaos that may break out when several persons vie for the highest position. Shen Tao's alleged words go on:

An emperor is enthroned to avert suspicion among state rulers. State rulers are enthroned to avert suspicion among the great officers. A legal spouse is designated to avert suspicion among the concubines, and the designation of the heir apparent is to avert suspicion among the other sons. With suspicion there will be action by ambitious ones; with two persons of equal status there will be a quarrel; with people mixed together they will injure one another. The problem is that there are too many and not that there is only one. Therefore when a minister holds two positions the state must be in disorder; if the state is not in disorder it is only because there is still the ruler. That the state does not fall into disorder depends upon the ruler. If the ruler is lost, the state must be in disorder.[32]

On the other hand, the ruler gains his power by occupying his position. Shen Tao compares this with the extraordinary powers of the dragon and the flying serpent, who take advantage of the clouds and the mist that bear them aloft, powers without which these mysterious creatures would be no different from other serpents.[33]

A section of the *Han Fei Tzu* that probably stems from the ideas of Shen Tao develops more fully the concept of the ruler's position and function as follows:

Indeed, the possessor of talent who has no position, even though he is worthy, cannot control the unworthy. For example, when a stand of timber is placed on the top of a high mountain, it overlooks the ravine a thousand fathoms below. It is not that the timber is long but that its position is high. When Chieh was the Son of Heaven, he could rule over all under heaven; it is not that he was worthy but that his position was influential. Yao, when a commoner, could not administer three families; it is not that he was unworthy but that his position was low. A weight of one thousand *chün* floats if aboard a ship, but the smallest farthing sinks if overboard. It is not that one thousand *chün* is light and the smallest farthing is heavy, but that the former has a favorable position while the latter does not. Therefore a short thing can look down on the tall because of its position; the unworthy man can rule over the worthy also because of his position.

The lord of men, because he is supported by all under heaven with united forces, is safe; because he is upheld by the masses of the people with united heart, he is glorious. The minister, because he maintains his specialty and exerts his ability, is loyal. If a glorious sovereign rules loyal ministers a state of constant enjoyment and meritorious reputation will be achieved. Name and reality, keeping pace with each other, will reach fruition. Form and shadow, coinciding with each other, will take shape. Hence the sovereign and the minister have the same desire but different functions.[34]

The members of this branch of the *Fa Chia* thus seem to have held that the ruler is needed to keep society from degenerating into anarchy and that the authority of a sovereign is derived from his position. The ruler exists to perform a function that is necessary for social order; his existence has nothing to do with the will of heaven. Also, anyone on the throne may perform the function as well as anyone else; hence the position of sovereign is also not necessarily given by the endorsement of heaven. Compared with Mencius's idea that the ruler is less important than the people he rules, the analysis by *Fa Chia* members such as Shen Tao is more penetrating and is presented more systematically. The doctrine of Hsün Tzu, who said that the ruler is given his power for the good of the state, was probably influenced by this concept. We can see that these scholars did not believe that sovereigns had any charismatic rights. It follows that a psychological block against social mobility seems to have been lifted from the minds of the Chan Kuo people.

Changes in the Concept of the Shih

The rise of respect for ability and personal worth coincided with the appearance of a self-respect among the members of the new *shih* class. The *shih* were still the lowest order of the ruling group, usually functionaries in various positions, but they now differed from their Ch'un Ch'iu predecessors, who were most likely to be retainers to their lords and who therefore were hardly conscious of their status as a group. In the Ch'un Ch'iu period the conduct of the *shih* was guided by a sense of familial loyalty as well as by his attitude toward his seigneur. But after the idea of putting able men into office gained currency, the *shih* realized that they were a new select group, a new elite, and they cultivated their sense of self-respect. They constituted a "layer" that extended beyond the state boundaries and spread over all of China. This was indicated by interstate friendships among *shih*, by their transfers from one court to another, and, most significant of all, by their awareness of themselves as one educated, intellectual group.[35] They looked down on those who gained high social position because of noble birth, and asserted that virtue and competence were what one could be proud of. On the other hand, the *shih* had their own moral code, which stressed having a sense of responsibility and integrity among other virtues. This is illustrated in a passage from the *Analects* that goes, "The philosopher Tseng said, 'The *shih* may not be without breadth of mind and vigorous endurance. His burden is heavy and his course is long. Perfect virtue is the burden which he considers his to sustain; is it not heavy? Only with death does his course stop; is it not long?' "[36] Mencius thought that virtue was at least as important as competence and noble rank, and insisted that with virtue as his qualification, a *shih* ought not to bow before worldly vanity. Therefore he did not like to answer those who came to him conscious of their noble rank. He maintained that it was the ruler who should show respect for worthy persons, and not the worthy who needed to respect the sovereign.[37]

The general attitude of a *shih* is denoted by the following passage of the *Hsün Tzu*:

The ancient worthy man, even if he had no rank, no property, and no good food or clothing, yet would not advance [in rank] without propriety nor accept gain without righteousness. Why? Tzu-hsia was so poor that his clothes had worn to pieces. People asked him, "Why do not you serve in the government?" He answered, "To a ruler who is a peacock over me, I would not be subject. [As for] ministers who are peacocks over me, I would not see them again."[38]

It was thought natural that a highly qualified *shih* would look down on a ruler, because a clever ruler should know that the *shih* would come to him if he were in the habit of treating them well and respecting them. Support by this elite group would cause the rest of the world to come to the ruler, who would therefore be ill-advised to look down on the *shih*.[39]

The social function of the lowest class of the ruling group may have remained about the same during Ch'un Ch'iu and Chan Kuo times, but the *shih* themselves changed in attitude because of their new self-consciousness. It is this group that gave Chinese civilization the form it has since retained, that paved the way for a unified China, and that provided Chan Kuo courts as well as the future imperial government with administrators, clerks, and courtiers; it is this group that was the forerunner of the "gentry" layer of Chinese society for centuries to come.

Changes in the Concept of the Ruler-Official Relationship

When the relationship between the ruler and his officials was familial, each party took his position as an obligation. When the ruler began to give offices to persons because of their ability, an employer-employee relationship was set up even though such persons may have been kinsmen of the ruler. The official might regard his post as a source of wages. Mencius said, "Office is not sought on account of poverty; yet there are times when one seeks office on this account."[40] The new contractual relation was naturally looser than the obligatory relationship between the ruler and his hereditary ministers. Mencius described the difference between the two kinds of ministers:

King Hsüan of Ch'i asked about the office of high ministers. Mencius said, "Which high ministers is Your Majesty asking about?" "Are there differences among them?" enquired the king. "There are," was the reply. "There are the high ministers who are nobles and relatives of the prince, and there are those who are of a different surname." The king said, "I beg to ask about the high ministers who are noble and relatives of the prince." Mencius answered, "If the prince has great faults, they ought to remonstrate with him, and if he does not listen to them after they have done so again and again, they ought to dethrone him." . . . The king . . . then begged to ask about high ministers who were of a different surname from the prince. Mencius said, "When the prince has faults, they ought to remonstrate with him, and if he does not listen to them after they have done this again and again, they ought to leave the state."[41]

By "ministers of a different surname" Mencius must have meant not the hereditary ministers of Ch'un Ch'iu times, whose surnames may not have been the same as the ruler's, but newly advanced subjects such as himself who served temporarily and as employees. Since they were not obliged to stay in any particular state, they were free to offer their services to any ruler who could or would use them. There developed a concept of reciprocity that Mencius described, saying, "When the prince regards his ministers as his hands and feet, his ministers regard their prince as their belly and heart; when he regards them as his dogs and horses, they regard him as any other man; when he regards them as the ground or as grass, they regard him as a robber and an enemy."[42] Such a radical statement would have astonished a loyal Ch'un Ch'iu minister, but Mencius in the Chan Kuo period said it to the king of Ch'i as if it were a self-evident truth.

Han Fei discussed the same ideas even more unequivocally; the "Five Vermin" chapter of the *Han Fei Tzu* says of the uselessness of the familial concept of state,

In these days the *ju* and the Mohists all say that the former kings practiced impartial love for the world, that is to say, they looked upon the people as parents [look upon their own children]. . . . If one supposes that when ruler and subject act like father and son there must always be order, this implies that there is never disorder in the relationship between father and son. In human nature, nothing surpasses [the affection of] parents. [Nevertheless, even when] both parents show love [for their children] order does not necessarily [result]. [Similarly] even though the ruler should deepen his love [for his subjects], how [could one expect] disorder thereupon to end?[43]

The remedy given in the *Han Fei Tzu* for the error of relying on familial relations to keep order is to understand that the first concern of any individual is his own interest. It was written that if a son did not receive good care during childhood from his parents, then when he grew up he would show resentment and provide rather scantily for their future well-being, and the parents would grow angry and reprimand him. On the other hand, the *Han Fei Tzu* defined the reciprocity between master and hired hand; no love existed between them, but the employee, expecting good food and generous wages from his employer, would work hard, and the master, expecting good service from the hired man, would treat him well.[44] The book concludes, "Thus, in the master's treatment of the workman and in the workman's services to the master it seems as if there exists the compassion of father and son. But really their minds are attuned to utility since they both cherish self-seeking motives."[45]

The services of the people were bought by the ruler with wages, as the *Han Fei Tzu* makes clear by the following description of a father's instruction to his son: "The sovereign sells ranks and offices; the subject sells wisdom and strength. Hence the saying, 'Rely on nobody but yourself!' "[46] According to the *Han Fei Tzu*, a state can be kept in good order only if the familial relationship is replaced by calculations of mutual profit. This was expressed as follows:

The enlightened sovereign . . . learns what the people want in order to gain services from them; he bestows ranks and emoluments to encourage them. [Similarly] he learns what the people dislike in order to prevent them from committing villainy; he inflicts punishment to overawe them. As rewards are sure and punishments are definite, the ruler can promote meritorious persons to office, and no malefactor is used in the government. . . . Moreover, ministers in bartering with the ruler offer their full strength; the ruler in bartering with the ministers dangles ranks and emoluments before them. Thus the relationship of ruler and minister is not as intimate as the bond of father and son; it is an outcome of mutual calculation.*

The reciprocal relationship played an important part in the bureaucratic machinery established to meet the demands of new patterns of government and monarchy. A kind of contractual concept probably emerged from the idea of mutual profit.[47] Reward or punishment from the ruler and service from the ministers are the items of exchange, i.e., the price and the commodity.[48] Inspection and examination are necessary to ensure a satisfactory exchange; according to Shen Pu-hai, the whole process resembles striking a bargain. A passage of the *Han Fei Tzu* uses such words as "covenant" and "warrant" in explaining the relationship between ruler and minister:

Whenever an action is performed pursuant to a statement, the ruler holds its covenant. Whenever any task is performed, he holds its warrant. And on the basis of coincidence and discrepancy between covenant and action, and warrant and performance, reward and punishment are born. Therefore, the ministers set forth their statements, and the ruler assigns them tasks and demands performance according to the task. When the performance matches the task and the task matches the statement, there is reward; when they do not match, there is punishment.[49]

The employer-employee relationship was also reflected in the salary system of the Chan Kuo officials. In the Ch'un Ch'iu period it seems that officials received no income other than that from the estates that they inherited or that were bestowed upon them by rulers, although they occasionally received presents from rulers. In the Chan Kuo pe-

---

* HFT, 15/5. The *Han Fei Tzu* used the idea of trade or barter in a market as a simile for the mutual calculation of profit by the ruler and ministers. This translation is a modification of Liao, II, 145–46.

riod, however, the officials began to receive salaries, which were often paid in grain. It is written in the *Mo Tzu* that one of his disciples was promised a salary of one thousand *p'en* of grain to serve in Wey, but received only five hundred *p'en*.[50] In the *Mencius*, payments given by states are often recorded in terms of grain measures. Mencius was once offered a salary of one hundred thousand *chung* by the state of Ch'i to take office along with his disciples, but he declined the offer.[51] Another time, in discussing the behavior of an obscure scholar, he mentioned that the scholar's brother had received a salary of one hundred thousand *chung* of grain in Ch'i.[52] Salary systems may have been established in many states. The king of Yen, intending to abdicate and enthrone his chancellor, ordered the appointments of all officials who received three hundred or more *shih* of grain to be canceled so that they could receive new appointments from the chancellor.[53] The later Ch'in and Han dynasties designated official rank by the number of *shih* of grain received as salary.

In summary, a contractual relationship seems to have replaced the familial relationship during the Chan Kuo period. The rewards or salary from the ruler were exchanged for the services of the officials on a barter basis. The relationship of officials to the ruler appears to have been voluntary, but it also appears far less definite and constant than the obligatory relationship among family members bound together by kinship. Hence the contractual relationship made for greater social mobility.

The Trend Against Tradition

As I have already said, the general attitude of the Ch'un Ch'iu period was respect for tradition and the past; witness the lines, "Erring in nothing, forgetful of nothing, / Observing and following the old statutes."[54] Innovation and novelty are indeed seldom acclaimed in the Ch'un Ch'iu period. Such conditions resemble those subsumed in the concept of *Gemeinschaft,* a social order based upon consensus of wills, resting on harmony, and developed and ennobled by folkways, mores, and religion.[55] No legislation was needed. Tradition determined the criterion of propriety, which in Ch'un Ch'iu China was called *li.* Thus we read in the *Tso Chuan,* "It is *li* which governs states and clans, gives settlement to the tutelary altars, secures the order of the people, and provides for the good of one's future life."[56] The best expression of the revolutionary Chan Kuo spirit can be found in a quotation attributed to Shang Yang, the Ch'in reformer. The first chapter of the book bearing his name contains an argument between the reformer and the conservatives. At one point in it, the conservatives told the king:

Now if Your Highness alters the laws without adhering to the old customs of the Ch'in state and reforms the rites in order to teach the people, I am afraid that the empire will criticize Your Highness and I wish that you would reflect maturely.

Part of Shang Yang's answer was as follows:

Indeed, ordinary people abide by old practices and students are immersed in the study of what is reported from antiquity. These two kinds of men are ... not the kind who can take part in a discussion which goes beyond the law. The three dynasties have attained supremacy by different rites, and the five Lords Protector have attained their protectorship by different laws. Therefore a wise man creates laws, but a foolish man is controlled by them; a man of talent reforms rites, but a worthless man is enslaved by them.... Let Your Highness not hesitate.

A conservative replied:

I have heard it said that in taking antiquity as an example, one makes no mistakes, and in following established rites one commits no offence. Let Your Highness aim at that.

Shang Yang's answer was:

Former generations did not follow the same doctrines, so what antiquity should one imitate? The emperors and kings did not copy one another, so what rites should one follow? ... King Wen and King Wu both established laws in accordance with what was opportune and regulated rites according to practical requirements; as rites and laws were fixed in accordance with what was opportune, regulations and orders were all expedient and weapons, armor, implements, and equipment were all practical. Therefore I say, "There is more than one way to govern the world and there is no necessity to imitate antiquity in order to take appropriate measures for the state." T'ang and Wu succeeded in attaining supremacy without following antiquity, and as for the downfall of Yin and Hsia—they were ruined without rites having been altered. Consequently those who acted counter to antiquity do not necessarily deserve blame, nor do those who followed established rites merit much praise. Let Your Highness not hesitate.

The king of Ch'in was thereupon convinced and declared:

One should, in one's plans, be directed by the needs of the times—I have no doubts about it.[57]

Interestingly enough, the same argument, phrased similarly, appears in the *Chan Kuo Ts'e* attributed to King Wu-ling of Chao and his ministers, who discussed the adoption by Chao of the costume, archery, and cavalry techniques of the northern nomadic peoples. The similarity is such that the main parts of both tracts coincide line by line and phrase by phrase.[58]

It is difficult to decide which of the two books contains the original; moreover, it is possible that neither is the original and that both were taken from a third source. However, in the Chan Kuo period there seems to have been an entire set of ideas that the reformers believed in and defended against the attacks and objections of the conservatives, who felt that the way of the ancestors was the best way. Arguments similar to those quoted above may have been raised in the courts of the various states whenever new policies or institutions were proposed.

A more thorough and logical discussion of the reformers' ideas can be found in the *Han Fei Tzu*, as follows:

Those who do not know the right way to political order always say, "Never change ancient traditions, never alter existing institutions." The sage does not heed injunctions either to change or not to change; he merely rectifies the government. Whether or not ancient tradition should be changed, whether or not existing institutions should be altered, all depends upon whether or not they are suitable. . . . Generally speaking, men hesitate to change ancient traditions because they are afraid of disturbing the people. Not to change ancient traditions is to perpetuate the path of disorder; to accord with the mind of the people is to give free rein to wicked conduct. If the people are stupid and do not know what constitutes disorder, and the superior is weak and unable to make reforms, this constitutes a breakdown of the government.[59]

When a tradition or institution had outlived its usefulness, a change was inevitable and necessary. Another passage of the *Han Fei Tzu* is:

In high antiquity the people were few; the animals were many. And the people could not overcome the animals and reptiles. Then there came a sage who made wooden scaffolds to use for tree-huts in order to avoid the multitude of dangers. And the people were pleased with him and caused him to rule All-Under-Heaven, calling him, "Lord of the Huts." The people ate raw foods that were foul smelling and harmed their stomachs so that many fell ill. There came a sage who made fire drills to obtain a flame that transformed the foul smell. And the people were pleased with him and caused him to rule All-Under-Heaven, calling him "Lord of the Fire Drills."

In middle antiquity there was a great flood in the world, and Kun and Yü opened ditches to drain it.

In recent antiquity the vicious kings Chieh and Chou created tyrannical disorder, and the virtuous kings T'ang and Wu led punitive expeditions against them.

Now if somebody had made wooden scaffolds or fire drills in the age of the Hsia Hou Lords, he would certainly have been ridiculed by Kun and Yü. Again if somebody had opened ditches to drain the waters in the age of the Yin and Chou dynasties, he would certainly have been ridiculed by T'ang and Wu. That being so, if somebody in the present age were to praise the ways of Yao, Shun, Kun, Yü, T'ang, and Wu, he would no doubt be ridiculed by new sages. Therefore, the sage neither seeks to conform to the ways of the ancients nor does he follow any constant standard, but considers the contemporary situation in order to deal with it.[60]

Those discussed above were reformers who denounced traditions that were obstacles in the way of social and political reform. A more radical attitude was represented by the skeptical philosophers who derided the traditional values by which the behavior of men was evaluated. In a possibly spurious chapter called "Robber Chih" of the *Chuang Tzu* the author ridicules many moral standards and belittles many model personages of the past. The passage is supposedly a conversation between Confucius and an imaginary character, Robber Chih, the leader of a bandit troop, who mocks and ridicules Confucius. The sage emperors Huang Ti, Yao, Shun, T'ang, and King Wu of Chou, who are traditionally held up as examples of perfect virtue, are condemned by Robber Chih as "promoters of disorder and confusion." He accuses Confucius of practicing "deceitful speech and hypocritical conduct" and of "seeking for riches and honors," and therefore calls the sage "Robber Ch'iu."[61] Robber Chih also criticizes four persons whom the world called virtuous because they gave their lives in order to safeguard their moral integrity, as follows:

[The deaths of] these four men were not different from those of the dog that is torn to pieces, the pig that is borne away by a current, or the beggar [drowned in a ditch] with his alms gourd in his hand. They were all caught as in a net by [their desire for] fame, not caring to nourish their lives to the end as they were bound to do.[62]

The two loyal ministers Pi Kan and Tzu-hsü sacrificed their lives and won nothing but ridicule; therefore, concludes Robber Chih, from the most ancient times down to the period of Pi Kan and Tzu-hsü there have been none deserving of honor.[63]

The latter part of the same chapter is allegedly a discussion between Tzu-chang, a disciple of Confucius, and an imaginary person called Man Kou Te, which means literally "full of recklessly gotten gain." Tzu-chang advised Man Kou Te to practice virtue in order to gain a good reputation and told him that righteousness was the true key. Man Kou Te answered, "He who has no shame becomes rich, and he who is talkative becomes illustrious. Thus great fame and gain would seem to spring from being without shame and being talkative." Tzu-chang countered with the assertion that virtuous persons such as Confucius and Mo Tzu received more respect than monarchs did, and that it is moral quality that makes people worthy or unworthy. Man Kou Te's cynical reply was, "Small robbers are put in prison; a great robber becomes a feudal lord; and in the gate of the feudal lord your righteous scholars will be found. . . . Who is bad? Who is good? The successful is regarded as the head and the unsuccessful as the tail."[64]

Another section of the *Chuang Tzu* ridicules the virtues advocated by Confucius and others by comparing them to the conduct of a robber:

That the robber in his recklessness comes to the conclusion that there are valuable deposits in an apartment shows his sageness; that he is the first to enter it shows his bravery; that he is the last to quit shows his righteousness; that he knows whether [the robbery] may be attempted or not shows his wisdom; and that he makes an equal division of the plunder shows his benevolence. Without all these five qualities no one in the world has ever . . . become a great robber.[65]

The "Robber Chih" chapter reflects disillusionment with the moral standards that sanctioned behavior in society before the Chan Kuo period. After the disorder and disturbances of the Ch'un Ch'iu and Chan Kuo periods these moral standards disintegrated. Before order was restored and new values were established to fit the new society, there was no standard to live up to and no course to follow. The strong, if low in status, were now released from the social bondage of the old morality, while the weak, if high in position, were exposed to social struggle without the old sanctions to protect them and sank downward in society.

In conclusion, in the Chan Kuo period respect for the past was replaced by a revolutionary spirit that justified the reformation that was taking place in many states. New ideas were to be praised and new institutions were to be erected; the phases of society were changed and social mobility accompanied the transformation. The values and standards of the old society became meaningless, and the old moral sanctions were under suspicion by the people and could no longer function. In such a society more channels were available to the social climber. Greater social mobility existed than could have obtained in a static society.

The Changing Meaning of Chün Tzu

The word *chün* means "lord" and *tzu* "son"; thus the compound *chün tzu* may originally have meant "children of lords." The scope of this meaning enlarged to include all the persons related to the ruling group by kinship, which makes *chün tzu* a synonym for "noble." However, in the Chan Kuo period this term came primarily to mean a person possessing certain moral qualities. A *chün tzu* was then an admirable person whose virtues entitled him to a high moral position no matter what his social status was. This reflects two aspects of social mobility; the hereditary noble class may have declined or even almost disappeared, and birth was no longer so important in deciding a man's future. These two points may have caused the change in the meaning of *chün tzu*.

The *Shih Ching* contains 189 occurrences of the term *chün tzu* in the sense of "noble" or something similar; many of these, of course, are repetitions in the same verse. The different shades of meaning of *chün tzu* can be classified into three categories:

1. lord, sovereign;
2. son of a ruler, princely man, gentleman, nobleman, or officer;
3. host, husband.

The first two groups are social positions and the third is a social relationship; none of them connote anything about the moral level of the person referred to.

The following are some illustrative quotations from the *Shih Ching*. The first verse uses *chün tzu* to mean "lord" or "sovereign":

> Look at the Lo,
> With its waters broad and deep.
> Thither has come our *chün tzu*,
> In whom all happiness and dignity are concentrated.
> Red are his madder-dyed knee covers,
> In which he might raise six armies.
>
> .   .   .
>
> Look at the Lo,
> With its waters broad and deep.
> Thither has our *chün tzu* come,
> In whom all happiness and dignities are united.
> May our lord live myriads of years,
> Preserving his clans and states.[66]

We are able to identify the *chün tzu* in question as a ruler by the references to "six armies" and "states."

The following poem from the Odes of Wei is an example of the meaning "prince":

Look at those recesses in the banks of the Ch'i,
With their green bamboos, so fresh and luxuriant!
There is an elegant and accomplished *chün tzu,*
As from the knife and the file,
As from the chisel and the polisher!
How grave is he and dignified!
How commanding and distinguished!
Our elegant and accomplished *chün tzu*
Never can be forgotten.

. . .

There is our elegant and accomplished *chün tzu,*
With his ear-stoppers of beautiful pebbles,
And his cap, glittering as with stars between the seams!

. . .

Look at those recesses in the banks of the Ch'i,
With their green bamboos, so dense together!
There is our elegant and accomplished *chün tzu,*
[Pure] as gold or as tin,
[Soft and rich] as a sceptre of jade!
How magnanimous is he and gentle!
There he is in his chariot with its two high sides!
Skillful is he at quips and jokes,
But how does he keep from rudeness in them![67]

This vivid picture of the well-dressed, merry *chün tzu,* presumably a young prince, hardly calls to mind the idea of beauty of the soul alone.

The next poem uses *chün tzu* to mean "general" or "officer":

What is that so gorgeous?
It is the flowers of the cherry tree.
What carriage is that?
It is the carriage of our *chün tzu.*
His war carriage is yoked;
The four steeds are strong.
Dare we remain inactive?
In one month we shall have three victories.
The four steeds are yoked,
The four steeds, eager and strong;
The confidence of the *chün tzu,*
The protection of the men.
The four steeds move regularly, like wings;
There are the bow with its ivory ends, and the sealskin quiver.
Shall we not daily warn one another?
The business of the Hsien-yün is very urgent.[68]

This poem depicts the valiant warrior, driving his fast war chariot with determination, concerned only with victory.

The third category of the meanings of *chün tzu*—husband or host—differs greatly from the other meanings. It seems to have little connection with the original sense, but it is understandable that a woman would consider her husband to be her master and that guests would use the term as a polite form of address to the head of the household whose hospitality they enjoy. If the guests were actually retainers, this usage would be even more natural. The following two verses illustrate the use of *chün tzu* to mean "husband":

> My *chün tzu* is away on service,
> And I know not when he will return.
> Where is he now?
> The fowls roost in their holes in the walls;
> And in the evening of the day,
> The goats and cows come down [from the hills];
> But my *chün tzu* is away on service,
> How can I but keep thinking of him?[69]

Here only "husband" or "sweetheart" would fit the context. The second verse is the song of a honeymooning bride:

> My *chün tzu* looks full of satisfaction.
> In his left hand he holds his reed-organ,
> And with his right he calls me to the room.
> Oh, the joy!
> My *chün tzu* looks delighted.
> In his left hand he holds his screen of feathers,
> And with his right hand he calls me to the stage.
> Oh, the joy![70]

The meaning of this poem would be ambiguous if *chün tzu* were not translated "husband" or "lover." These examples show that the term as used in the *Shih Ching* denotes either a social position such as "prince" or "ruler," or a social relationship such as "husband." None of the occurrences give a clear impression that *chün tzu* had any moral or behavioral connotations.

The *Analects* appears to be the earliest work in which *chün tzu* was used to imply high moral standards in a person; here it denotes the ideal man whom all men should cultivate their characters to imitate. However, there are still a very few occurrences of the phrase in the *Analects* with its conventional, older meaning of "noble." The three following passages use *chün tzu* to define the social status of a person:

The border-warden at I requested to be introduced to the Master, saying "When *chün tzu* have come to this, I have never been denied the privilege of seeing them."*

The master, having come to Wu-ch'eng, heard there the sound of stringed instruments and singing. Well-pleased and smiling, he said, "Why use an ox-knife to kill a fowl?" Tzu-yu replied, "Formerly, Master, I heard you say, 'When the *chün tzu* is well instructed, he loves men; when the man of low station [*hsiao jen*] is well instructed, he is easily ruled.' " The Master said, "My disciples, Yen's words are right. What I said is only in sport."[71]

Tzu-lu said, "Does the *chün tzu* esteem valor?" The Master said, "The *chün tzu* holds righteousness to be of highest importance. A *chün tzu* having valor without righteousness will be guilty of insubordination; one of the lower people [*hsiao jen*] having valor without righteousness will commit robbery."†

Only the last two of these occurrences of *chün tzu* are clearly about social status, the first being somewhat ambiguous; this is quite different from the usages in the *Shih Ching*. On the other hand, all the other occurrences of *chün tzu* in the *Analects*—sixty-five passages in all—definitely denote persons superior in virtue without regard to social rank. A considerable number of the passages are exclusively discussions of the definition of the *chün tzu* and his conduct. So much space has been devoted to this subject that one suspects the meaning "virtuous man" may then have been a new concept and hence still lacking precise definition. The passages in question paint a picture of a superior person who integrates these three cardinal virtues: "Virtuous, he is free from anxieties; wise, he is free from perplexities; bold, he is free from fear."[72] The *chün tzu* therefore feels no discomposure even though men take no note of him.[73]

A *chün tzu* was most anxious about maintaining his virtue: "If a *chün tzu* abandons virtue, how can he fulfill the requirements of that name?" He always remains virtuous, even in moments of haste or in time of danger.[74] He is always satisfied and composed, whereas a mean man is always full of distress.[75] This is so because there is nothing to

---

* Legge, *Analects*, 3.24. It is not easy to decide whether the emphasis in this passage is on moral significance or social status. However, it seems to make more sense to assume that the officer on the border asked to see the dignitaries who were en route to their assigned district, rather than to see a person of superior virtue, who is not readily visible. The assumption that Confucius was already well known at the time is also needed here.

† Legge, *Analects*, 17.22. The translator surmises from context that the *chün tzu* here is a person superior in rank as well as in virtue. The third mention of *chün tzu*, translated as "the man in a superior station," particularly supports this idea since it is parallel with "one of the lower people" (Legge, *Analects*, p. 193, n. 3). Moreover it would be contradictory to hold that a man of superior virtue could not have been righteous.

be anxious about and nothing to fear if inner examination shows nothing wrong.[76] He does not set his mind for or against anything, but follows what is right.[77] Therefore his mind is conversant with righteousness, but the mind of a mean man is conversant with gain.[78] The *chün tzu* is critical of his own conduct but tolerates faults in others; hence the saying "What the *chün tzu* seeks is in himself. What the mean man seeks is in others."[79] He "honors the talented and virtuous, bears with all, praises the good, and pities the incompetent," according to one disciple of Confucius.[80] He is critical of himself and prudent in what he says; thus he is "modest in his speech but exceeds in his actions."[81] The *chün tzu* should "act before he speaks, and afterwards speak according to his actions."[82]

The *chün tzu* is a righteous man, considers principle to be the most important of all considerations, and will not allow private interest to influence him. Confucius thus said, "The *chün tzu* is affable but not adulatory; the mean man is adulatory but not affable."[83] This means that the *chün tzu* may disagree among themselves but will still maintain harmonious relations. Thus the *chün tzu* is "dignified, but does not wrangle. He is sociable, but not a partisan."[84] From all this it can be seen that a *chün tzu* is trustworthy and bold enough in his moral courage to face any trial. Tseng Tzu, a disciple of Confucius, said,

Suppose that there is an individual who can be entrusted with the charge of a young orphan prince, and can be commissioned with authority over a state of a hundred *li,* and whom no emergency however great can drive from his principles: is such a man a *chün tzu?* He is a *chün tzu* indeed.[85]

The *chün tzu* values not only achievement of great personal morality but also service to the world. In a passage of the *Analects* Confucius tells Tzu-lu of the three stages of the moral self-cultivation of the *chün tzu,* the final step of which is very difficult to reach:

Tzu-lu asked what constituted a *chün tzu*; the Master said, "The cultivation of himself in reverential carefulness." "And is that all?" said Tzu-lu. "He cultivates himself so as to give rest to others," was the reply. "And is this all?" again asked Tzu-lu. The Master said, "He cultivates himself so as to give rest to all the people—even Yao and Shun were still solicitous about this!"[86]

In summary, the term *chün tzu,* except for a few occurrences, is used in the *Analects* to mean a person of virtue, principle, righteousness, and tolerance, a person who loves people and cultivates his own character in order to serve people. Such a man, noble in virtue, was not necessarily a noble in social status.

The *Tso Chuan,* a great annalistic history, is a compilation of early writings that may be historical records by contemporary Ch'un Ch'iu scholars and of materials inserted by later men, perhaps of the Chan Kuo period. Thus it is natural that in this work we find both the old and the new meanings of the phrase *chün tzu*, meanings with connotations both of social rank and of virtue. The old meaning of the term will be examined first; the implication of social status is obvious in the following:

"I have heard that the *chün tzu* [divides the day] into four periods: the morning to hear the affairs of the government, noon to make full inquiry about them, the evening to consider well and complete the orders [he has resolved to issue], and the night for rest."[87]

Kung-tzu Ch'i-chi went to Chin. . . . He forbade his foragers, grooms, and fuel collectors to go into the fields. No trees were to be cut down for fuel; no grain nor vegetables were to be gathered; no houses were to be unroofed; there was to be no violent begging. He made a declaration that whoever should violate orders, if he were a *chün tzu*, he should be dismissed, and if he were a small man, he should be reduced still lower.[88]

In the first of these two passages Legge translated *chün tzu* as "superior man," and in the last, as "officer"; to avoid confusion, the transliteration has been used here. In the former a *chün tzu* seems to be anyone of the ruling group who takes part in government affairs; in the latter he is in a high position since he is subject to dismissal and thus is taken to be an officer. Neither of the meanings has the slightest connotation of virtue.

The *chün tzu* (in the sense of social status) should also behave according to the moral code befitting his position. A passage of the *Tso Chuan* indicates that this moral code included respect for seigniory and for the past; in other words, respect for the established and hierarchical social order. The passage in question records a conversation between the Chin ruler and a Ch'u captive who answered the ruler's inquiries properly, whereupon a minister of Chin told his ruler,

That prisoner of Ch'u is a *chün tzu*. He told you of the office of his father, showing that he is not ashamed of his origin. He played an air of his country, showing that he has not forgotten his old associations. He spoke of his king when he was a prince, showing his own freedom from mercenariness. He mentioned the two ministers by name, doing honor to your lordship. His not being ashamed of his origin shows the man's virtue; his not forgetting his old associations, his good faith; his freedom from mercenariness, his loyalty; and his honoring your lordship, his intelligence.[89]

The concept of virtue as the criterion of a *chün tzu* seems to have been introduced here, but what the passage reveals is the conduct expected of a person of the social status in question. This is slightly different from the idea of behavior guided by general moral concepts that is discussed in the *Analects*.

Nevertheless, *chün tzu* does appear in the *Tso Chuan* with the meaning that it possesses in the *Analects*. These occurrences will be discussed in three groups. The first group consists of commentaries that begin with the words "The *chün tzu* will say," followed by a moral discussion that often has nothing to do with the subject of the narrative. As early as the Sung dynasty, annotators doubted the authenticity of such commentaries; we shall therefore leave this group without further discussion.[90] The second group consists of quotations from Confucius, for example, a comment on the conduct of a forester that says, "To keep the rule [of answering a ruler's summons] is not so good as to keep [the special rule for] one's office. The *chün tzu* will hold this man right."[91] What Confucius means by *chün tzu* is obvious here.

The third group consists of occurrences of *chün tzu* in the sense of a person of superior virtue that do not mention Confucius, who may or may not have influenced the development of this meaning of the phrase. It is possible that the idea that a noble should behave with propriety gave rise to the abstract idea of a person superior in virtue; it is also possible that Confucius did help establish this concept. The highest probability is that both possibilities were involved. The following is one of the several occurrences of *chün tzu* that definitely mean a gentleman in more than the social sense:

Tsu-p'i said, "Good. I have shown myself unintelligent. I have heard that what the *chün tzu* makes it a point to know is the great and the remote, while the *hsiao jen* [small man] is concerned to know the small and near. I am a *hsiao jen*. The garment which fits to my body I know and am careful about, but the great office and the great city on which my body depends for protection were far off and slighted by me."[92]

This is part of a conversation between Tzu-p'i, a chancellor of Cheng, and his assistant Tzu-ch'an. Tzu-p'i was higher both in rank and in seniority, and thus could not have called himself *hsiao jen* and referred to Tzu-ch'an as *chün tzu* if the two terms referred only to social status.

Therefore the *Tso Chuan* contains some occurrences of *chün tzu* that refer to social rank and also some in which the term is used to mean a person who has outstanding moral qualifications. The latter meaning may or may not have been originated by Confucius. If Confucius was the sole inventor of the latter meaning, the quotation attributed to Tzu-p'i, who lived before Confucius, would be an obvious anachronism. It is possible that the *Tso Chuan* passages using that meaning were later interpolations or modifications. It is, however, more likely that the new usage of the term had already begun to arise around the time of Confucius, who may nevertheless have helped make the new connotation explicit. In any case, the meaning of *chün tzu* was expanded in the *Tso Chuan* to include moral considerations.

We shall now consider a non-Confucian work in order to see whether or not the term *chün tzu* also took on moral emphasis outside the Confucian school or kept only the meaning of high social status. It may be possible by this means to determine the extent of Confucian influence on the conceptual development of the term. An analysis of the use of *chün tzu* in the *Mo Tzu* shows that there are about thirty passages in which the term either is associated with *shih*, the lowest order of the aristocracy, or clearly denotes a social status.[93] The following are a few examples:

The *shih chün tzu* of today all exalt the virtuous in their private speech and conduct. But when it comes to the administration of the government for the public, they fail to exalt the virtuous and [to] employ the capable. Then I know the *shih chün tzu* understand only trifles and not things of significance.[94]

The boats are to be employed on water and the vehicles on land, so that the *chün tzu* can rest their feet and the laborers can rest their shoulders and backs.[95]

Now when the big bell, the sounding drum, the *ch'in* and the *she*, the *yü* and the *sheng* are provided, it is yet no pleasure for the lords alone to listen to the playing. Therefore they must enjoy it with either common people or the *chün tzu*. If with the *chün tzu*, it will interfere with their attending to government. If with the common people, it will interfere with their work.[96]

Thus the *chün tzu* referred to in these passages is a person, different from the common people and laborers, who attends to government affairs. The meaning here is apparently the conventional one of social rank and has nothing to do with moral achievements.

The usages of *chün tzu* in a moral sense appear mostly in the three chapters *Fei Ju* (Anti-Confucianism), *Keng Chu,* and *Kung Meng.* One example from each chapter, respectively, is given:

Again the Confucianist says, "The *chün tzu* conforms to the old but does not make innovations." We answer him, "In antiquity, I invented the bow, Yü invented armor, Hsi Chung invented vehicles, and Ch'iao Ch'ui invented boats. Would he say the tanners, armorers, and carpenters of today are all *chün tzu*, whereas I, Yü, Hsi Chung, and Ch'iao Ch'ui were all ordinary men?

Moreover, some of those whom he follows must have been inventors. Then his instructions are after all the ways of ordinary men."[97]

A pupil of Tzu-hsia asked Mo Tzu whether there could be any struggle among the *chün tzu*. Mo Tzu said, "The *chün tzu* do not struggle." The pupil of Tzu-hsia said, "There is a struggle even among the dogs and hogs; how can there be no struggle among men?" Mo Tzu said, "What a shame! T'ang and Wu are praised with words, but dogs and hogs are brought into comparison in conduct. What a shame!"[98]

Kung-meng Tzu said that there were no ghosts and spirits; again, he said that the *chün tzu* must learn sacrifice and worship. Mo Tzu said, "To hold that there are no spirits and [yet to] learn sacrificial ceremonials is comparable to learning the ceremonials of hospitality while there is no guest or to making fishing nets while there are no fish."[99]

All three instances are about the idea of proper conduct for the *chün tzu*; there is no connotation of social rank. Note that the three passages are all debates between Mohists and Confucianists about the definition of *chün tzu*.[100] Although the arguments of the Mohists were not always fair, since they distorted some of the Confucian ideas about men of superior virtue, the discussion of the *chün tzu*'s conduct is basically on a moral level.

In summary, this investigation of the usages of *chün tzu* in the *Mo Tzu* discloses that in the twenty-four chapters in which the terms *chün tzu* or *shih chün tzu* are used, the moral implications only appear in two of the spurious first seven chapters and in the three chapters that discuss Confucianism; in the remaining nineteen chapters *chün tzu* or *shih chün tzu* always means the "learned people who are the officials and advisers to the ruler."[101] Therefore the Confucian school should perhaps be given credit for having helped develop a new meaning for this term that refers only to the virtue of the person in question.

The most important Confucian of the Chan Kuo period was Mencius. In the *Mencius* the term *chün tzu* is generally taken to mean a person of superior morals, regardless of his social standing. However there are four passages in which the term still clearly implies nobility:

Moreover, when the *chün tzu* of old had errors, they reformed them. The *chün tzu* of the present time, when they have errors, persist in them.... But do the *chün tzu* of the present day only persist in their errors? They go on to apologize for them likewise.[102]

Although the territory of T'eng is narrow and small, yet there must be in it *chün tzu* and countrymen. If there were not *chün tzu*, there would be none

to rule the countrymen. If there were no countrymen, there would be none
to support the *chün tzu*.[103]

Thus the *chün tzu* of Shang took baskets full of black and yellow silks to
meet the *chün tzu* of Chou, and the lower classes of the one met those of the
other with baskets full of rice and vessels of congee.[104]

Chün tzu violate the laws of righteousness, and inferiors violate the penal
laws. It is only by fortunate chance that a state in such a case is preserved.[105]

Though the translations in each of the four passages differ, it is clear
that no moral concepts enter into the definition of *chün tzu* as used
in them.

However, most of the occurrences of *chün tzu* in the *Mencius* definitely stress the virtue of the persons concerned and sometimes even
their intellectual capabilities. Mencius's concept of the ideal *chün tzu*
is suggested by the following quotations:

The *chün tzu* will not manifest either narrowmindedness or the want of self-
respect.[106]

The *chün tzu* does not murmur against heaven nor grudge against men.[107]

So a *chün tzu* is ashamed of a reputation beyond his merits.[108]

These quotations show us a man of modesty, honesty, and inner peace,
who achieves these qualities by regarding principle as his only concern, as in the following passage:

The *chün tzu* makes his advances in what he is learning with deep earnest-
ness and by the proper course, wishing to get hold of it in himself. Having
got hold of it in himself, he abides in it calmly and firmly. Abiding in it
calmly and firmly, he is secure in his deep reliance on it.[109]

Thus he should behave according to the *tao*, a proper course, which
is also his goal. Mencius said, "Flowing water is a thing that does not
proceed until it has filled the hollows in its course. The *chün tzu* who
has set his mind on the *tao* does not advance to it but by completing
one stage after another."[110] However the final goal of the *chün tzu* is
not only to accomplish his own virtuous self-cultivation, but also, and
perhaps more importantly, to extend his influence to the people, the
state, and the whole world. Mencius said:

When a *chün tzu* resides in a country, if its sovereign employs his counsels,
he comes to tranquility, wealth, honor, and glory. If the young in it follow
his instructions, they become filial, obedient to their elders, true-hearted,

and faithful. What greater example can there be than this of not eating the bread of idleness?[111]

Wherever the *chün tzu* passes through, transformation follows; wherever he abides, his influence is of a spiritual nature. It flows abroad, above and beneath, like that of heaven and earth. How can it be said that he mends society but in a small way![112]

The principle which the *chün tzu* holds is that of personal cultivation, but the kingdom is thereby tranquilized.[113]

The *chün tzu* presumably extends his good influence by serving a ruler and teaching him the principle of *jen*; thus we read, "The way in which a *chün tzu* serves his prince contemplates simply the leading of him in the right path, and directing his mind to benevolence [*jen*]."[114] *Jen* is also one of the most basic virtues of the *chün tzu*:

That whereby the *chün tzu* is distinguished from other men is what he preserves in his heart, namely, benevolence and propriety. The benevolent man loves others. The man of propriety shows respect to others. . . . Thus it is that the *chün tzu* has a life-long anxiety and not one morning's calamity.[115]

In the *Mencius* the term *chün tzu*, with a few exceptions in which it denotes social standing, implies high moral criteria. The *chün tzu* is a man of virtue and principle who loves people and is willing to help them to achieve a tranquil existence.

Next we will investigate the occurrences of *chün tzu* in the *Chuang Tzu*, a work attributed to the great Taoist of the same name, since it is also a non-Confucian work. The *Chuang Tzu* shows that the moral meaning of *chün tzu*, presumably developed most fully among Confucians, was adopted by scholars of other schools as well. Nowhere in the entire book is there a single passage in which this term is used unquestionably to mean "a member of the nobility," a situation that is quite remarkable when the book is compared with the *Mencius*. It may be that the older meaning had been largely replaced by the newer one by the time of Chuang Tzu (ca. 365–290 B.C.), which was more than a century after the death of Confucius. None of the fourteen occurrences of the phrase implies social rank; they all mean a person of superior moral cultivation, as follows:

The Master said, "It is the *Tao* that overspreads and sustains all things. How great it is in its overflowing influence! The *chün tzu* ought by all means to remove from his mind [all that is contrary to it]. Acting without action is called Heaven[-like]. Speech coming forth of itself is what is called [a mark of] the [true] Virtue. Loving men and benefiting things is what is called

Benevolence. Seeing wherein things are different but agree is what is called being Great. Conduct free from the ambition of being distinguished above others is what is called being Generous. The possession in himself of a myriad points of difference is what is called being Rich. Therefore to hold fast the natural attributes is what is called the Guiding Line [of government]; the perfecting of these attributes is called its Establishment; accordance with the *Tao* is what is called being Complete; and not allowing anything external to affect the will is what is called being Perfect. When the *chün tzu* understands these ten things, he keeps all matters as it were sheathed in himself, showing the greatness of his mind; and through the outflow of his doings, all things move [and come to him].[116]

Chuang Tzu's criteria for calling a man *chün tzu,* which stress a kind of transcendental comprehension instead of conduct in accordance with the moral code, are obviously different from the Confucian scholar's definition of the term. The author of the *Chuang Tzu* did not regard the ideal Confucian *chün tzu* highly and saw him as merely one who was to "regard benevolence as [the source of all] kindness, righteousness as [the source of all] distinctions, propriety as [the rule of all] conduct, and music as [the idea of all] harmony, thus diffusing a fragrance of gentleness and goodness."[117] The *chün tzu* in the *Chuang Tzu* is usually listed after the heavenly man, the spirit-like man, the perfect man, and the sage-like man, and thus was presumably considered to be inferior to these four classes.[118] One passage seems to have used *chün tzu* in the social sense:

Yes, in the age of perfect virtue, men lived in common with birds and beasts, and were on terms of equality with all creatures, as forming one family—how could they know among themselves the distinctions of *chün tzu* and small men? Equally without knowledge, they did not leave [the path of] their natural virtue; equally free from desires, they were in the state of pure simplicity.[119]

Though the meaning of *chün tzu* is ambiguous here, it seems more likely that it refers to social status than to moral level.

Despite the great difference between the Confucian and Taoist estimations of the *chün tzu,* it is beyond question that the earlier meaning of the term seldom appears in the *Chuang Tzu.* Though Chuang Tzu disagreed with the ideals of the Confucian school, the use of the term in a moral rather than in a social sense in the book was probably the result of Confucian influence.

The work attributed to Hsün Tzu, a Confucian scholar who lived a little after Chuang Tzu, contains hundreds of occurrences of the phrase *chün tzu.* Most of these mean a person superior in both virtue and intellect, but there are four uses of the term in its social sense, as follows:

[Tzu-ssu said] this is really the saying of my former *chün tzu*.[120]

When a horse hitched to a carriage is restless, a *chün tzu* is not secure in the carriage. When the common people are restless under the government, then a *chün tzu* is not secure in his position. . . . When the common people are satisfied with his government, then only is a *chün tzu* secure in his position.[121]

Besides the two above examples, of which the first is admittedly dubious, *chün tzu* appears occasionally with its older meaning in quotations from such earlier works as the *Shih Ching*.[122]

Uses of *chün tzu* other than in the above-mentioned two groups seem to mean something quite distinct from social status. From the first sentence of the *Hsün Tzu* onward the moral dicta in the text are voiced by the *chün tzu*, who is considered the ideal man. The criteria for a *chün tzu* are expressed as follows:

Therefore the *chün tzu* is noble though he has no title; he is rich though he has no official emoluments; he is trusted though he does not advertise himself; he is majestic though he does not rage; he is glorious though he be poor and retired; he is happy though he lives alone; do not his circumstances of being most honorable, most wealthy, most important, and most dignified all increasingly show this to be true? . . . Therefore the *chün tzu* pays attention to developing his inner capacities, but yields to others in external matters; he pays attention to cultivating virtue himself and dwells in it by his modesty; in this way his fame arises like the sun and the moon; the country responds like an echo to the thunder. Hence it is said: "The *chün tzu* is retired and yet manifest; he is subtle and yet clear; he yields to others and yet conquers."[123]

As for social rank, the *chün tzu* began in a low station; hence the proper criterion for his status is his cultivation of virtue in himself. This is discussed further:

A man who practices hoeing and ploughing becomes a farmer; if he practices chopping and shaving wood, he becomes an artisan; if he practices trafficking in goods, he becomes a merchant; if he practices the rules of proper conduct [*li*] and justice [*i*], he becomes a *chün tzu*. . . . Hence if a man knows how to pay attention to his choices and rejections, to be careful of his habits, and to magnify profuse cultivation, he will become a *chün tzu*. If he follows his nature and emotions, and his scholarship is restricted, he will become a small-minded man. If a person is a *chün tzu* he is usually peaceful and honored; if he is a small-minded man, he is usually in danger and disgrace.[124]

Good education, by which one acquires an appreciation of proper conduct, is also a criterion for a *chün tzu*. "Now the people who are influenced by good teachers and laws, who accumulate literature and knowledge, who are led by the rules of proper conduct and justice become *chün tzu*."[125]

The *Hsün Tzu* distinguishes between just glory and circumstantial glory, and just shame and circumstantial shame. The many virtuous actions and brilliant thoughts of the cultivated man constitute just glory, which comes from within. High noble rank, generous tribute or emolument, and great power, from the emperor down to the officers of low rank—these are the glory of circumstance, which comes from without. The shame that follows licentiousness, filth, transgressions of duty, evil principles, pride, oppression, and avarice is just; circumstantial shame comes from being reviled, insulted, abased physically, and tortured. The text says:

Hence the *chün tzu* can have the shame of circumstances, but cannot have just shame. The mean-minded man can have the glory of circumstances, but cannot have just glory.... Only a *chün tzu* can have both just glory and glory of circumstances. Only a mean-minded man can have both just shame and the shame of circumstances.[126]

It is obvious that in fact the glory or the shame of circumstances has nothing to do with whether one is a *chün tzu*. Thus the term *chün tzu* as it appears in the *Hsün Tzu* does not normally denote social status; the few times that this term is used to refer also to social rank can perhaps be considered exceptions to the general rule that the term is used with the meaning stressed by Confucius.

The last work to be examined, the *Han Fei Tzu*, contains twenty-two instances of *chün tzu* in seventeen passages. Only three of them use the term to refer to membership in the nobility, and two of the three, including one quotation from the *Tao Te Ching*, are found in the chapter on the teachings of Lao Tzu, a chapter whose attribution to Han Fei Tzu is dubious.[127] The other one uses the term in the sense of "the nobility": " 'The Wu people have made a round trip of sixty *li*,' remarked the Left Court Historiographer. 'By this time their *chün tzu* must be resting, and their *hsiao jen* eating.' "[128] It is obvious from the context that *chün tzu* here implies officers. The *Han Fei Tzu* indicates a *chün tzu* is not a violent person; in one passage a person said,

What a dolt Tseng Tzu is! If he took me for a *chün tzu* how could he afford to be disrespectful? If he took me for a *pao jen* [violent person] how could he afford to insult me?[129]

One passage makes righteousness the distinction between a small man and a *chün tzu*:

> The listener is either a *hsiao jen* or a *chün tzu*. The *hsiao jen*, having no concern for righteousness, must be unable to estimate the speeches from the standpoint of righteousness; whereas the *chün tzu*, estimating them from the standpoint of righteousness, is certainly not delighted by them.[130]

Lack of righteousness is thus a great shame to the *chün tzu*. The *Han Fei Tzu* criticizes the actions of Duke Huan of Ch'i and Kuan Chung, saying,

> Thus, though in the eyes of the *hsiao jen* he wiped away the disgrace of dropping his hat, yet in the eyes of the *chün tzu* there was still the disgrace of dropping righteousness.[131]

In the *Han Fei Tzu* there is not a single case in which a direct quote is introduced by the phrase "the *chün tzu* said," an idiom that appears frequently in Confucian works, including the *Mencius* and the *Hsün Tzu*.[132] In addition, discussion of the definition of *chün tzu* seems to be a favorite topic in the Confucian writings, but such discussions hardly appear at all in the *Han Fei Tzu*. Although Han Fei Tzu was a disciple of Hsün Tzu, his ideas diverged from those of his master, which may explain the relatively few occurrences of the term *chün tzu* in the *Han Fei Tzu*. In summary, the *Han Fei Tzu* uses the term *chün tzu* in both its meanings; most of the occurrences are in the sense adopted by the Confucian school and only a very few are in the older sense.

This discussion of *chün tzu* shows that the term underwent a development like that of the English term "gentleman."[133] In early works such as the *Shih Ching*, *chün tzu* denotes a social status such as membership in the nobility. It may have been Confucius who helped transform it from a title of social rank to a title that referred to superior virtue. Use of the new meaning then gradually increased. Both meanings appear frequently in the *Tso Chuan*, but the new sense of *chün tzu* is not only accepted but more frequent in the Chan Kuo non-Confucian books *Chuang Tzu* and *Han Fei Tzu*, as well as in the Confucian works *Mencius* and *Hsün Tzu*. One possible reason for this shift is that the old society, which was ruled by a hereditary noble class, had changed radically in structure. When the highborn social elite could no longer hold their positions at the top of society, the scholars began to develop the concept of morally and intellectually outstanding men who owed their superiority not to their hereditary rank but to their personal qualities. The name stayed the same, but in the old bottle there was new wine.

Summary

The Chan Kuo period witnessed great changes in the ideas that justified social relationships. The divine charisma of rulers and ruling groups was no longer recognized, and respect for the past was replaced by attention to present expediency. The familial bond between the ruler and his ministers was replaced by a contractual relationship like that between employer and employee. It was believed that able and virtuous persons should be selected to carry on the business of government rather than relatives of the ruler, who was no longer the father-figure of a familial state but the head, functional or nonfunctional, of a bureaucratic administration. Those who served in the court belonged to a universal layer of experts, administrators, and scholars; that is, a layer of educated intellectuals with a clear group-consciousness that went beyond state boundaries. These changes greatly influenced concepts and meanings. One manifestation of this was the gradual change in the meaning of the term *chün tzu* from a title that referred to high social station to one that referred to superiority in virtue; the name that had denoted the social elite was now used for the moral elite. The changes in these concepts may have helped the people of the Chan Kuo period adjust themselves to great social mobility by facilitating it psychologically. On the other hand, social mobility helped bring about an ideological remodeling.

Chapter 7   Conclusion

The following questions were posed in the first chapter:
1. How free was social mobility during the Ch'un Ch'iu and Chan Kuo periods?
2. Did this mobility occur within an unchanged social structure?
3. If the social structure remained unchanged, what correlated the greater mobility of individuals within it?
4. If there were changes in the social structure, what were they, when did they occur, and how were they related to the changes in social mobility?

In answering these questions, let us first consider social stratification, which was principally by political rank in the society of ancient China. Before the changes that occurred in the Ch'un Ch'iu period the top stratum was occupied by rulers of states, including Chou; the next lower one consisted of ministers and great officers who were lords of their own fiefs. The lowest order of the ruling group was the *shih*. Persons in these three strata, except for a few of the *shih,* may be classified as landlords, at least from a purely economic viewpoint. They were all at least classificatory kin to one another; hence their sociopolitical relationships before and during the early Ch'un Ch'iu period were predominantly familial. Below the ruling group were the masses who tilled the soil and supported the upper strata. There were also merchants and artisans, but these were usually retainers of aristocratic families. The peasants, merchants, and artisans formed three occupational divisions but only one social class, the *hsiao jen* or small men, in contrast to the *chün tzu* or "sons of lords." At the very bottom of the social scale were the slaves, about whom very little is known; there is almost no information about their role in the economy of ancient China, and their numbers, though unknown, appear to have been few.

Chapter 2 offers answers to the first and second questions. Though the rulers always held nominal sovereignty, their descendants gradually became less and less active politically, whereas the hereditary ministers who headed great families became quite powerful after the middle of the seventh century B.C., when the *shih* also began to participate in political affairs. After about a century, the ministerial group began to lose political power, while the same period witnessed the growing influence of the *shih*. Since social and political stratification in ancient China were closely linked, the fluctuations in political power reflected to a great degree the rise and decline of social groups.

At the beginning of the Chan Kuo period, in the fifth century, the number of persons who rose from obscurity greatly increased; the ministerial families of the previous period had disappeared. The new ministers who filled the vacant political positions do not seem to have established powerful families to fill the social vacancy. The class of noble ministers largely disappeared from Chan Kuo society. Thus the first two questions can be answered. There was a great deal of social mobility in the Ch'un Ch'iu and Chan Kuo periods, and after the fifth century B.C. the social structure appears to have changed, since the class of hereditary nobles almost disappeared. We find both the movement of individuals between strata and the disintegration of some social groups.

The answer to the third question required an investigation of political institutions, economics, and ideology. In the third and fourth chapters we saw that when the Chou feudal system collapsed, any unity that China may have had dissolved and a multi-state system emerged. Power was then the decisive factor in interstate relations and conflict concentrated power; the few strongest states extinguished their small, weak neighbors and absorbed them. The members of the upper strata of the defeated states were summarily dropped to the bottom of the social scale. Since there were scores of extinguished principalities, nobility was abased on a grand scale.

Elimination by conquest also went on inside the states. In a situation in which several powerful noble families had for generations overshadowed the sovereign of their state, there were struggles, usually violent, between the nobles and the ruler as well as among the noble houses. The result of such struggles was either eventual domination and survival by one or a few aristocratic families, or the victory of the ruling house by suppression of the unruly nobility. The nobles who were defeated in the struggle for power faced complete social abasement, as did all their kinsmen and associates. So it was that the upper classes in the Ch'un Ch'iu period were disintegrated and shrunken by the internecine warfare of their members.

On the other hand, the rise of individuals from the lower to the upper classes was also made possible by these struggles. The frequency of wars increased because of the intensity of the struggles, and new tactical and strategic concepts of warfare were introduced. New types of strategists, field officers, and career soldiers were in demand; the old art of war with its chariots and its code of gallantry disappeared along with the noble, gentlemanly warriors. Those who could master the new techniques of warfare were promoted no matter what their origins or birth, as were those skilled in the complicated diplomacy demanded by the frequent contacts among the states.

Individuals passed between classes with especial frequency in the Chan Kuo period, when all of the seven surviving powerful states strove to consolidate their home governments and to win battles abroad. These states were headed by monarchs of a new type, who were assisted by bureaucratic officials instead of by a corps of nobles; hence experts in government were greatly in demand. Meanwhile the more highly developed warfare and the more effective diplomacy of Chan Kuo times required more persons to fill military and diplomatic offices. Many of those who held office in Chan Kuo states may have been descendants of the *shih* class of the previous period, which furnished the state functionaries after the class of noble ministers had declined. They occupied a position between the ruler at the top and the ruled at the bottom, a social space so broad that it could not be considered a homogeneous social stratum. Therefore it would be misleading to describe the enlargement of the *shih* class as the movement of an entire group into a higher social plane.

Changes in the economy, discussed in Chapter 5, led to a new, economically stratified social structure that challenged the domination of the society by those of high political rank. By the later part of the Ch'un Ch'iu period, the use of serf labor by manorial lords seems to have largely given way to a system in which the users of the land paid rent or taxes. At this point the feudal lord became a landowner and his subjects became tenants. The next stage was the appearance of men who owned land but did not necessarily have a concomitant noble rank. Some landowners became very rich by buying up land and the landless peasants grew poorer still—an economic stratification that was also a social differentiation and caused a basic change in the structure of society.

The increase in commercial activity gave rise to wealthy men who were neither of the nobility nor associated with political power. As the states grew larger during the Ch'un Ch'iu and Chan Kuo periods, inter-regional contact became easier because of relative order within large areas and frequent contacts, either warlike or friendly, between states. The wide circulation of money, the specialization of production, and progress in technology all facilitated the prosperity of commerce. It is impossible to date precisely the appearance of rich businessmen, but the sudden appearance of much varied coinage during the fifth and fourth centuries B.C. indicates that active commerce had begun at the start of the Chan Kuo period. In the fifth and fourth centuries B.C., there was a class of rich men in the newly developed cities who wielded political influence with their wealth and, by investing their capital in land, speeded up the widening of the gap between the rich and the poor classes. They were nobles without rank and lords without scepters—a completely new social group.

Along with new political and economic institutions, there appeared new concepts about morals, patterns of social relationships, and even religious beliefs. The problem of ideological evolution was discussed in Chapter 6. The first chapter pointed out that the Chou and pre-Chou nobles justified their superior rank by the idea that their ancestors had had charismatic power bestowed upon them by heaven or at least were associated in some extraordinary way with the deities, and that they in turn passed this charismatic power on to their descendants. The familial concept of the feudal system, which stressed blood ties, served to ensure inheritance of the divine superiority; hence the ancestors cast their shadows on their posterity, and the past commanded the present. Tradition was honored and the status quo preserved. A person's birth, which depended on the past, decided his life; his own personality and capabilities counted for little. However, the last part of the Ch'un Ch'iu period saw a change in these views.

The first important person to focus new light on the changing world was Confucius, who, perhaps because he witnessed the abrupt ascents and descents of his contemporaries and became aware of the inequities of his society, began to teach that the most important aspect of a man was his moral caliber. His ideal was a person having humanitarian views, a moral conscience, and the ability to carry out his convictions. Confucius dreamed of a world peopled by men of this sort or at least ruled by them, but he never saw the fulfillment of his dream. Nevertheless he contributed much to the overthrowing of the feudal system by undermining its cornerstone, the belief of the inborn superiority of the noble. His ideas were advocated, taught, and developed by scholars of his own school, and also by other men who were inspired by his thoughts and agreed with him in general but who had various reservations and revisions—Mohists, *Fa Chia* scholars, and others. What seems to have concerned the *Fa Chia* most was the practical process of putting the capable and the competent into office to meet the urgent demands of the new bureaucratic state. This is a case in which political institutions and ideology influenced one another.

The growth of commerce also seems to have influenced the basic pattern of social relations. In the familial relationship of the feudal society, the lord corresponded to the father and his vassal to the son; it was not a contractual matter. But at the high tide of commercial activities in the Chan Kuo period, the ruler-minister relationship often took on the characteristics of an employer-employee contract. Such a reciprocal concept seems to have became basic to social relationships and may have greatly influenced the development of commerce. Again one sees here a connection between ideological change and change in more concrete phenomena, in this case, in economic development.

Hence the principal changes in views were twofold. First, the emphasis on a man's birth gave way to an emphasis on the importance of his personal character; second, a system of contractual reciprocity replaced the familial relationship in society. Both changes increased social mobility, the first by making possible personal competition for high positions, and the second by loosening the tight familial bonds between members of society.

Our investigation of the term *chün tzu* shows that the change in its meaning reflected the disappearance of the class of hereditary nobles. In Ch'un Ch'iu writings *chün tzu* usually meant a nobleman, but during and after the time of Confucius, it came to mean a person of superior moral character. Perhaps the later writings merely reflect the change in the meaning, but it is possible that the scholars helped change the meaning of the term and thus helped destroy the hereditary nobility, of whose existence in Chan Kuo times there is little evidence.

The fourth question, concerning the nature and the dates of these changes, has been answered in the preceding paragraphs. We have seen that the change in political institutions gathered its principal momentum in the sixth century B.C., the middle of the Ch'un Ch'iu period, when upward social mobility generally consisted of the rise of individuals and downward mobility was found mainly in the social disintegration of the upper strata. In the Chan Kuo period, the change in political institutions was completed and mobility between political strata became relatively free. Meanwhile, a social stratification that was economic as well as political appeared in the fifth century B.C., at the end of the Ch'un Ch'iu period, when economic development brought about the emergence of wealthy men and great landowners to compete with persons of political consequence. The reformation in ideology began in the fifth century B.C., the time of Confucius.

Therefore the period comprising the sixth to the third centuries B.C. is of the greatest significance in Chinese history. The final stage of the struggle among the states of these times brought the unification of China. The methods evolved for consolidating state governments gave to unified China the means to maintain her cultural and political unity for centuries. The idea of selecting only the best men for public service led to the philosophy of giving every man a fair chance to rise in the social scale. These four centuries were indeed the decisive period in the formation of China and her culture.

Appendix

Appendix   Authenticity and Dating of Pre-Ch'in Texts

The *Shih Ching,* or *Book of Songs,* is a collection of early folk and ritual songs. Confucius is traditionally supposed to have selected the now extant three-hundred-odd songs from a total of about three thousand.¹ The evidence is, however, that the *Shih Ching* was the same in Confucius's day as it is now; he himself at least twice referred to "the three hundred songs."² During the Ch'un Ch'iu period quotations from the *Shih Ching* were used in the indirect and decorous language of diplomacy, and most of the quotations of poetry appearing in the *Tso Chuan* can be located in the extant version of the *Shih Ching.* If there had been three thousand songs before they were edited, one would expect to find far fewer of the *Tso Chuan* quotations among the later three hundred.³ The *Shih Ching* consists of folk songs, love songs, songs of praise, feasting songs, and songs used in sacrificial rites. The last group is particularly interesting because it contains epics about the origins of ruling houses, references to the mandate of heaven and religious attitudes, and other informative material. The folk songs also reveal much about the daily life of the people. The ritual songs appear mostly in the *Sung* section, the folk songs in the *Kuo Feng* part, and the songs in praise of the lords or for the entertainment of the nobles in the *Ya* section.⁴

The time span of the *Shih Ching* is about six or seven centuries. Fu Ssu-nien suggests that the earliest part of the *Chou Sung* be attributed to the beginning of the Chou dynasty and the latest parts of *Shang Sung* and *Lu Sung* to a period just before the time of Confucius, when the Ch'un Ch'iu period was already more than half over. According to Fu, most of the *Ta Ya* and *Hsiao Ya* and several of the poems of the *Kuo Feng* appeared in late Western Chou times and in the first half of the Ch'un Ch'iu.⁵ I have used information from the *Shih Ching* for two main purposes, to discuss various little-known aspects of life under the Ch'un Ch'iu feudalism that the pre-Ch'un Ch'iu and early Ch'un Ch'iu parts of the book throw light on, and to

discuss early religious concepts that are found in the epics and sacrificial songs.

The work most heavily used in this study is the *Tso Chuan*. Today
the historical student need not seriously consider the theory that the
Tso Chuan was written to interpret the supposed hidden meanings
put into the *Ch'un Ch'iu* by Confucius.[6] Nor is there adequate ground
for the theory that the *Tso Chuan* was deliberately forged in the Former Han dynasty by Liu Hsin or his colleagues for alleged political
ends.[7] Even though most of the events in the *Ch'un Ch'iu* coincide
with happenings reported by the *Tso Chuan,* there are many that do
not. The *Tso Chuan* may not even have been written as a counterpart to the *Ch'un Ch'iu*; though it is similar to the *Ch'un Ch'iu* its
sources of information are somewhat different. For instance, accounts
of affairs in Chin appear more often in the *Tso Chuan* than in the
Ch'un Ch'iu, which chiefly records the affairs of Lu.[8] Its grammatical
differences from other works reveal that the *Tso Chuan* was written
in a style so unique, natural, and consistent that later forgers could
not likely have created it.[9] Bernhard Karlgren gives the date of the
Tso Chuan as probably 468–300 B.C., based on his study of the comparative grammar of this and other pre-Ch'in texts.[10] A study of the
supposed prophecies contained in the *Tso Chuan* shows that some
were astonishingly accurate but others were not. The emergence of
Wei as a state from one part of Chin as well as the division of Chin
into three states (403 B.C.), the usurpation of the Ch'i throne by the
house of T'ien (386 B.C.), and the ruin of the Cheng state (375 B.C.)
were predicted in the chronicles for the years 659 and 543 B.C., 533
B.C., and 543 B.C., respectively.[11] On the other hand, the chronicle for
the year 605 B.C. foretold that the life span of the Chou dynasty would
be seven hundred years, but it actually lasted eight hundred and sixty-
seven years.[12] The capital of the state of Wey, according to the *Tso
Chuan,* was supposed to be moved from Ti-chiu three hundred years
after its establishment there in 627 B.C., but Wey did not move its
capital until 241 B.C.[13] It was also predicted in the chronicle for 620
B.C. that Ch'in could expand no further to the east, but that state won
its first great victory against Wei in 340 B.C.[14]

Using these cases as evidence, Liu Ju-lin argued that the author of
the *Tso Chuan* did not witness the eighth centennial of the Chou
dynasty (ca. 322 B.C.), the third centennial of the Wey capital after its
settlement, or the expedition of Ch'in to to the east in 340 B.C. Hence
Liu deduced that the author of the *Tso Chuan* wrote the book before

340 B.C. and after 375 B.C., the year that Cheng was destroyed.* Notice
that both Liu and Karlgren assume that the *Tso Chuan* was written at one particular time. However, several passages clearly contain
later ideas, which William Hung's remarkable study of this aspect
has shown.[15] Regardless of when the *Tso Chuan* was completed, much
of the material on which it is based appears to be quite old. This material seems to be a body of data similar to (but much more detailed
than) that used in the *Ch'un Ch'iu,* which is a brief chronicle of the
state of Lu containing records of events that the historians of Lu
either considered important or were ordered to write down. The author or authors of the *Tso Chuan* edited such sources; it may be that
they, or other later persons, slightly revised the material or added
something to the text. It is also possible that some commentaries
found their way into the text during the long process of copying and
recopying the book by hand. It is difficult to settle all of these points,
but it can be said that accounts of historical events are not easily invented whole-cloth, since they must be consistent with other events.
It is relatively easy, however, to invent passages dealing with moral
teachings, for which reason caution must be exercised in using such
passages as, for example, the sayings attributed in the *Tso Chuan* to
Tsang Hsi-po.[16] There are passages that are usually attributed to such
spokesmen of moral teachings as Shih Mo, Shu-hsiang, and Tzu-ch'an.
Any moral discussion that appears to have no intimate connection
with the development of a particular historical event should be regarded with reasonable skepticism.[17] Also passages beginning "The
chün tzu said" or with words to that effect should be treated with caution. The authenticity of this phrase was doubted as early as the Sung
dynasty; it has been considered to date from the Han dynasty.[18] Today no critical scholar holds that the *Tso Chuan* was written to supplement the *Ch'un Ch'iu* and to answer the riddles supposedly contained in that work, such as whether it is meant as praise or censure
of the actions of the rulers of Lu. Hence I have avoided the frequent
doubtful passages in seeking reliable sources.

Another work closely associated with the *Tso Chuan* is the *Kuo Yü.*
During the Later Han dynasty some scholars considered the *Kuo Yü*

* *WSTK,* I, 408–9. Using the same evidence combined with a theory based on calculations of the calendar system of the *Tso Chuan,* Maspero concluded that the
Tso Chuan could not have been written earlier than the end of the fourth century
B.C. He then combined his deductions with those of Karlgren to suggest that it was
written around the end of the fourth century B.C. See Maspero, "La Composition,"
pp. 137–208, and the preface by Hung to *CCYT,* pp. lxx–lxxi.

to have been written by the same author who wrote the *Tso Chuan*.[19] In the Sung dynasty the differences between the two were pointed out.[20] Some recent scholars, such as Ts'ui Shu, have said that the two were not written by the same author; others have maintained that the *Tso Chuan* was a part of the *Kuo Yü* that was cut out of it by Liu Hsin.[21] It can be seen that the two books are indeed closely related in style and content. For this reason William Hung sought to date the *Kuo Yü* before the *Tso Chuan* and concluded that the former was compiled near the close of the Chan Kuo period, before the unification of China by Ch'in.[22] Bernhard Karlgren made a careful study of the grammar of both books and of other pre-Han texts and came to the conclusion that the *Kuo Yü* and the *Tso Chuan* have similar but not identical grammar. The similarity caused him to attribute both to the same school, but a difference in one important point indicated that they were not written by the same hand. He concluded that the date of the *Kuo Yü* is the same as that of the *Tso Chuan*.[23] Some old material was preserved and used in the *Kuo Yü* as well as in the *Tso Chuan*. This material is a valuable source of information for discussing Ch'un Ch'iu or even earlier times, but it must be used with great care.

The *Lun Yü*, or the *Analects of Confucius*, is another important source. The two versions of this work that existed in the Former Han dynasty were merged into the single standard version by the end of that period.[24] Liu Tsung-yüan of the T'ang dynasty doubted the theory current in Han times that the disciples of Confucius edited the *Analects* from their notes; he said it was the second generation of Confucian disciples who edited this work.[25] Ts'ui Shu, who agreed with this idea, contributed to the study of the subject by showing the difference between the last five chapters and the preceding fifteen.[26] Doubtful passages were carefully pointed out both by H. G. Creel and by Ts'ui Shu, although they differ over some chapters.[27] Most of the *Analects*, except for the chapters ruled out by critical scholars, is considered to be authentic and to have been edited by students of the Confucian school about one generation after the time of the Master. They are treasured as the finest source of information on the ideas of Confucius and the history of his period.

The book of Mo Tzu (ca. 479–390 B.C.) is one of the earliest of what we consider to be Chan Kuo materials.[28] Like the *Analects of Confucius*, the *Mo Tzu* was not written by the Master himself. It seems to consist of notes written by his disciples and other essays prepared by the Mohist school.[29] Hu Shih divides the material of the *Mo Tzu* into five groups. The first seven chapters, and especially the first three, are suspected of being spurious. The second group consists of the chapters *Shang Hsien, Shang T'ung, Chien Ai, Fei Kung, Chieh Yung, Chieh Tsang, T'ien Chih, Ming Kuei, Fei Yüeh, Fei Ming,* and *Fei Ju,* a total of thirty-two counting the duplicates (eight have been lost). This group constitutes the main body of the book and expresses the principal concepts of the Mohist school; as Hu Shih suggests, it may have been written by scholars of the school. The third group is made up of the *Ching, Ching Shuo, Ta Ch'ü,* and *Hsiao Ch'ü,* the canonical chapters and their supplements. Hu Shih doubted that they were written in the time of Mo Tzu and attributed them to a later period. The fourth group is the five chapters *Keng Chu, Kuei I, Kung Meng, Lu Wen,* and *Kung Shu,* which Hu Shih suggests are similar to the *Analects of Confucius,* that is, fragmentary speeches and accounts concerning the Master edited by his disciples. The last group is the eleven chapters on military tactics and engineering, which Hu Shih also attributes to the Mohist school.[30] The authenticity of this last group was questioned by the Ch'ing scholars, and it has now been fully proven that these chapters were forged by Han tacticians.[31] Originally there were twenty chapters in this section, but the extant version contains only eleven.[32] The canonical chapters in the third group are apparently discussions of logic; the two *Ching Shuo* chapters are obviously supplements to the *Ching* chapters, as shown by their title and content, but it is not certain whether they are of the same period as the *Ching* chapters. Liang Ch'i-ch'ao considered the *Ta Ch'ü* and *Hsiao Ch'ü* to have been written later, but he disagreed with the conclusions of Hu Shih on the authenticity of the *Ching* sections and suggested that the canonical chapters were prepared by Mo Tzu himself for the instruction of his disciples.[33] I do not agree with Liang on this point; the canonical chapters may or may not have been from the hand of Mo Tzu and very little can be said about them since they include scant historical material.[34]

The chapters of the second group are in duplicate and even triplicate with very little difference between the versions of the same chapter. They seem to be notes on Mo Tzu's teachings taken by different disciples, which implies that they indeed consist of the speeches and instruction of the Master. On this supposition the group could not be dated much later than one generation after Mo Tzu and may even have been written during his lifetime; the same argument applies to the chapters of the fourth group. Therefore only the chapters of these two groups are used in this study.[35]

The *Mencius* seems to be in the same category as the *Analects*, although its authenticity is less in question and it is relatively free of interpolations. It is reported that there were originally eleven chapters in the Han catalogue instead of the extant seven. The commentator Chao Ch'i (born ca. A.D. 108) of the Han dynasty examined the book carefully and threw out four chapters, leaving the seven that he considered authentic.[36] The authorship of *Mencius* has been attributed to the Master himself by Ssu-ma Ch'ien, who made the first judgment on this subject.[37] The T'ang scholar Han Yü asserted that the book was written by Mencius's disciples.[38] This conclusion is supported by the facts that the posthumous names of rulers contemporary with Mencius occur in the book and that many passages read like accounts by a narrator instead of memoirs by the Master himself.[39] Whether or not Mencius actually wrote the book, it can still be considered one of the most valuable sources for the history of the Chan Kuo period.

The *Chuang Tzu* is generally attributed to the philosopher Chuang Chou (ca. 365–290 B.C.) but it appears to be the work of more than one author.[40] By the time of the commentator Kuo Hsiang (died ca. A.D. 311) the book had been divided into three parts, *Nei P'ien, Wai P'ien,* and *Tsa P'ien.* Kuo excluded as spurious nineteen chapters of the fifty-two in existence at that time. The *Nei P'ien* section of seven chapters is practically the same in all versions and therefore, he thought, probably genuine.[41] Hu Shih concurs on this point but suspects possible later interpolations in them. He strongly doubts the authenticity of the remaining chapters.[42] Ku Chieh-kang suggested that the *Chuang Tzu* is an anthology of the writings of Taoist scholars; the writings are not consistent and, according to Ku, some of them might date from as late as the end of the Chan Kuo period.[43] T'ang Lan questioned the uniformity and the authorship of the book, doubted that the *Nei P'ien* is authentic, and asserted that all the rest is spurious. Some chapters and even some sections of chapters of the *Nei P'ien,* he says, were not written by the same hand. T'ang nevertheless concluded that the writings of Chuang Tzu's disciples and of their followers in turn may have been included in the book and are still valuable, since they are from pre-Ch'in times.[44] We may accept the opinion of T'ang Lan and treat the *Chuang Tzu* as a book written by Taoist scholars rather than as the work of the one man Chuang Chou. We must therefore exclude chapter xxx, which has no connection with the Taoist philosophy and which seems to be about a certain Chuang Hsin, who was active in politics. Chuang Chou, the real

Chuang Tzu, probably was never involved in worldly affairs like Chuang Hsin, who once instructed a ruler in the strategy of winning in interstate struggles.[45]

The *Hsün Tzu* is attributed to the last great pre-Ch'in Confucian philosopher, Hsün Tzu (ca. 340–245 B.C.). Most of the book appears to be authentic; chapters xxiv and xxvii–xxxii of the extant version are considered to be fragmentary records of his sayings written down by his disciples, a view that was held by the T'ang commentator Yang Liang, who rearranged the book into its present order.[46] Liang Ch'i-ch'ao doubted the authenticity of chapter xxiv and pointed out that chapters ix, xv, and xvi all contain the term "Master Hsün Ch'ing," which led him to believe that these chapters were interpolations by the disciples of Hsün Tzu.[47] Hu Shih doubted the integrity of the entire book and suggested that it might be a melange of all kinds of materials. He came to the conclusion that only four chapters, xvii and xxi–xxiii, are genuine. He stated that the last six chapters are spurious, that some chapters contained passages unrelated to the subject matter, and that many passages of the *Hsün Tzu* had appeared in other books.[48] It seems to me that Hu Shih is somewhat overcautious in asserting that only four chapters were written by Hsün Tzu.

Chang Hsi-t'ang, after studying the consistency of the ideas in the various chapters, suggested that fourteen chapters can be safely ascribed to Hsün Tzu: i–iii, vi, ix–xi, and xvii–xxiii. He thought that four other chapters—iv, v, xii, and xiii—are from the pen of Hsün Tzu but contain possible late interpolations, that chapters viii, xv, and xvi were written by disciples of the Master, and that chapters vii, xiv, and xxiv are of doubtful authenticity. He ruled out entirely the two chapters of poems and the last six chapters.* It is perhaps permissible to say that the *Hsün Tzu* consists of writings by Hsün Ch'ing and his disciples. At any rate the work seems to be made up of pre-Ch'in materials, and even the dubious last six chapters may be helpful if used with due caution.

The *Han Fei Tzu* is named for Han Fei (?–233 B.C.), the last great

---

* *HTCH*, pp. 149–50. Dubs translated twenty-three chapters and left out the seven dubious ones, the two chapters of poems, and chapters xxv and xxvi. The last paragraph of chapter xxxii in the current version is translated as an answer by a disciple of Hsün Tzu to the criticism of an unknown person. Dubs also doubted the genuineness of parts of chapters viii, xv, and xvi and pointed this out either by omitting the entire passage or by noting it in the text. See Dubs, p. 91, n. 1; p. 162, n. 1; p. 170, n. 4; and p. 171, in which only one passage of chapter xvi is translated. For some unspecified reason Dubs omitted chapters xii–xiv and only partially translated chapter xi.

thinker of the Chan Kuo period. The *Han Fei Tzu* is for the most part a collection of works by him, his followers, and people with similar ideas. However, some parts are so far away from his philosophy that they must be interpolations, although the integrity of the book as a whole has not been questioned in the past. Using the two chapters xlix, *Wu Tu* ("Five Vermin"), and l, *Hsien Hsüeh* ("Learned Celebrities"), both of which are generally considered to be by Han Fei, as a standard of comparison, Jung Chao-tsu classified the chapters of the *Han Fei Tzu* into several groups. The first group includes only the aforementioned traditionally genuine chapters. The second group is made up of six chapters that the evidence proves, he believes, to be contemporaneous with the first group; these are chapters xl, xli, xlv, xlvi, liv, and xxxvi. The rest he considers to be insertions by other groups of people such as the *Fa Chia* and Taoists, accounts about Han Fei, or dubious chapters that Jung felt unsure of but that he could neither prove nor disprove to be connected with Han Fei.*

Ch'en Ch'i-t'ien in his textual criticism of the *Han Fei Tzu* re-evaluated the authorship of all its chapters and rearranged the order of the entire book. Most of the chapters he ascribed to Han Fei. Ch'en said that thirty of the fifty-five are definitely his work and ten others probably are, though he had doubts about the latter ten because of suspicious terminology or concepts contained in them.[49] Ch'en attributed eight chapters to the followers or fellow *Fa Chia* scholars of Han Fei, since they contain ideas similar to Han Fei's.[50] Six whole chapters and one half chapter Ch'en held to be definitely by other persons or schools.[51] I have generally accepted Ch'en's conclusions for use in this study; material relating to Han Fei is taken primarily from those chapters that Ch'en considered to be Han Fei's work. However, since most of the *Han Fei Tzu* was written before or shortly after the unification of China under Ch'in, it is a valuable source of information on various aspects of late Chan Kuo history. The most interesting parts are chapters xxii, xxiii, and xxx–xxxv, which seem to be collections of various histories and anecdotes probably culled by Han Fei

---

* *HFCT*, pp. 653–74. Liao in his translation does not mention the authorship of the various chapters, with a few exceptions. Chapter i, which Jung considered to be the work of an unknown career strategist-diplomat, was attribtued to Han Fei by Liao; cf. *HFCT*, pp. 665–66, and Liao, I, 1, n. 1. Liao considered the first half of the second chapter to contain the work of Han Fei, whereas Jung said that the entire chapter was an account concerning Han Fei but not written by him; cf. *HFCT*, p. 668, and Liao, I, 13, n. 1. Chapters xxiv–xxix are doubted by Jung, but Liao held that these six chapters give a summation of the theories of Han Fei; cf. *HFCT*, pp. 672–73, and Liao, I, 258, n. 4.

from whatever literature he read. Many useful data are preserved in them, so I have depended greatly upon them in this study.

The *Lü Shih Ch'un Ch'iu* is a collection of writings by scholars of various schools that was edited under the patronage of the Ch'in chancellor Lü Pu-wei. According to a postscript that occurs at the middle of the book, it was finished in 239 B.C.[52] The book is organized integrally even though the ideas in it seem to be inconsistent.[53] There seems to be little doubt as to its authenticity, and the postscript clearly gives the date of composition. One must agree that it is a complete and readable book with no serious defects.[54] The materials preserved in the book have indeed been very helpful in studies of the Chan Kuo period.

The *Chan Kuo Ts'e* is neither a history nor the work of any philosopher or school. It is obvious from the preface by the editor, Liu Hsiang, that this book was compiled by him from sources in the Han Imperial Library. He selected what he considered to be discussions of the plans and stratagems of diplomats, strategists, and politicians of the Chan Kuo period. According to Liu, the book covers two hundred and forty-five years (453–209 B.C.), from the end of the Ch'un Ch'iu period to the beginning of the Han dynasty.[55] However, the current version of the book seems to differ from the edition of Liu Hsiang. Some parts of it were lost in the period between the Han and Sung dynasties, and some Sung scholars endeavored to complete it by making an edition from the then extant versions. The current book is believed to be the result of their work.[56] The inconsistencies, duplications, and contradictions in the different chapters of the *Chan Kuo Ts'e* show that it could not have been written by one person.[57] Many passages, such as the stories of Su Ch'in and Chang I, are obviously anachronistic and hence unreliable as historical accounts.[58] However, much of the *Chan Kuo Ts'e* seems to consist of the notes or records of persons who were seeking official positions. Some of these notes, for example the lengthy discussions attributed to Chang I, may be speeches that were put in the mouths of diplomats of former times to show the persuasive skills of the real author.[59] Others, such as the passage concerning Shang Yang, seem to be accounts of historical events that the writers thought useful for future reference.[60] It seems that many of these accounts were well-known in the Chan Kuo period for they also appear in other books, such as the *Han Fei Tzu* and the *Lü Shih Ch'un Ch'iu*.[61]

The materials used in the *Chan Kuo Ts'e* may have existed as separate works in the Chan Kuo period before they were acquired by the

Han Imperial Library and edited into the book *Chan Kuo Ts'e* by
Liu Hsiang. These materials should be treated with care, since they
may be quite unreliable as sources for the reconstruction of political
or other history. They constitute, nevertheless, a valuable treasury for
social and institutional history, since in large part they were written
by Chan Kuo people and are therefore reflections of the times.[62]

Notes

Notes

For complete authors' names, titles, and publication data of works in Western languages and Japanese, see the Bibliography, pp. 221–24. Chinese titles are cited in abbreviated form; for complete publication data, see the Bibliography, pp. 225–29.

Chapter 1

1. Maine, p. 134; cf. Redfield, p. 301.
2. Weber, *Theory*, pp. 136–38, 329ff, 341ff; also Introduction (ed. by T. Parsons), pp. 56ff.
3. Weber, *Protestant Ethic*. Cf. Bendix, pp. 86–90.
4. The *Shu Ching* is another valuable source of both Western and Eastern Chou materials. One should be extremely scrupulous, however, when quoting from it, owing to its heterogeneity of authenticity and difficulty of dating. A useful comparison of various styles in the collection is contained in Creel, "Bronze Inscriptions." On the general nature of the *Shu Ching* and its translations, see Karlgren, "The Book of Documents," pp. 1–81.
5. *TCCI*, 3/3 (Yin 3), 6/5 (Huan 5).
6. Walker, pp. 98ff.
7. Creel, *Birth of China*, pp. 278–79.
8. Legge, *Tso Chuen*, p. 41.
9. *LC*, 10/14. The *Li Chi* is a collection of writings presumably completed as late as the Han dynasty; cf. *WSTK*, I, 327ff. A passage such as this may contain quite old material, since formal phrases are likely to be handed down from the past.
10. Granet, *Chinese Civilization*, pp. 227, 238.
11. *TCCI*, 15/4 (Hsi 23), says that one should not change masters after submitting oneself. Cf. *KY*, 14/3, 15/2, which gives examples of loyalty to the lord.
12. One captured *shih* chose to die because a eunuch was sent by his captors to negotiate for his life. *TCCI*, 33/4 (Hsiang 17).
13. *TCCI*, 30/15 (Hsiang 9), 32/2 (Hsiang 13). Cf. Eberhard, *Conquerors*, pp. 10–11.
14. *LCCW*, p. 34.
15. Some information should be given here about the so-called well-field system, which was first mentioned in *Meng Tzu* in a passage so ambiguous

that later scholars never have agreed on its interpretation. The traditional depiction of a well-field shows eight families cultivating eight square fields that surround a square piece of the lord's land that they also cultivate, so that the whole field resembles a tic-tac-toe board, or the Chinese character for "well," 井. Some consider the well-field system to have been imagined by Mencius; others say it was a remnant of an ancient commune system, or an irrigation layout in which the square field and the well are important components. See Legge, *Mencius*, 3.1.3; cf. *HSWT*, pp. 581–618, which includes letters from those who believed in the existence of the well-field system; *CTCT*, pp. 121–56; *YCST*, pp. 184–87; and *CKFC*, pp. 127–34. Mencius used the imperative mood in his statement about the system, "Please let there be ...," and therefore did not claim that it was a historical account. One scholar rejected the existence of such a system on the grounds that it would have been unworkable in practice. Mencius's mention of it could mean either that he had some little knowledge of its past existence, or that he was more interested in presenting his own proposal than in giving an account of a past system. Since a system existed until recently among a few minority groups in China in which the land of a chieftain was tilled by his subjects without other pay than the produce of assigned lands that they cultivated themselves, it is possible that a similar system should have existed in ancient China, even though its details have been forgotten. See also *CTCT*, pp. 149–53. Cf. Levenson, pp. 268–87; Granet, *Chinese Civilization*, pp. 149–50; Bodde, "Feudalism," p. 64; Miyazaki, "Taxation," pp. 491, 499 (n. 28); Amano, pp. 100ff; *MTCT*, pp. 101–27; *HCLH*, pp. 102–11; Yang, "Notes," pp. 531–43; and Maspero, "Le Régime féodal," pp. 124–26. The papers by Levenson, Amano, Ch'i (*MTCT*), Bodde, and Yang contain convenient summaries of other theories.

16. *KY*, 5/16.

17. *Ibid.*, 10/18. See also *CKFC*, pp. 232–34.

18. *SC*, 8/1–4. This translation is based on those of Legge and Waley, with modifications. See Legge, *She King*, 1.15.1, and Waley, pp. 164–67. This poem is traditionally dated at the beginning of the Chou dynasty; see Legge, *She King*, pp. 226–27, note under the title of the book. Waley says, however, that the date falls in the eighth or seventh centuries B.C.; see Waley, p. 164. Hsü Chung-shu considers the date to be in Ch'un Ch'iu times; see *PFS*, pp. 435–39.

19. The state of Ch'u built the city of I (*TCCI*, 22/9, Hsüan 11) and Chin built the royal capital for the Chou king (*ibid.*, 53/13–14, Chao 32), both tremendous projects involving the erection of city walls. On another occasion when Chin built a city wall for the home state of the duchess, a seventy-three-year-old peasant was drafted with the others to help in the work (*ibid.*, 40/2–3, Hsiang 30). As for palaces, when Duke P'ing of Sung called the peasants to build a terrace during the busy part of the farming season, the work-

ers complained (*ibid.*, 33/4, Hsiang 17). King Lin of Ch'u built terraces year after year until the overworked people deposed him (*KY*, 17/7–9).

20. Legge, *Mencius*, 5.2.7.

21. *KY*, 10/18.

22. *TCCI*, 55/8 (Ting 8). Hereafter I romanize 衛 as Wey in order to distinguish this state from Wei, 魏 .

23. *Ibid.*, 47/10 (Chao 16).

24. *Ibid.*, 25/12 (Ch'eng 2).

25. *Ibid.*, 9/12 (Chuang 22), 30/11 (Hsiang 9), 42/18 (Chao 4), 56/3 (Ting 4).

26. Wang, pp. 55ff.

27. Legge, *Confucian Analects*, 6.3.

28. For example, a slave who had been an official of Kuo was bought for five pieces of sheepskin; see *LSCC*, 14/16–17. Horses, silk, and slaves were used for transactions according to one bronze inscription; see *LCCW*, pp. 96–97.

29. *TCCI*, 44/2 (Chao 7). The definitions of some of the eight terms are so doubtful that it is better to leave them untranslated.

30. *KY*, 13/7. The women here were sent as tribute from Cheng to Chin.

31. *TCCI*, 12/9 (Hsi 5).

32. *Ibid.*, 26/15 (Ch'eng 10).

33. *Ibid.*, 24/7 (Hsüan 15).

34. *LCCW*, p. 203. According to Kuo, the possible date of this bell is about 565 B.C. (*ibid.*, p. 205).

35. *Ibid.*, p. 97. The unit *lieh* 爰 varies with time and place, and its value here is unknown; see *ibid.*, pp. 12–13. The probable date of this vessel is the ninth century B.C.

36. *Ibid.*, p. 97.

37. *TCCI*, 53/1 (Chao 29).

38. Legge, *Analects*, 3.1–2.

39. *TCCI*, 14/9–10 (Hsi 16).

40. Creel, *Birth of China*, p. 184.

41. Wilson, p. 46; Herodotus, I, 321; Xenophon, II, 674; Frazer, I, 46–47.

42. Granet, *Chinese Civilization*, pp. 249ff. Gustav Haloun made a classical study of the ancestries claimed by "clans" in China; see Haloun, pp. 76ff, and esp. 84ff.

43. Creel, *Birth of China*, p. 184.

44. Legge, *She King*, 4.3.3, with slight revisions.

45. *Ibid.*, 4.3.4, with slight revisions.

46. *LCCW*, p. 203.

47. Legge, *Shoo King*, 5.12.9 (p. 425), 5.14.4–14 (pp. 454–56, 459), 5.16.2–3 (pp. 474–75).

48. Legge, *She King*, 3.2.1 (p. 1).

49. Haloun doubts the Chou genealogy, which seems to be fabricated to justify the Chou rule; Haloun, pp. 596–99.

50. Legge, *She King*, 3.2.1 (pp. 2–3).

51. *Ibid.*, 3.2.1 (pp. 4–8).

52. For examples of this idea, see Legge, *Shoo King*, 5.3.5 (pp. 310–11), and *She King*, 3.1.1, 3.1.7, 4.1.6, 4.1.9, and 4.2.4.

53. *Ibid.*, 4.1.7.   54. *Ibid.*, 3.1.1.

55. *Ibid.*, 3.1.9.   56. *Ibid.*, 3.3.5.

57. *Ibid.*, 3.3.6.   58. *Ibid.*, 3.1.1.

59. *Ibid.*, 3.1.9.   60. *LCCW*, p. 1.

61. *Ibid.*, p. 51.   62. *Ibid.*, p. 83.

63. *LCCW*, p. 127.   64. Haloun, p. 127.

65. *LCCW*, p. 219. This is the first occurrence of Huang Ti in bronze inscriptions.

66. *SCHI*, 5/1, 43/1.

67. *LCCW*, pp. 247, 250. The dates of these two vessels are still in doubt. Though the context clearly refers to their having been cast during the reign of the thirteenth duke of Ch'in, we cannot be sure which duke was the first ruler of that state. Kuo Mo-jo suggests that the thirteenth duke was Duke Ching (576–534 B.C.); *ibid.*, pp. 247–48.

68. *TCCI*, 27/6 (Ch'eng 13).

69. Legge, *Tso Chuen*, p. 441.

70. *TCCI*, 8/9 (Chuang 7), 11/7 (Min 2).

71. *Ibid.*, 28/4 (Ch'eng 16).

72. Legge, *Tso Chuen*, p. 799.

73. *TCCI*, 3/13 (Yin 5), 48/5 (Chao 17).

74. Legge, *Tso Chuen*, p. 453.

75. *Ibid.*, p. 618. Cf. Granet, *Chinese Civilization*, pp. 250–53.

76. Legge, *Tso Chuen*, p. 466.   77. *TCCI*, 32/10 (Hsiang 14).

78. Legge, *Tso Chuen*, p. 523.   79. *Ibid.*, p. 466.

80. *Ibid.*, p. 297.   81. *Ibid.*, p. 211.

82. *Ibid.*, p. 275.   83. *LCCW*, pp. 33–34.

84. *TCCI*, 25/13 (Ch'eng 2).

85. Legge, *She King*, 3.2.5, p. 2.

Chapter 2

1. *TCCI*, 52/11 (Chao 27), 55/2, 5, 9 (Ting 5, 6, 8).

2. *Ibid.*, 58/11 (Ai 11).   3. *Ibid.*, 42/5–6 (Chao 3).

4. *Ibid.*, 53/14 (Chao 32).   5. *KY*, 15/8.

6. *CHSP*, 20. Most of the corrections of names are according to the annotations by Wang Hsien-ch'ien.

7. *TCCI*, 2/9–11 (Yin 1).

8. *Ibid.*, 3/6, 9, 10 (Yin 3, 4, 5).

9. *Ibid.*, 3/11–12 (Yin 5).

10. *Ibid.*, 3/9–10 (Yin 3–4), 4/15 (Yin 11).

11. *Ibid.*, 7/12 (Huan 16), 8/7 (Chuang 6).
12. *Ibid.*, 21/12 (Hsüan 16), 6/9–10 (Chuang 6).
13. *Ibid.*, 9/12 (Chuang 22).
14. *Ibid.*, 10/13 (Chuang 32), 11/4–5 (Min 2).
15. *Ibid.*, 10/13 (Chuang 32), 10/6–8 (Chuang 27–28), 12/9 (Hsi 5), 13/1–3 (Hsi 6–8), 14/9 (Hsi 16).
16. *Ibid.*, 13/4 (Hsi 8).
17. *Ibid.*, 19a/5–6 (Wen 6).
18. *Ibid.*, 13/3 (Hsi 8), 16/1–2 (Hsi 25).
19. *Ibid.*, 16/15 (Hsi 28).
20. *Ibid.*, 21/3, 10 (Hsüan 1, 4).   21. *Ibid.*, 22/2 (Hsüan 6).
22. *Ibid.*, 28/7 (Ch'eng 16).   23. *Ibid.*, 24/6 (Hsüan 15).
24. *Ibid.*, 21/11 (Hsüan 4), 23/2 (Hsüan 12), 26/1–2, 8–9, 15 (Ch'eng 3, 7, 10), 27/9 (Ch'eng 13).
25. *Ibid.*, 27/9 (Ch'eng 13).
26. *Ibid.*, 29/5 (Hsiang 3).
27. *Ibid.*, 37/2 (Hsiang 26).
28. *Ibid.*, 34/8 (Hsiang 21), 27/12 (Ch'eng 15), 32/12 (Hsiang 15).
29. *Ibid.*, 39/5 (Hsiang 29), 52/8–9 (Chao 27).
30. *Ibid.*, 27/9 (Ch'eng 13), 29/4 (Hsiang 2), 30/7 (Hsiang 8), 31/5 (Hsiang 10).
31. *Ibid.*, 41/4 (Chao 1), 44/12 (Chao 8).
32. *Ibid.*, 50/7 (Chao 22), 52/4 (Chao 26), 55/1 (Ting 5).
33. *Ibid.*, 48/12 (Chao 19), 49/2 (Chao 20), 60/2 (Ai 16).
34. *Ibid.*, 51/9 (Chao 25), 53/2 (Chao 29), 58/11 (Ai 11).
35. *Ibid.*, 52/3 (Chao 26), 54/14 (Ting 4), 55/4 (Ting 7), 58/2 (Ai 6), 60/2 (Ai 16).
36. *Ibid.*, 57/5 (Ai 2).
37. *Ibid.*, 58/2 (Ai 6), 60/3 (Ai 16).
38. The names of powerful noble families of the various states are given on pp. 33 ff.
39. Radcliffe-Brown and Forde, pp. 39–41, esp. p. 40. Cf. Murdock, p. 46. For cases of polysegmentation in Africa, specifically among the Zulu, see Hughes, pp. 35–45; Krige, pp. 34–35.
40. A similar process has occurred in southeastern China in modern times; see Freedman, p. 49.
41. *CCST*, 1/22 ff.
42. *TCCI*, 38/13–15 (Hsiang 28), 35/6, 10 (Hsiang 23).
43. *Ibid.*, 15/9 (Hsi 24).   44. *Ibid.*, 20/7 (Wen 18).
45. *Ibid.*, 21/6 (Hsüan 2).   46. *Ibid.*, 28/12 (Ch'eng 17).
47. On Chih Ch'o, see *ibid.*, 33/7 (Hsiang 18); on Ch'in Chin-fu and Ti Ssu-mi, see *ibid.*, 31/2 (Hsiang 10); on Shu-liang Ho, see *ibid.*, 31/2 (Hsiang 10) and 33/4 (Hsiang 17); on Chi Liang and Hua Chou, see *ibid.*, 35/10 (Hsiang 23).

48. *Ibid.*, 33/4 (Hsiang 17).

49. *Ibid.*, 44/5 (Chao 9).

50. *Ibid.*, 45/16–17 (Chao 12), 47/1 (Chao 17).

51. *Ibid.*, 49/3–4 (Chao 20).

52. *Ibid.*, 52/9 (Chao 27).

53. Legge, *Mencius*, 5.2.5:4. Confucius also spoke of his humble background; see Legge, *Analects*, 9.6.

54. For instance, Tzu Kung praised him as a man whom no one could surpass; see *ibid.*, 19.23–25.

55. *TCCI*, 58/14 (Ai 11), 59/3 (Ai 12), 60/1 (Ai 16).

56. *Ibid.*, 56/5 (Ting 12).

57. *Ibid.*, 59/12–13 (Ai 15).

58. Legge, *Analects*, 11.25.

59. *TCCI*, 58/7 (Ai 8).

60. *Ibid.*, 58/11 (Ai 11).

61. *Ibid.*, 52/11 (Chao 27), 55/2, 5, 9 (Ting 5, 7, 8).

62. *Ibid.*, 56/5 (Ting 12).

63. *Ibid.*, 56/7–8 (Ting 13–14).

64. *Ibid.*, 58/11 (Ai 11).

65. *Ibid.*, 56/5 (Ting 12).

66. Legge, *Analects*, 11.18.

67. *Ibid.*, 11.2; *TCCI*, 56/10 (Ting 15), 58/4, 13 (Ai 7, 11).

68. *Ibid.*, 58/11 (Ai 11).

69. Legge, *Analects*, 11.24.

70. *TCCI*, 59/12–13 (Ai 15), 60/6 (Ai 17).

71. *Ibid.*, 59/12–13 (Ai 15).

72. *Ibid.*, 59/9 (Ai 15).

73. Lipset and Bendix, pp. 3–5.

74. Ch'i Ssu-ho published an article on this subject that has been of great assistance in this connection; see *CKTH*. Concerning dating, see *HCCT*, Appendix, pp. 61–88.

75. *SCHI*, 43/11. For complete groupings of these names, see Cho-yun Hsu, Appendixes B and C.

76. *Ibid.*, 43/12, 14; *CKT*, 26/1.

77. *SCHI*, 43/14.

78. *Ibid.*

79. *Ibid.*, 43/20, 22.

80. *Ibid.*, 43/22.

81. *Ibid.*

82. *Ibid.*, 43/25.

83. *Ibid.*, 76/8, 79/11.

84. *Ibid.*, 43/27; *CKT*, 20/1.

85. *SCHI*, 15/25, 29, 30, 76/1, 4.

86. *Ibid.*, 43/29.

87. *CKT*, 18/10.

88. *Ibid.*, 20/10.

89. *SCHI*, 15/18, 46/7–8; *CKT*, 8/4.

90. *SCHI*, 75/1; *CKT*, 8/2–3.

91. *SCHI*, 40/22; his name appears as Han Min in *CKT*, 28/6.

92. *SCHI*, 15/25, 75/4, 5; *CKT*, 11/2.

93. *SCHI*, 75/5.

94. *Ibid.*, 46/13.

95. *CKT*, 13/3.

96. *Ibid.*, 46/15.

97. *SY*, 8/9.

98. *SCHI*, 15/21, 70/16.

99. His biography appears in *ibid.*, 70. See also *ibid.*, 15/22–23.

100. *Ibid.*, 5/20.

101. *HFT*, 9/10.
102. *SCHI*, 43/15.
103. His biography is in *ibid.*, 71/1–3. See also *ibid.*, 5/20–22, 15/24.
104. His biography appears in *ibid.*, 71/3–7. See also *ibid.*, 5/21–22, 15/24.
105. *Ibid.*, 71/4, 7.
106. *Ibid.*, 75/3. See also *ibid.*, 5/22.   107. *Ibid.*, 5/22.
108. *CKT*, 43/16.   109. *SCHI*, 5/22, 72/1–2.
110. See his biography, *ibid.*, 72/1–5. See also *ibid.*, 79/7–8.
111. *Ibid.*, 72/2.
112. See his biography, *ibid.*, 79/1–12.
113. See his biography, *ibid.*, 79/12–17.
114. See his biography, *ibid.*, 85. See also *ibid.*, 15/30, 32.
115. *Ibid.*, 6/4.
116. *Ibid.*, 6/7.   117. *Ibid.*
118. *Ibid.*, 6/4.   119. *Ibid.*, 6/8.
120. *HFT*, 4/14. Also see his biography in *SCHI*, 65/3–6.
121. *CKT*, 22/8.
122. *SCHI*, 15/23, 70/6.
123. *Ibid.*, 44/9.
124. See his biography in *ibid.*, 78. Ch'ien Mu cites the account in the *Han Fei Tzu* as evidence that he was a prince of Ch'u. See *HCCT*, pp. 370–71.
125. See biography in *SCHI*, 78.
126. *CKT*, 17/1–2; *HFT*, 10/4.
127. *SCHI*, 40/26.
128. For information concerning Chia Lei as chancellor and uncle of the ruler, see *CKT*, 27/6–7, and *SCHI*, 86/6. The date of the assassination is given as 397 B.C., in the reign of Marquis Lieh (*ibid.*, 15/13). Another version placed this event in the reign of Marquis Ai in 371 B.C. (*ibid.*, 15/16). For a third version, see *CKT*, 28/4.
129. *Ibid.*
130. For information on his life see the brief account in *SCHI*, 63/4. For his term as chancellor see *ibid.*, 15/18, 20.
131. *Ibid.*, 55/1.
132. *Ibid.*, the annotation *So Yin* by Ssu-ma Cheng.
133. *SCHI*, 55/1.
134. *CKT*, 26/3.
135. *SCHI*, 5/21.
136. *Ibid.* For his career in Ch'in see p. 43.
137. *CKT*, 28/2, 5. If Han Mei and Han Min are the same, then he was also once chancellor of Ch'i.
138. *Ibid.*, 28/5–6. Cf. *SCHI*, 71/4 for the date.
139. *Ibid.*, 87/15.
140. *HFT*, 10/6–7.
141. For instance, Chang Hou is mentioned in *TCCI*, 25/6. For more

information on the genealogy of the Chang family in the *Tso Chuan,* see
CCST, 2/18–19.

142. *LSCC,* 19/19. A more detailed account is given in *HSWC,* 3/3–4.

143. *SCHI,* 15/12. Also see under annotation by Wang Hsien-ch'ien in
CHSP, 30/40. Li Kuei is generally considered to be an alternative form of
Li K'o; see *HCCT,* pp. 121–33. Some scholars, however, still insist that the
two names are not identical; see *CKTH,* pp. 191–92. Li K'o was also a chancellor; see Wang's annotation in *CHSP,* 30/28.

144. *LSCC,* 15/10.

145. *Ibid.,* 17/20; also known as T'ien Wen in *SCHI,* 65/5.

146. *Ibid.,* 65/5.

147. *CKT,* 22/3.

148. *HFT,* 10/6–7.

149. *SCHI,* 15/19; also *HCCT,* pp. 234–36.

150. *SCHI,* 44/2.

151. *Ibid.,* 44/4.

152. *Ibid.,* 15/20, 44/6.

153. *LSCC,* 18/13–16; *HNT,* 1/2. Cf. *HCCT,* pp. 264–65.

154. *CKT,* 22/10.

155. *Ibid.,* 23/1–2.   156. *SCHI,* 44/9.

157. *CKT,* 23/6; *SCHI,* 44/9.   158. *Ibid.,* 15/22–24, 70/4, 14.

159. *Ibid.,* 70/16.   160. *CKT,* 15/1. Cf. *SCHI,* 71/6.

161. *Ibid.,* 75/5.   162. *Ibid.,* 79/1, 9.

163. *Ibid.,* 79/10–11.   164. *Ibid.,* 44/12.

165. *CKT,* 23/6.   166. *Ibid.,* 24/3–4; *SCHI,* 44/11.

167. *Ibid.,* 15/23; *CKT,* 29/6.   168. *SCHI,* 15/30, 34/6.

169. *Ibid.,* 34/7.   170. *Ibid.,* 71/8.

171. *TCCI,* 26/3 (Ch'eng 3). The number of Chin armies varied before 587
B.C., but after this time Chin always had six armies.

172. *CCTS,* 22/5–16.

173. *TCCI,* 26/2 (Ch'eng 3).

Chapter 3

1. *HT,* 4/1, 8/12. Cf. Granet, *Chinese Civilization,* pp. 209ff, and *Categories.*

2. *SCIC,* p. 84.

3. Legge, *Mencius,* 6.2.7. I have made alterations in the arrangement and
wording of Legge's translation.

4. *KY,* 2/9.   5. *Ibid.,* 9/4.

6. *TCCI,* 34/3 (Hsiang 19).   7. *Ibid.,* 44/8 (Chao 7).

8. *KY,* 4/5.   9. *TCCI,* 28/5, 6 (Ch'eng 16).

10. *SCHI,* 14; *TCCI,* 26/9 (Ch'eng 7).

11. *Ibid.,* 14/1 (Hsi 15).

12. *Ibid.,* 38/3–6 (Hsiang 27).

13. *Ibid.*, 29/7 (Hsiang 3).
14. *Ibid.*, 25/5 (Ch'eng 2), 32/6 (Hsiang 14).
15. *Ibid.*, 38/3–6 (Hsiang 27), 13/4–5 (Hsi 8).
16. *Ibid.*, 24/7 (Hsüan 15).   17. *Ibid.*, 31/2–3 (Hsiang 10).
18. *Ibid.*, 11/2 (Min 1).   19. *Ibid.*, 12/12–15 (Hsi 5).
20. *Ibid.*, 8/7–8 (Chuang 7).
21. Based on *CCTS*, 5. The dates of extinction of 40 other states are not recorded. According to other sources, Duke Hsien of Chin annexed 17 states and subjugated 38; Duke Huan of Ch'i occupied 30; King Chuang of Ch'u conquered 36; and Ch'in conquered 12 states in the reign of Duke Mu. See *HFT*, 2/1, 3/11, 3/50, 15/17.
22. *TCCI*, 13/1 (Hsi 6), 42/15 (Chao 4). Cf. Granet, *Danses*, p. 135.
23. *TCCI*, 14/12 (Hsi 19), 45/11 (Chao 11).
24. Legge, *Tso Chuen*, p. 316. I have made some revisions in the translation and transliteration. The original text is in *TCCI*, 23/2 (Hsüan 12).
25. Ch'en and Ts'ai were conquered by Ch'u in 534 B.C. and 531 B.C., respectively. Both states were allowed to re-establish a degree of autonomy in 529 B.C. Hsü was conquered by Cheng in 504 B.C. The year of the re-establishment of Hsü is not known, but we may infer that it was some years before 482 B.C., when the death of a Hsü ruler is reported. See *ibid.*, 44/13 (Chao 8), 45/11 (Chao 11), 46/11 (Chao 13), 55/3 (Ting 6), 59/3 (Ai 12).
26. *Ibid.*, 36/5 (Hsiang 25).   27. *Ibid.*, 10/10, 11 (Chuang 31).
28. *Ibid.*, 6/12 (Huan 6).   29. *Ibid.*, 12/14 (Hsi 5).
30. *Ibid.*, 16/12–13 (Hsi 28).   31. *Ibid.*, 24/7–8 (Hsüan 15–16).
32. *Ibid.*, 26/8 (Ch'eng 7).   33. *Ibid.*, 55/3 (Ting 6).
34. *Ibid.*, 24/7 (Hsüan 15).   35. *Ibid.*, 56/6 (Ting 13).
36. Legge, *Mencius*, 5.1.9; also *LSCC*, 14/16–17; *SCHI*, 5/8. Though Mencius doubts the story, it seems to have been widely circulated, since there are several versions of it in the three sources cited here.
37. *LSCC*, 16/5.
38. "Liu Kuo Nien Piao," *SCHI*, 15.
39. An example is a war between Ch'u and Wu that started with a trifling dispute about people living along their common border (*ibid.*, 31/9).
40. *TCCI*, 16/5–12 (Hsi 27–28).
41. *Ibid.*, 54/12–14 (Ting 4), 55/1–2 (Ting 10).
42. *CKT*, 27/1.   43. *Ibid.*, 8/8–9.
44. *Ibid.*, 28/7.   45. Legge, *Mencius*, 1.2.10.
46. *SCHI*, 46/14, 80/2, 82/2.   47. *TCCI*, 2/11 (Yin 1).
48. *Ibid.*, 11/5–6, 8 (Min 2).   49. *Ibid.*, 16/5 (Hsi 27).
50. *Ibid.*, 44/13 (Chao 8), 46/6 (Chao 13).
51. *Ibid.*, 58/6 (Ai 8).
52. Annotation by Tu Yü in *ibid.*, 2/11 (Yin 1). Tu Yü, a general of the third century A.D., based this statement on an alleged Chan Kuo tactical code that has since been lost.

53. *Ibid.*, 11/6 (Min 2), 16/12–13 (Hsi 28).

54. Legge, *She King*, 4.2.4.   55. *TCCI*, 6/6 (Huan 6).

56. *Ibid.*, 41/10 (Chao 1).   57. *Ibid.*, 25/5 (Ch'eng 2).

58. *Ibid.*, 29/6 (Hsiang 3).   59. *Ibid.*, 33/4 (Hsiang 17).

60. *Ibid.*, 58/11 (Ai 8).   61. *Ibid.*, 59/4 (Ai 13).

62. *SCHI*, 15/1. Cf. Bodde, *China's First Unifier*, pp. 4–5.

63. *SCHI*, 5/25, 73/2–3.

64. *CKT*, 31/3.

65. *Ibid.*, 20/1.

66. The other four arts are music, poetry or literature, arithmetic, and *li*. *Li* seems to have meant, at least in the Confucian usage, the theory and practice of right conduct. A good explanation of this concept is found in Creel, *Confucius*, pp. 82–88. For the structure of the war chariot of ancient China, see Cheng Te-kun, pp. 265ff.

67. *TCCI*, 29/6 (Hsiang 29).

68. *Ibid.*, 23/8 (Hsüan 11).

69. *Ibid.*, 28/6 (Ch'eng 16), 52/3 (Chao 26).

70. *Ibid.*, 23/8 (Hsüan 12).

71. *Ibid.*, 16/12 (Hsi 28).

72. Granet, *Chinese Civilization*, pp. 263ff, esp. p. 270.

73. *KY*, 19/8.   74. *TCCI*, 58/11 (Ai 11).

75. *Ibid.*, 35/3 (Hsiang 22).   76. *CKT*, 19/1–2.

77. *Ibid.*, 19/7–8, 10/11.   78. *Ibid.*, 19/2.

79. *TCCI*, 4/8 (Yin 9).   80. *Ibid.*, 14/3 (Hsi 15).

81. *Ibid.*, 41/10 (Chao 5).   82. Bodde, "Feudalism," p. 59.

83. *TCCI*, 31/9 (Hsiang 11), 43/1 (Chao 5).

84. *SCHI*, 68/3, 73/3.

85. *CKT*, 15/4.

86. *Ibid.*, 29/6. A *ch'ih* of the Chan Kuo period is equivalent to 23 centimeters; see *CSKC*, no. 3–8. Five *ch'ih* equal three feet ten inches. As a minimum height for conscription, this measurement seems somewhat dubious.

87. *CKT*, 19/11.   88. *Ibid.*, 24/2, 26/2.

89. *Ibid.*, 14/1, 5, 26/2.   90. *Ibid.*, 8/8.

91. *TCCI*, 34/11 (Hsiang 21).   92. *Ibid.*, 35/7 (Hsiang 23).

93. *HT*, 10/5–6. A *li* in the Chan Kuo period was about 1,800 *ch'ih*, or just over a quarter-mile.

94. For information about Chang I, see his biography in *SCHI*, 70/4–14; for Kung-sun Yen, see *ibid.*, 5/19–21.

95. Legge, *Mencius*, 3.2.2.   96. *SCHI*, 65/2–3.

97. *HFT*, 19/8.   98. *TCCI*, 35/6 (Hsiang 23).

99. *Ibid.*, 57/6 (Ai 2). A *mou* in the Chou dynasty equaled 3,600 square *ch'ih*, or about 2,100 square feet. The reward of 100,000 *mou* equaled about 4,820 acres. See *CKTL*, p. 97.

100. *HT*, 10/7. The five families were probably captives rather than Ch'in subjects. Moriya Mitsuo has suggested, however, that the five families, far

from being awarded as slaves, were obligated only to work six days each month for their new master; in this case they might possibly have been Ch'in subjects. Moriya, pp. 59–116, esp. p. 115; *SLSY*, pp. 43–63.

101. *SCHI*, 68/3.

102. *CHSP*, 19a/25–26.

103. *SCHI*, 65/2–3.

104. *Ibid.*, 65/4–5.

105. *Ibid.*, 70/1–14.

106. *Ibid.*, 71/1–3.

107. *Ibid.*, 71/3–7.

108. *Ibid.*, 72/1–5.

109. *Ibid.*, 73/1–5.

110. *Ibid.*, 73/5–7.

111. *Ibid.*, 75/1.

112. *Ibid.*, 77/1–6.

113. *Ibid.*, 78/5. For information on the origin of Lord Ch'un-shen, see *HCCT*, pp. 371–73.

114. *SCHI*, 80/1–2, 5–6.

115. *Ibid.*, 81/1, 3–4, 7.

116. *Ibid.*, 81/5–6.

117. *CKT*, 20/1.

118. *SCHI*, 81/8–9.

119. *Ibid.*, 82/1–2.

120. *Ibid.*, 88/1.

121. *CCTS*, 22/1–16.

Chapter 4

1. *TCCI*, 7/4 (Huan 10). Shih Fu is not mentioned otherwise and his descendants seem never to have achieved any importance.

2. *Ibid.*, 8/3 (Chuang 2).

3. *Ibid.*, 10/13 (Chuang 32), 11/4 (Min 2).

4. *CCST*, 1/15.

5. Legge, *Tso Chuen*, p. 466.

6. *TCCI*, 20/6 (Wen 18).

7. *CKSH*, II, 233–35.

8. *Ibid.*, II, 235–36.

9. *TCCI*, 24/11 (Hsüan 18).

10. *Ibid.*, 51/9 (Chao 25); Legge, *Analects*, 3.1, 3.2, 3.6.

11. *TCCI*, 30/5 (Hsiang 7).

12. *Ibid.*, 32/12 (Hsiang 15).

13. For instance, in 562 B.C. the Chi family occupied the neighboring small vassal state of Yün; see *ibid.*, 31/13 (Hsiang 12). Also the *Analects* records the annexation of Chuan-yü by the Chi family; see Legge, *Analects*, 16.1. The occupation in 544 B.C. of Pien, previously a part of the ducal domain, was the most serious threat to the authority of the ducal house; see *TCCI*, 39/2–3 (Hsiang 29).

14. *Ibid.*, 43/1 (Chao 5).

15. *Ibid.*, 45/16–17 (Chao 12).

16. *Ibid.*, 51/9–12 (Chao 25).

17. Legge, *Mencius*, 5.2.3.

18. *TCCI*, 4/1 (Yin 6), 54/10 (Ting 4).

19. *Ibid.*, 10/1, 3, 5 (Chuang 23, 24, 26), 21/7 (Hsüan 2).

20. *Ibid.*, 19a/6 (Wen 6).

21. *Ibid.*, 21/7 (Hsüan 2).

22. *Ibid.*, 28/13–15 (Ch'eng 17–18).

23. *Ibid.*, 34/8 (Hsiang 21), 35/5–6, 10 (Hsiang 23).

24. *Ibid.*, 52/14 (Chao 28); Bodde, *China's First Unifier*, p. 134; Eberhard, *Conquerors*, p. 12; Masubuchi, pp. 411ff.

25. *TCCI*, 56/7–8, 9, 12 (Ting 13–15), 57/4–8, 12 (Ting 1–2, 5).

26. *KY*, 15/10–11; *SCHI*, 4/26.

27. *TCCI*, 58/1 (Ai 6).

28. On Yen, see *ibid.*; on Ts'ui, see *ibid.*, 38/8–9 (Hsiang 27); on Luan and Kao, see *ibid.*, 42/9 (Chao 4), 45/7 (Chao 10).

29. *Ibid.*, 9/12–15 (Chuang 22).

30. *Ibid.*, 45/7–8 (Chao 10), 58/1, 2–3 (Ai 6).

31. *Ibid.*, 59/8–10 (Ai 14).

32. *Ibid.*, 39/3 (Hsiang 29).

33. *HFT*, 14/3–4. It is also possible that the usurper Tzu Han was of the Huang family; see *ibid.*, 10/12.

34. *CCTS*, 23/16.

35. *TCCI*, 21/11–12 (Hsüan 4).

36. *Ibid.*, 45/15 (Chao 12).

37. *Ibid.*, 35/3 (Hsiang 22).

38. *Ibid.*, 26/9 (Ch'eng 7).

39. *Ibid.*, 52/10–11 (Chao 27).

40. *Ibid.*, 8/11 (Chuang 9), 16/11 (Hsi 28).

41. *Ibid.*, 28/11 (Ch'eng 17).

42. *Ibid.*, 38/14 (Hsiang 28).

43. *Ibid.*, 35/7 (Hsiang 23).

44. *Ibid.*, 5/2 (Huan 1).

45. In this year Hua Yü-shih was named to the office of *ssu k'ou*; see *ibid.*, 19a/7 (Wen 7).

46. *Ibid.*, 19a/7 (Wen 7), 30/15 (Hsiang 9), 27/13 (Ch'eng 15), 44/13 (Chao 8), 20/11 (Wen 18), 13/8 (Hsi 4), 27/12 (Ch'eng 15). Another important family was founded by Duke Wen (reigned 610–589 B.C).

47. *Ibid.*, 51/10 (Chao 25).

48. *Ibid.*, 28/9 (Ch'eng 16).

49. *Ibid.*, 41/4, 7–8 (Chao 1).

50. *KY*, 15/8.

51. *TCCI*, 42/6 (Chao 3).

52. Legge, *Mencius*, 6.2.7:3. The same agreement as recorded in other sources does not include this particular stipulation concerning the status of *shih*; see *KLC*, 5/9–10, and *KYC*, 5/6.

53. For instance, the noble Hou family of Lu, who apparently took their name from the fief they possessed, lost their land in 517 B.C., when the minister Hou was killed by the Shu-sun family. Seventeen years later the area Hou was mentioned as a part of the Shu-sun domain governed by a steward of that household; see *TCCI*, 51/10 (Chao 25), 56/3 (Ting 10).

54. *Ibid.*, 45/16–17 (Chao 12), 46/2 (Chao 13), 47/1 (Chao 14).

55. *Ibid.*, 56/3–4 (Ting 10).

56. *Ibid.*, 56/5 (Ting 12).

57. *Ibid.*, 59/10–11 (Ai 15).

58. *Ibid.*, 51/9–11 (Chao 25).

59. *Ibid.*, 56/5 (Chao 12).

60. *Ibid.*, 58/11 (Ai 11), 60/9 (Ai 23).

61. *Ibid.*, 55/1, 3–4, 5, 8–9 (Ting 5, 6, 7, 8).

62. *Ibid.*, 51/10 (Chao 25).

63. *Ibid.*, 30/18 (Hsiang 9).

64. *KY*, 4/14.

65. *TCCI*, 19b/8 (Wen 14).

66. *HFT*, 13/2–3.

67. *TCCI*, 42/5 (Chao 3), 52/7 (Chao 26); *HFT*, 13/3.

68. *TCCI*, 45/7 (Chao 10), 58/1 (Ai 6).

69. *Ibid.*, 39/3 (Hsiang 29).

70. *Ibid.*, 20/2–3 (Wen 16).

71. *HNT*, 12/2, 18/20–21.

72. *TCCI*, 57/6 (Ai 2).

73. *Ibid.*

74. *Ibid.*, 35/6 (Hsiang 23).

75. *CCTS*, 10/29, 45/46.

76. *TCCI*, 52/16 (Chao 28).

77. For a brief history of the emergence of local administrative units, see *CKCT*, pp. 213–18. In a lengthy discussion on the beginning of local administration, Creel suggests that Ch'u was the first to develop the *hsien* system; see Creel, "The Beginnings of Bureaucracy," pp. 155–83. Masubuchi gives a good case on the evolution of Chin local administration; see Masubuchi, pp. 328ff. See also Bodde, "Feudalism," p. 68, and Eberhard, *Conquerors*, pp. 12–13. Eberhard has offered a convincing argument that the peripheral states such as Ch'u and Ch'in had a better chance than the central states to develop a local administrative system which gave them full authority in the conquered territory, a theory supported by Creel.

78. *HCCT*, pp. 118–26.

79. *SCHI*, 65/5–6; *HFT*, 4/14.

80. *SCHI*, 68/3–4; *HFT*, 4/14, 17/9.

81. *Ibid.*, 17/7, trans. by Creel in "The *Fa Chia*," p. 609.

82. *CSCY*, 36/25–26.

83. *Ibid.*, 36/26; *ST*, 71/48. A more detailed account of the reforms carried out by Wu Ch'i, Shang Yang, and Shen Pu-hai is beyond the scope of this study, which is limited to social mobility, but some of their theories will be discussed in Chap. VI. Good sources for further information on this subject are *CKCT*, pp. 197–218; *SYPF*, pp. 163–94; Creel, "The *Fa Chia*," pp. 607ff, and "The Meaning of *Hsing-Ming*," pp. 200–207.

84. *CKT*, 21/10.

85. *Ibid.*, 30/5–6.

86. *LSCC*, 14/12–13.

87. *CKT*, 8/2; *HFT*, 14/11.

88. *Ibid.*, 12/9, 15/15–16; *HNT*, 18/9.

89. *SCHI*, 46/6.

90. *Ibid.*, 87/2–3.

91. *CCTS*, 23/1–15; *CCST*, 5/1–13.

92. *TCCI*, 39/4 (Hsiang 29).

93. *Ibid.*, 58/11 (Ai 11).

94. *Ibid.*, 55/5 (Ting 7).

95. *Ibid.*, 52/14 (Chao 28).

96. *Ibid.*, 20/7–11 (Wen 18).

97. *Ibid.*, 40/11 (Hsiang 31).

98. Legge, *Analects*, 11.24.

99. *CKT*, 20/11.

100. Gerth and Mills, pp. 215–16, 235–37. Weber, in the chapter on bureaucracy in his *Wirtschaft und Gesellschaft*, pointed out the nature and value of the specialized experts.

101. Legge, *Mencius*, 1.1.3:4, 1.1.7:23–24, 1.2.5:3, 3.1.3:13–20.

102. *CKT*, 3/5–8.

103. For instance, in 251 B.C., Yen suffered a major defeat by Chao because the chancellor of Yen underestimated the strength of Chao; see *ibid.*, 31/1.

104. An excellent reference for the life of Confucius and sources of information about him is Creel, *Confucius and the Chinese Way*, pp. 25–56.

105. *Ibid.*, p. 32.

106. Legge, *Analects*, 12.5, 13.20; *TCCI*, 59/12 (Ai 15), 60/13 (Ai 27).
107. Legge, *Analects*, 13.17, 12.19, 12.7.
108. *Ibid.*, 13.9. 109. *Ibid.*, 12.14, 13.1.
110. *Ibid.*, 13.2. 111. *Ibid.*, 5.7, 6.6.
112. Creel, *Confucius and the Chinese Way*, pp. 31, 67, 299, n. 9, 10.
113. *Ibid.*, pp. 30–31. Legge translates one passage in the *Analects*, 8.12, as follows: "The master said, 'It is not easy to find a man who has learned three years without coming to be good.' " In fact, the character 祿 here seems to mean salary or emolument, as Legge translated it in the *Analects*, 14.1. Hence the passage seems to mean: "It is not easy to find a man who has learned three years without thinking of salary."
114. *Ibid.*, 7.7.
115. *Ibid.*, 6.12, 17.4.
116. *SCHI*, 67, 44/2, 3, 4, 121/1–2; Legge, *Mencius*, 4.2.31.
117. *SCHI*, 65/3. 118. *Ibid.*, 74/5, 83/9–10.
119. *MOT*, 13/10. 120. *MTHK*, pp. 448–53.
121. *MOT*, 12/10. 122. *SCHI*, 44/2, 3, 4.
123. *Ibid.*, 74/3, 4. 124. *HCCT*, pp. 330–31.
125. *SCHI*, 43/11–12.
126. For reliable research information on the date of Su Ch'in, see *HCCT*, pp. 268–78.
127. *SCHI*, 69/1–3, 12–13; *CKT*, 3/3–4.
128. *CHT*, 4/24. 129. *HFT*, 19/8.
130. *Ibid.*, 11/2. 131. *LSCC*, 4/6.

Chapter 5

1. Legge, *She King*, 1.9.6, 1.15.1, 4.1(2).5, 4.1(2).2.
2. *Ibid.*, 1.5.4.
3. *TCCI*, 2/10 (Yin 1). This passage compares the sizes of cities in terms of a unit of 100 battlements, each of which was, according to Tu Yü and K'ung Ying-ta, either 200 *ch'ih* or 30 *ch'ih*; one *ch'ih* equaled 23 cm. in the Chou dynasty. Cf. *LTCT*, p. 44; *CSKC*, nos. 2, 3–8; Oshima, pp. 39–50, 59–60; Miyazaki, "The Age of City-States," p. 4, "Les villes en Chine," p. 386; Chang, pp. 180ff, esp. pp. 190–91.
4. Legge, *Mencius*, 3.1.3:13–20. 5. *KY*, 5/16; *LC*, 4/8.
6. *TCCI*, 24/7 (Hsüan 15). 7. *Ibid.*, 31/9 (Hsiang 11).
8. *Ibid.*, 57/8 (Ai 2). 9. *HFT*, 14/11.
10. *CHSP*, 24a/7–8. One Chan Kuo *mou* was 3,600 square *ch'ih*. One *shih* weighed 120 *chin*, which equaled 228.8 grams. Cf. *CSKC*, nos. 3–8; *CKTL*, pp. 97, 109, 73. Sekino figures there were two linear measures in the Chan Kuo period, the shorter *ch'ih* being equivalent to 18 cm., the longer to 22.5 cm. Cf. Sekino, *Chinese Archaeology*, p. 402. Until there is more convincing evidence, however, I will reserve judgment.

11. *MOT*, 9/10.

12. Legge, *She King*, 2.6.1–2.

13. *TCCI*, 39/3 (Hsiang 29).

14. *Ibid.*, 31/5 (Hsiang 10).

15. *Ibid.*, 40/6 (Hsiang 30); *LSCC*, 16/11.

16. *TCCI*, 59/3 (Ai 12).

17. Legge, *Mencius*, 4.1.1:9, 4.1.14:3; cf. *ibid.*, p. 306, n. 14, in which the quoted annotation by Chu Hsi misses the meaning of the text.

18. *HFT*, 12/11.

19. Maspero, "Le Régime féodal," p. 138.

20. *HT*, 10/6.

21. *HFT*, 9/13–14.

22. *SCHI*, 5/18, 15/19, 68/4; *SYPF*, pp. 182–85.

23. *CHSP*, 24a/16. The context of this passage, which quotes a memorial to the throne by Tung Chung-shu, shows that the concentration had been in existence before the Han dynasty.

24. See the arguments of both the leftists and the rightists in *HSWT*, pp. 587–97. Cf. Levenson, pp. 268–87.

25. *HFT*, 11/14–15.

26. *SCHI*, 81/7.

27. *LSCC*, 19/14; *CHSP*, 24a/9, 16.

28. *LC*, 4/8.

29. *HFT*, 11/10.

30. *Ibid.*, 19/2.

31. *CKT*, 13/1.

32. *CHSP*, 24a/16.

33. *HFT*, 17/19, 19/11.

34. Legge, *Mencius*, 7.2.27; *HT*, 6/8, 7/25.

35. Legge, *Analects*, 12.9.

36. Legge, *Mencius*, 1.1.5:4; *MOT*, 5/2.

37. *CHSP*, 24a/16.

38. *CKT*, 6/4; *CHSP*, 24a/7–8.

39. Legge, *Mencius*, 1.1.7:22.

40. *HNT*, 6/8.

41. *KT*, 15/11–12. The *Kuan Tzu*, allegedly written by the Ch'un Ch'iu statesman Kuan Chung, is a compilation of writings generally believed to be of Chan Kuo times; see *WSTK*, II, 767–71.

42. *KT*, 24/7. The interest period is not specified in the text.

43. Legge, *Mencius*, 3.1.3:7.

44. *KY*, 10/17; *TCCI*, 28/15 (Ch'eng 18), 49/7 (Chao 20); *KT*, 24/8.

45. *CKT*, 11/1–2; *SCHI*, 75/6–7.

46. *LSCC*, 19/14; *CHSP*, 24a/16.

47. *SCHI*, 129/15. In the *Han Shu* there is a passage on this topic. Though it is about the early Han, the Chan Kuo picture was probably similar. Cf. *CHSP*, 24a/14.

48. *LSCC*, 10/6; Legge, *Mencius*, 3.1.3:3.

49. See also *KY*, 10/18.

50. *TCCI*, 19b/2 (Wen 11).

51. *Ibid.*, 18/8 (Wen 2).

52. *KY*, 6/14.

53. *TCCI*, 27/3 (Ch'eng 12).

54. *CKT*, 3/1.

55. *SCHI*, 46/6, 8.

56. Legge, *She King*, 2.5.9.

57. *KY*, 2/12.

58. *Ibid.*, 2/10.

59. *TCCI*, 2/3–15 (Yin 1).

60. *Ibid.*, 42/3, 4 (Chao 2, 3).

61. *Ibid.*, 40/8 (Hsiang 31).

62. *Ibid.*, 45/8 (Chao 10).

63. *Ibid.*, 40/8–9 (Hsiang 31).

64. The *Chan Kuo Ts'e* contains so many such occurrences that they cannot all be mentioned here. One example will suffice. A Wei diplomat was sent to Ch'u with one hundred chariots; another asked to visit Yen and Chao with thirty chariots (*CKT*, 22/6).

65. *Ibid.*, 28/2; *SCHI*, 46/13. Shang Yang, Chang I, and Kan Mou, for example, all came from other states to Ch'in (*ibid.*, 68/1–2, 70/1, 71/3).

66. Creel, *Confucius*, p. 43.
67. Legge, *Mencius*, 3.2.4:1, 3.1.4:1.
68. *CKT*, 22/3.
69. *TCCI*, 58/9 (Ai 9); *KY*, 19/6.
70. *SCHI*, 29/2.
71. *Ibid.*, 29/2–3; *CKT*, 14/7, 18/9.
72. *TCCI*, 54/12 (Ting 4).
73. *Ibid.*, 58/10 (Ai 10).

74. The *Yü Kung* is believed to have been written in the later part of the Chan Kuo period, because the geographical information in it does not correspond with the statements of the *Mo Tzu* and the *Mencius*, and because it mentions southwest China, which was not a part of the middle kingdom until it was conquered by Ch'in; see *WSTK*, I, 125–26.

75. *SS*, 3/1–6.

76. The *Chou Li* is a large, well-organized book that contains a great many fascinating though often impractical ideas. According to one theory it was written by an anonymous scholar of the Chan Kuo period to describe a utopia governed by a gigantic bureaucracy; see *WSTK*, I, 316–27. However, further research concerning the nature of the *Chou Li* is still needed.

77. *CLCI*, 63/3–64/4.
78. *CKT*, 16/2; *MOT*, 13/9.
79. *HT*, 5/10.
80. *HFT*, 9/10.
81. *MOT*, 13/9; *CKT*, 16/2.
82. *HT*, 5/10.
83. *SCHI*, 32/3, 129/2, 7; *HT*, 5/10–11.
84. *CKT*, 29/1.
85. *TCCI*, 14/10 (Hsi 18), 15/6 (Hsi 23), 37/7 (Hsiang 26), 42/10 (Chao 4).
86. *HT*, 2/12, 10/16; *CKT*, 26/1.
87. *Ibid.*, 29/9.
88. *CLCI*, 74/6–7. The *K'ao Kung Chi* was not a part of the *Chou Li* until it was added to repair a shortage in the last part of that book (*CHSP*, 30/11–12). The *K'ao Kung Chi* is dated in the Chan Kuo period, since it mentions Yen, a state that became active in China in late Ch'un Ch'iu times, and Hu, the name applied to some nomadic tribes on record for the late Chan Kuo period; see *WSTK*, I, 313.
89. *CLCI*, 74/9.
90. *SCHI*, 86/12; *CKT*, 31/6.
91. *HT*, 5/10–11.
92. Cheng, p. 70; *CKHP*, p. 70; cf. Sekino, *Chinese Archaeology*, Map 3, pp. 451–52.
93. Menger, pp. 257–62, 272–80.
94. Wang, p. 22.
95. *CICI*, 8/2. Translation based on Yang, *Money and Credit*, 2:2. Cf.

Legge, *Mencius*, 2.2.10:7. The *Hsi Tz'u* may not have been written before the late Chan Kuo period; see *WSTK*, I, 71.

96. *CKKT*, pp. 16–17; Wang, pp. 55–61.

97. Yang, *Money and Credit*, 5:2–3; cf. Wang, pp. 209–11. One Chou catty (or *chin*) was probably 228.86 grams (*CKTL*, p. 73). Sekino (*Chinese Archaeology*, pp. 436ff) thinks that a *lu* (= *lieh*) should be equivalent to six *liang* and sixteen *chu*, or slightly less than half a catty.

98. *LCCW*, pp. 26, 11–14.

99. The *Tsa Chi* chapter of the *Li Chi* contains a passage that gives the length of a unit of cloth money, which was calculated by the Han annotator, Cheng Hsüan, to be forty *ch'ih* (*LC*, 12/19). A phrase in the Chou Li refers to *pu*, which Sun I-jang, a Ch'ing annotator, took to be a piece of cloth with a length of two *ch'ih* and width of one-twentieth of a *ch'ih*, marked with three stamp imprints (*CLCI*, 24/16). Despite the ambiguity of the *Li Chi* and *Chou Li* passages, the Han commentator gives detailed information, which implies that cloth money began to have a standardized form during Han times.

100. *LCCW*, p. 96.

101. *TCCI*, 52/1–2 (Chao 26). A *chang* equals ten *ch'ih*.

102. *Ibid.*, 21/4 (Hsiang 2).

103. *Ibid.*, 52/1–2 (Chao 26). According to the annotation, I figure that this amount equaled approximately 155 kiloliters (*CKTL*, p. 70).

104. *LSCC*, 14/16–17.

105. *MOT*, 12/4. Pi Yuan considered the character *p'en* 盆 to be a misprint for *i* 盁 , a weight of metal. There is no way to prove or disprove this hypothesis.

106. Legge, *Mencius*, 3.2.10:5. The same amount of salary had been offered to Mencius himself (*ibid.*, 2.2.10:3).

107. *CKT*, 32/2. The volume of a *chung* equaled 640 *sheng*, which perhaps equaled 193.7 milliliters (*CKTL*, p. 70). The weight of an *i* traditionally was equal to either twenty or twenty-four *liang*. One *liang* equaled 1,493 grams (Yang, *Money and Credit*, 5:6; *CKTL*, p. 73).

108. Yang, *Money and Credit*, 1:3. Wang suggests that metallic money could have appeared as early as the eleventh century B.C.; see Wang, pp. 113, 153. His argument is mainly based on the interpretation of *pu* as metallic money, which I feel is dubious. His interpretation of the date of the Ch'i state is also unsatisfactory.

109. Yang, *Money and Credit*, 4:10; Kato, pp. 1ff. Two other passages concerning the weight relationship of coins exist. One, in *SCHI*, 119/1, records the issue of coins in large denominations during the reign of King Chuang of Ch'u (613–591 B.C.). The other account, in *ICS*, 2/7, claims that King Wen of Chou invented the concurrent use of large and small coins. However, the *Shih Chi* is from quite a late date, and the existing version of *Chi Chung Chou Shu* is generally considered of doubtful authenticity;

see *WSTK*, I, 506–8. Therefore these alleged early dates cannot be accepted.

110. According to Wang, fully developed spade money appeared about 400 B.C., which seems an improbably long time after the appearance of its prototype, which he dates in the twelfth or eleventh century B.C. (Wang, p. 129).

111. *MOT*, 10/12. Here the inverse ratio between commodity prices and the value of money is discussed.

112. Legge, *Mencius*, 2.1.5:5; *HT*, 2/20, 6/8, 7/25; *HFT*, 11/10, 19/18.

113. Wang, pp. 123ff; Yang, *Money and Credit*, 2:12, 2:15–20. So many denominations of money were used that even a brief list of their characteristics would take several pages; see Wang, pp. 131–35. A clear synopsis of Chan Kuo numismatic studies is given in Yang, *Money and Credit*, chap. II. Cf. *HCHP*, chap. III; *CKHP*, pp. 69–71; Cheng, pp. 260–62; Amano, p. 150; Sekino, "Remarks," pp. 101–27; Kato, pp. 15ff, 20ff.

114. *MOT*, 10/12.

115. *HFT*, 11/10.

116. Legge, *Mencius*, 2.1.5:5; *HT*, 6/8, 7/25.

117. *SCHI*, 6/4.

118. Yang, *Money and Credit*, 5:6. One *chin* comprised 16 *liang* and was therefore a little smaller than the *i*, which comprised 20 to 24 *liang*. One *liang* equaled 14.93 grams (*CKTL*, p. 73). Sekino figures that one Ch'in dynasty *liang* equaled 16 grams, but that one pre-Ch'in *liang* equaled 9.6 grams in Ch'u; Sekino, *Chinese Archaeology*, pp. 432–33.

119. Wang, pp. 180ff; Yang, *Money and Credit*, 5:5.

120. *KT*, 23/15.

121. *CHT*, 1/15–16.

122. For a reference to property valued at one thousand pieces of metal, see *ibid.*, 10/16. Ten thousand pieces are mentioned in *CKT*, 28/7–8, and *HFT*, 18/12.

123. Legge, *She King*, 1.15.1.

124. Legge, *Mencius*, 3.1.4:4–5.

125. *CHT*, 2/26.

126. *Ibid.*, 1/15–16.

127. *Ibid.*, 1/17, 2/22, 3/17.

128. *Ibid.*, 10/22.

129. Legge, *Mencius*, 6.1.14:3.

130. *HFT*, 11/9.

131. *LSCC*, 20/10.

132. *Ibid.*, 17/5.

133. *CLCI*, 74/11–12.

134. *LYHN*, pp. 38–39.

135. *CTTC*, p. 95; Cheng, pp. 44–45.

136. *HMKT*, pp. 222–28; Cheng, pp. 29–30.

137. Legge, *Mencius*, 3.2.4:3.

138. *CKT*, 11/3–4.

139. Legge, *Mencius*, 2.2.10:7.

140. *CKT*, 6/4.

141. *KY*, 14/14.

142. Legge, *Analects*, 11.18.

143. *SCHI*, 129/2–3.

144. *Ibid.*, 129/4.

145. *Ibid.*, 129/5.

146. *Ibid.*, 85/1–2; *CKT*, 7/3.

147. *Ibid.*, 28/7–8.

148. *HFT*, 19/11.

149. *KT*, 15/11.

150. *CKTT*, 5/6.

151. *CTTC*, p. 104; *CSCM*, p. 56; *HHPK*, pp. 82–83; *SNKK*, p. 507.
152. Legge, *Mencius*, 3.1.4:4.
153. *CKCT*, p. 167; *CKS*, p. 240.
154. *CTTC*, p. 95; *HMKT*, p. 225; *HPSC*, p. 88; *SSCC*, p. 111.
155. *CTTC*, p. 104; Amano, pp. 125–27; *CTTC*, p. 104; Cheng, pp. 246–49.
156. *Ibid.*, pp. 248–49.
157. *LSCC*, 16/13; *SCHI*, 29/2, 126/12.
158. *Ibid.*, 29/2; *SHCC*, 33/4.
159. *CHT*, 5/12, 42.
160. Legge, *Mencius*, 3.1.3:7; *CLCI*, 30/11–12.
161. *LSCC*, 26/6–12; *SS*, 3/1–5, 9.   162. *CHSP*, 24a/7–8.
163. *TCCI*, 2/10 (Yin 1).   164. *Ibid.*, 38/3 (Hsiang 27).
165. Legge, *Analects*, 5.27.   166. *TCCI*, 56/5 (Ting 12).
167. *KY*, 15/4.
168. Max Weber, *The City*, pp. 77–80.
169. *CKT*, 20/1. One *chang* is equal to ten *ch'ih*, one of which then equaled twenty-three centimeters. Therefore the normal Chan Kuo city occupied an area of 2,300 meters square, which was approximately the size of a large city in the Ch'un Ch'iu period.
170. Chang, pp. 18off, 257ff; Miyazaki, "Origin," pp. 187ff.
171. Chang, pp. 194–95; Miyazaki, "Towns and Cities," pp. 342ff.
172. Legge, *Mencius*, 2.1.5:5. For information on the taxes in Chao cities, see *SCHI*, 81/8.
173. *CKCC*, p. 249.
174. *YTL*, 1/8. The *Yen T'ieh Lun* is a record of discussions of the second century B.C., but it includes a great deal of information about the Chan Kuo period.
175. *SCHI*, 129/6–10.
176. *Ibid.*, 129/7–8.
177. Lipset and Bendix, pp. 217–18.

Chapter 6

1. The translation is from Creel, "The *Fa Chia*."
2. Linton, pp. 113ff, esp. pp. 127–31; cf. Merton, p. 382.
3. Legge, *Analects*, 6.1.1.   4. Creel, *Confucius*, pp. 119–20.
5. *TCCI*, 3/6 (Yin 3).   6. Mei, pp. 32–33.
7. *Ibid.*, p. 36.   8. *Ibid.*, p. 44.
9. Legge, *Mencius*, 1.2.7.   10. *Ibid.*, 1.2.9.
11. *Ibid.*, 7.1.36, slightly altered. 12. *Ibid.*, 3.2.2:3, 4.1.10:2.
13. *Ibid.*, 4.2.32, 4.2.2.   14. *Ibid.*, 6.2.15.
15. Mei, pp. 33–34.   16. Dubs, p. 121.
17. *Ibid.*, p. 210, slightly altered; cf. *HT*, 12/23.

18. Dubs, pp. 60–61, slightly altered.

19. *HFT*, 17/7. This passage is translated by Creel; see "The *Fa Chia*," p. 609.

20. Liao, II, 58. Translation revised and in part from Creel, "The *Fa Chia*," p. 608; cf. *HFT*, 11/18–19. A similar story appears in *CKT*, 26/1.

21. *HFT*, 17/9.

22. *SCHI*, 68/3.

23. Liao, II, 222; the translation has been revised, cf. *HFT*, 17/13.

24. *LSCC*, 14/9.   25. *CKT*, 11/6.

26. Legge, *Mencius*, 7.2.14.   27. *Ibid.*, 1.2.8.

28. *Ibid.*, 6.1.16.   29. *HT*, 19/15.

30. *CSCY*, 36/26.   31. *Ibid.*, 37/8.

32. *Ibid.*, 37/12–13.   33. *Ibid.*, 37/7.

34. Liao, I, 276; translation revised, cf. *HFT*, 8/19.

35. I owe the concept of "layer" to Professor Wolfram Eberhard, who gave a speech on this general concept on May 6, 1964, at Academia Sinica, Nankang, Taipei, Taiwan. See Eberhard, "Concerns."

36. Legge, *Analects*, 8.7. *Shih* is preferable to Legge's translation of it as "scholar."

37. Legge, *Mencius*, 7.2.34, 2.2.2, 7.1.43.

38. *HT*, 19/22.   39. *LSCC*, 15/7.

40. Legge, *Mencius*, 5.2.5.   41. *Ibid.*, 5.2.9.

42. *Ibid.*, 4.2.3.

43. Liao, II, 280–81; translation revised, cf. *HFT*, 19/3–4.

44. Liao, II, 44.

45. *Ibid.*, II, 44–45; translation revised, cf. *HFT*, 11/10.

46. Liao, II, 127; translation revised, cf. *HFT*, 14/6.

47. Masubuchi thinks that reciprocity was the basis for a ruler's control over his subjects. See Masubuchi, pp. 212–31.

48. *HFT*, 17/7; translated in Creel, "The *Fa Chia*," p. 609.

49. *HFT*, 1/21; cf. Liao, I, 34.

50. *MOT*, 12/4; Mei, p. 227. *P'en*, which means literally a shallow container, was a measure for grain equal to 13 *tou*, according to Mei. One *tou* equaled 19.37 ml. in the Chou period (*ibid.*, p. 227, n. 3; *CKTL*, p. 7).

51. Legge, *Mencius*, 2.2.10. The *chung* equaled 64 *tou* in the Chou period (*CKTL*, p. 70).

52. Legge, *Mencius*, 2.2.10.

53. *CKT*, 29/6–7. A *shih* is a weight unit equal to 2746.32 grams (*CKTL*, p. 109).

54. Legge, *She King*, 3.2.5:2.

55. Tönnies, pp. 261–62.

56. Legge, *Tso Chuen*, p. 33.

57. Duyvendak, pp. 170–75. Proper nouns have been changed into the more common forms.

58. *CKT*, 19/5–6, 8–9. Ch'i Ssu-ho drew a three-column chart to compare the *Chan Kuo Ts'e* section, the first chapter of the *Shang Chun Shu*, and the corresponding part of the biography of Shang Yang in the *Shih Chi (SYPF*, pp. 172–75).

59. Liao, I, 154; translation revised, cf. *HFT*, 5/9.

60. Liao, II, 275–76; translation revised, cf. *HFT*, 19/1.

61. Legge, *Kwang-zze*, XL, 172–73. Ch'iu is the personal name of Confucius.

62. *CHT*, 9/39; cf. Legge, *Kwang-zze*, XL, 174.

63. *CHT*, 9/39.

64. *Ibid.*, 9/41. The translation is partly based on Legge, *Kwang-zze*, XL, 176, 177–78, with a different meaning for *to hsin*, which Legge translated "believed in." According to the commentary of Chen Hsüan-ying, *hsin* is the same as *yen* and *to hsin* should be taken as meaning "talkative," which is parallel to "without shame."

65. *Ibid.*, XXXIX, 283–84.

66. Legge, *She King*, 2.6.9. I have used the transliteration of *chün tzu* to replace Legge's various translations of it here and hereafter in order to avoid being misleading.

67. *Ibid.*, 1.5.1.
68. *Ibid.*, 2.1.7.
69. *Ibid.*, 1.6.2.
70. *Ibid.*, 1.6.3.

71. Legge, *Analects*, 17.4. The translator realized from context that *chün tzu* and *hsiao jen* here indicate rank and not character; his translation of *chün tzu* as "man of high station" is therefore correct. Transliterations of proper nouns have been changed into the Wade-Giles romanization.

72. *Ibid.*, 14.30.
73. *Ibid.*, 1.1.
74. *Ibid.*, 4.5.
75. *Ibid.*, 7.36.
76. *Ibid.*, 12.4.
77. *Ibid.*, 4.10.
78. *Ibid.*, 4.16.
79. *Ibid.*, 15.20.
80. *Ibid.*, 19.3.
81. *Ibid.*, 14.29.
82. *Ibid.*, 2.13.
83. *Ibid.*, 13.23.
84. *Ibid.*, 15.21.
85. *Ibid.*, 8.6.
86. *Ibid.*, 14.45.
87. Legge, *Tso Chuen*, p. 580.
88. *Ibid.*, p. 610.
89. *Ibid.*, p. 371.
90. *Ibid.*, "Prolegomena," pp. 34–35.
91. *Ibid.*, p. 684.
92. *Ibid.*, p. 566.

93. The first seven chapters of the *Mo Tzu* are not included in this investigation because they are spurious (Mei, pp. 1, 13, 17, 28). The canonical chapters and the chapter on military tactics are also excluded (*ibid.*, preface, xii).

94. *Ibid.*, p. 49. The combined term *shih chün tzu* is translated by Mei as "gentleman." The transliteration has been used here for the obvious reason that an interpretation of the term that may presuppose a certain meaning

should not be introduced into the discussion. This practice will be used in later quotations.

95. *Ibid.*, p. 176. Mei also translated *chün tzu* as "gentlemen."

96. *Ibid.*, pp. 177–78.   97. *Ibid.*, pp. 203–4.

98. *Ibid.*, p. 215.   99. *Ibid.*, p. 236.

100. Tzu-hsia and Kung-meng are both Confucianists (*ibid.*, pp. 231–33).

101. *Ibid.*, p. 49, n. 1. The only possible exception is the ambiguous quotation in chapter xviii (*ibid.*, p. 106). A similar proverb appears in the *Shu Ching*; it reads, however, "Let not men look into water; let them look into the glass of other people" (Legge, *Shoo King*, p. 409). Notice that in the *Motse, chün tzu* takes the place of *jen,* men.

102. Legge, *Mencius,* 2.2.9. Legge translates *chün tzu* here as "superior men."

103. *Ibid.*, 3.1.3. Legge here translates *chün tzu* as "men of a superior grade," which clearly implies high social rank.

104. *Ibid.*, 3.2.6. *Chün tzu* is translated as "the men of station."

105. *Ibid.*, 4.1.1. *Chün tzu* here is translated "superiors."

106. *Ibid.*, 2.1.9. The transliteration of *chün tzu* instead of Legge's translation "superior man" is used here for the reasons given above and will be used in the following passages.

107. *Ibid.*, 2.2.8.

108. *Ibid.*, 4.2.18.

109. *Ibid.*, 4.2.14, with modifications. This passage is quite ambiguous (*ibid.*, pp. 322–23, n. 14). What should be noted is the phrase "by the proper course," which implies compliance with a principle.

110. *Ibid.*, 8.1.24. The translation has been revised in order to fit the original meaning more closely.

111. *Ibid.*, 7.1.32.   112. *Ibid.*, 7.1.13.

113. *Ibid.*, 7.2.32.   114. *Ibid.*, 6.2.8.

115. *Ibid.*, 4.2.27.   116. Legge, *Kwang-zze,* XXIX, 309.

117. *Ibid.*, XL, 215.

118. *Ibid.* Cf. *ibid.*, p. 140, in which the sage-like man and the spirit-like man are made superior to the *chün tzu* or superior man, only the *hsiao jen* or small man being inferior to the latter.

119. *Ibid.*, XXXIX, 278.

120. *HT,* 3/14. The "former *chün tzu*" is Confucius, the grandfather of Tzu-ssu. This meaning for *chün tzu* is still in use today and implies that such a man is a person of dignity. However, this passage is considered dubious since it is not included in the quotation in *Han Shih Wai Chuan* (cf. Dubs, p. 77, n. 1).

121. *Ibid.*, pp. 124–25. Dubs translates the first *chün tzu* as "gentleman" and the last two as "prince."

122. For example, the first chapter of *Hsün Tzu* contains the following verse from the *Shih Ching:*

> Alas! *chün tzu!*
> You will not rest for long;
> Quietly fulfill your official duties;
> Love correctness and uprightness:
> Then the spirits will hear you
> And help you to great happiness.

(*ibid.*, p. 32; cf. Legge, *She King*, 2.6.3).

123. Dubs, pp. 100–101. 124. *Ibid.*, pp. 115–16.
125. *Ibid.*, p. 302. 126. *Ibid.*, p. 209.
127. *HFT*, 7/2, 7/7. The direct quotation is from 7/2.
128. Liao, I, 254; cf. *HFT*, 8/8.
129. *Ibid.*, 8/2.
130. Liao, II, 167; translation revised, cf. *HFT*, 15/16.
131. Liao, II, 159; translation revised, cf. *HFT*, 15/11.
132. The only occurrence of such a use is one in which the phrase is quoted from the *Tso Chuan*. Cf. *ibid.*, 16/11–12 and *TCCI*, 7/13 (Huan 17).
133. Creel, *Confucius*, pp. 77–78.

Appendix

1. *SCHI*, 47/18–19; *CHSP*, 30/9–10.
2. Legge, *Analects*, 13.5, 2.2.
3. *WSTK*, I, 214–16; *SCTW*, pp. 328–45.
4. *Ibid.*, pp. 320–45.
5. *SCCI*, pp. 94–95.
6. *SCHI*, 14/1–2.
7. *HHWC*, 3a/29–35. Cf. *WSTK*, I, 368–75; Tsuda, pp. 57–62, 470–71, 712–49.
8. *KSYC*, I, 72–160.
9. Karlgren, "Authenticity," pp. 64–65.
10. *Ibid.*, p. 64.
11. *TCCI*, 11/2 (Min 1), 39/6, 11 (Hsiang 29), 44/14 (Chao 14); cf. *WSTK*, I, p. 408.
12. *TCCI*, 21/9 (Hsüan 3).
13. *Ibid.*, 17/5 (Hsi 31); *SCHI*, 37/9, 15/31.
14. *TCCI*, 19a/5 (Wen 6); *SCHI*, 15/20, 68/4.
15. *CCYT*, pp. lxxi–xciii. However, his conclusion that the *Tso Chuan* was written by Chang Ch'ang at the beginning of the Former Han dynasty seems dubious.
16. *TCCI*, 3/12–14 (Yin 5) is the first occurrence of such sayings.
17. Tsuda, pp. 373–423.
18. Legge, *Tso Chuen*, pp. 34–35; p. 35, nn. 18–19.
19. *CHSP*, 62/24. 20. *SLCT*, 10/52.
21. *CSKY*, 3/3; *HHWC*, 4/6–7. 22. *CCYT*, p. lxxxv.

23. Karlgren, "Authenticity," pp. 58–59, 64–65.
24. *CHSP*, 30/20–21.
25. *LHSC*, 4/4–5.
26. *CSKL*, 2/17.
27. Creel, *Confucius*, pp. 293–94; cf. *LYYS*, pp. 24–35.
28. For information on dating Mo Tzu's life see *MTST*, pp. 271–78.
29. *SKCS*, 117/1.   30. *CKCH*, pp. 151–52.
31. *SKCS*, 117/1.   32. *MTPC*, pp. 261–71.
33. *TMYC*, pp. 253–61.
34. Mei did not include them in his translation (Mei, pp. xii–xiii).
35. Mei considers the first three chapters to be spurious, but seems to accept the others as authentic.
36. *CHSP*, 30/14; *MT*, preface; Legge, *Mencius*, p. 9.
37. *SCHI*, 74/1. Chao Ch'i concurs on this point (*MT*, preface).
38. *CLC*, 14/8.
39. Legge also cites these facts in the prolegomena to his translation of the *Mencius* (p. 12). He asserted, however, that the book was written under the guidance of Mencius himself.
40. The dates are based on the chart in *HCCT*, p. 102. Legge seems to have come to few definite conclusions about the 33 chapters of the *Chuang Tzu*. He questioned the authenticity of chaps. ix, xv, xvi, xxvi, xxix, and xxxiii, but accepted the very doubtful chap. xxx as genuine (Legge, *Kwang-zze*, XXXIX, 141, 146, 147, 155, 158, 159, 161).
41. *CTSW*, pp. 33–34.   42. *CKCH*, p. 254.
43. *TS*, p. 282.   44. *LTHM*, pp. 341–44.
45. For information about Chuang Hsin see *HCCT*, pp. 406–7.
46. *HTCC*, 19/1, 20/1.
47. *CTKS*, p. 74; *HCHT*, pp. 110–17.
48. *CKCH*, p. 306.
49. If the traditional order is used, the ten chaps. are xv (p. 116), vi (p. 249), xxx (p. 378), xxxv (p. 588), x (p. 654), v (p. 685), viii (p. 696), lv (p. 831), and iv (p. 837). Page numbers refer to *HFCS*.
50. In the traditional order, the chaps. are xix (p. 200), lii (p. 787), xxvii (p. 791), xxvi (p. 797), xxv (p. 808), liv (p. 813), li (p. 818), and xlii (p. 308). Page numbers refer to *HFCS*.
51. Ch'en thought chaps. xxix (p. 715) and xxiv (p. 718) to be Taoist writings. Chaps. xx (p. 721) and xxi (p. 764) are both obviously interpretations of the *Tao Te Ching*. The authenticity of chap. liii (p. 826) seems doubtful because the ideas in it do not fit in with the rest of the book. Chap. 1 has also been doubted by most critical scholars; Ch'en suggested that it had been included in the book by mistake. Chap. ii consists of two parts; the first half seems to be Han Fei's advice to the ruler of Ch'in, and the second half seems to be the objections to Han Fei's suggestions that were presented by one of his political opponents. Cf. *HFCT*, p. 654; *HFCS*, pp. 843–44, 866.

52. *LSCC*, 12/10. For informatiton about the editorship and patronage see *SCHI*, 14/2, 85/4.

53. For an analysis of the contents of the *Lü Shih Ch'un Ch'iu* see *LSCI*, pp. 321–39, and *LSFH*, pp. 340–58. Both works trace the ideas in the *Lü Shih Ch'un Ch'iu* back to their origins in the different schools of the Chan Kuo period.

54. *CTKS*, p. 104.

55. *CKT*, p. 1; cf. *CKTC*, pp. 257–59.

56. *Ibid.*, pp. 260–62.

57. *WSTK*, I, 541–43; *CKTC*, pp. 267–69.

58. *Ibid.*, pp. 268–71.

59. *CKT*, 3/5–8.

60. *Ibid.*, 3/1.

61. *CKTC* cites a number of examples on pp. 264–66.

62. Cf. *WSTK*, I, 543–44.

Bibliography

Bibliography

Works in Western Languages and Japanese

Amano, Motonosuke. "Development of Agriculture in Ancient China," *Toho Gakuho*, XXX (1959).

Bendix, Reinhard. Max Weber: An Intellectual Portrait. New York: Doubleday, 1960.

Bloch, Marc. Feudal Society. Translated by L. A. Manyon. London: Routledge and Kegan Paul, 1961.

Bodde, Derk. China's First Unifier: A Study of the Ch'in Dynasty as Seen in the Life of Li Ssu. Leiden: E. J. Brill, 1938. Vol. III of Sinica Leidensia.

———. "Feudalism in China," in Feudalism in History, edited by R. Coulborn. Princeton; Princeton University Press, 1956.

Chang, Kwang-chih. The Archaeology of Ancient China. New Haven: Yale University Press, 1963.

Cheng, Te-kun. "Chou China," in Archaeology in China, vol. III. Cambridge, Eng.: Heffer, 1963.

Creel, H. G. "The Beginnings of Bureaucracy in China: The Origin of the *Hsien*," *Journal of Asian Studies*, XXIII, no. 2 (1964).

———. The Birth of China. New York: John Day, Reynal & Hitchcock, 1937.

———. "Bronze Inscriptions of the Western Chou Dynasty as Historical Documents," *Journal of American Oriental Society*, LVI (1936).

———. Confucius and the Chinese Way. New York: Harper, 1960.

———. "The *Fa Chia*, Legalists or Administrators?" *Bulletin of the Institute of History and Philology*, extra vol. no. 4 (1961).

———. "The Meaning of *Hsing-Ming*," in Studia Sinica Bernhard Karlgren Dedicata, edited by Egerod Søren. Copenhagen: E. Munksgaard, 1959.

Dubs, H. H., trans. The Works of Hsüntze. London: Probsthain, 1928. Probsthain's Oriental Series, vol. XVI.

Duyvendak, J. J. L., trans. The Book of Lord Shang. London: Probsthain, 1928. Probsthain's Oriental Series, vol. XVII.

Eberhard, Wolfram. "Concerns of Historical Sociology," *Sociologus*, XIV, no. 1 (1964).

———. Conquerors and Rulers: Social Forces in Medieval China. Leiden: E. J. Brill, 1952.

———. History of China. Translated by E. W. Dickes. Berkeley: University of California Press, 1950.

Fairbank, John K. The United States and China. Cambridge, Mass.: Harvard University Press, 1961.

Frazer, James. The Golden Bough. New York: Macmillan, 1935.

Freedman, Maurice. Lineage Organization in Southeastern China. London: University of London, Athlone Press, 1958.

Gerth, H. H., and C. W. Mills, eds. and trans. From Max Weber: Essays in Sociology. New York: Oxford University Press, 1958.

Granet, Marcel. Catégories matrimoniales et relations de proximité dans la Chine ancienne. Paris: Alcan, 1939.

———. Chinese Civilization. New York: Meridian, 1958.

———. Danses et légendes de la Chine ancienne. Paris: Alcan, 1926.

Haloun, Gustav. "Contributions to the History of Clan Settlement in Ancient China," Asia Major, 1924.

Herodotus. Persian Wars, in Greek Historians, vol. I, edited by F. R. B. Godolphin. New York: Random House, 1942.

Ho, P. T. The Ladder of Success in Imperial China: Aspects of Social Mobility. New York: Columbia University Press, 1962.

Hsu, Cho-yun. "A Study of Social Mobility in Ancient China, 722–222 B.C." Ph.D. dissertation, University of Chicago, 1962.

———. "The Transition of Ancient Chinese Society," in International Association of Historians of Asia Second Biennial Conference Proceedings, 1962.

Hsu, Francis L. K. "Social Mobility in China," American Sociological Review, XIV (1949).

Hughes, A. J. B. Kin, Caste, and Nation among the Rhodesian Ndebele. Manchester: Manchester University Press, 1956.

Kaizuka, Shigeki. "The People's Assembly in the City-States of Ancient China," Tohogaku Ronshu, II (1954).

Karlgren, Bernhard. "The Authenticity and Nature of the Tso Chuan," Göteborg Hogskolos Årsskrift, XXXII, no. 3 (1926).

———. trans. "The Book of Documents," Bulletin of the Museum of Far Eastern Antiquities, XXII (1950).

Kato, Shigeshi. Studies in Chinese Economic History, vol. I. Tokyo: Toyo Bunko, 1952.

Kazuchika, Kumai, and Takeshi Sekino. Han Tan. Archaeologia Orientalis, series B, vol. VII. Tokyo: The Far Eastern Archaeological Society, 1954.

Krige, E. J. The Social System of the Zulu. 4th ed. Pietermaritzburg: Shutter and Shooter, 1962.

Lattimore, Owen. Inner Asian Frontiers of China. 2nd ed. New York: American Geographical Society, 1951.

Legge, James, trans. The Chinese Classics. Oxford: The Clarendon Press, 1865–95. Vol. I, The Confucian Analects. Vol. II, The Works of Mencius. Vol. III, The Shoo King. Vol. IV, The She King. Vol. V, The Ch'un Ts'ew with the Tso Chuen.

———. The Writings of Kwang-zze, in Sacred Books of the East, ed. by Max

Müller, vols. XXXIX and XL. London: Oxford University Press, 1891; reprinted, 1927.

Levenson, J. R. "Ill Wind in the Well-Field: The Erosion of the Confucian Ground of Controversy," in The Confucian Persuasion, ed. by Arthur F. Wright. Stanford: Stanford University Press, 1960.

Liao, W. K., trans. The Complete Works of Han Fei Tzu. London: Probsthain, 1939. Probsthain's Oriental Series, vols. XXV and XXVI.

Linton, Ralph. The Study of Man. New York: Appleton-Century-Crofts, 1936.

Lipset, S. M., and Reinhard Bendix. Social Mobility in Industrial Society. Berkeley: University of California Press, 1963.

Maine, Sir Henry. Ancient Law. London: John Murray, 1909.

Marsh, Robert M. The Mandarins: The Circulation of Elite in China. New York: Glencoe Free Press, 1961.

Maspero, Henri. La Chine antique. Revised edition. Paris: Imprimerie Nationale, 1955.

————. "La Composition et la date du Tso tchouan," in Mélanges chinois et bouddhiques, vol. I. Brussels, n.p., 1931–32.

————. "Le Régime féodal et la propriété foncière dans la Chine antique," in Mélanges posthumes sur les religions et l'histoire de la Chine, vol. III, Etudes historiques. Paris, 1950.

Masubuchi, Tatsuo. Society and State in Ancient China. Tokyo: Kobondo, 1960.

Mei, Y. P., trans. The Ethical and Political Works of Motse. London: Probsthain, 1929. Probsthain's Oriental Series, vol. XIX.

Meisner, Maurice. "The Despotism of Concepts: Wittfogel and Marx on China," The China Quarterly, XVI (1963), 99–111.

Menger, Carl. Principles of Economics. Translated and edited by James Dingwall and Bert F. Hoselitz. Glencoe, Ill.: The Free Press, 1950.

Merton, Robert. Social Theory and Social Structure. Revised edition. Glencoe, Ill.: The Free Press, 1957.

Miyazaki, Ichisada. "The Age of City-States in China," Shirin, XXXIII, no. 1 (1950).

————. "Origin of Inner Wall and Outer Wall of Chinese Cities," Rekishi To Chiri, XXXII (1933).

————. "Taxation in Ancient China," Shirin, XVIII, no. 2–3 (1933).

————. "Towns and Cities in the Warring States Period," in Eastern Studies Fifteenth Anniversary Volume. Tokyo: Toho Gakkai, 1962.

————. "Les Villes en Chine à l'époque des Han," T'oung Pao, XLVIII, no. 4–5 (1960).

Moriya, Mitsuo. "Shang Yang's Ideas on the Peerage System and the Origin of the Han Peerage System," Toho Gakuho, XXVII (1957).

Murdock, G. P. Social Structure. New York: Macmillan, 1949.

Oshima, Riichi. "On the Wall Cities in Ancient China," Toho Gakuho, XXX (1959).

Pulleyblank, E. G. "Review," *Journal of the Economic and Social History of the Orient,* VI, no. 3 (1963).

Radcliffe-Brown, A. R. Structure and Function in Primitive Society. 3rd ed. Glencoe, Ill.: The Free Press, 1959.

——— and D. Forde. African Systems of Kinship and Marriage. London: Oxford University Press, 1950; reprinted, 1958.

Redfield, Robert. "The Folk Society," *American Journal of Sociology,* LII, no. 4 (1947).

Rostovtzeff, M. The Social and Economic History of the Hellenistic World. Oxford: The Clarendon Press, 1941.

Sekino, Takeshi. A Study of Chinese Archaeology. Tokyo: University of Tokyo, 1956.

———. "Remarks on the Area of Distribution and Nature of Excavation of the Pu Coins," *Toho Gakuho,* XLI, no. 2 (1958).

Tönnies, Ferdinand. Fundamental Concepts of Sociology (Gemeinschaft und Gesellschaft). Translated by C. P. Loomis. New York: American Book Co., 1940.

Tsuda, Sakichi. A Study of the *Tso Chuan* in the Light of the Development of Confucian Thought. Tokyo: Toyo Bunko Ronso, 1935.

Utsunomiya, Kiyoyoshi. Studies on the Socio-Economic History of the Han Dynasty. Tokyo: Kobondo, 1954.

Waley, Arthur, trans. The Book of Songs. New York: Grove Press, 1960.

Walker, R. L. The Multi-State System of Ancient China. Hamsden, Conn.: The Shoe String Press, 1953.

Wang, Yü-ch'üan. Early Chinese Coinage. New York: American Numismatic Society, 1951.

Weber, Max. The City. Translated and edited by Don Martindale and Gertrud Neuwirth. Glencoe, Ill.: The Free Press, 1958.

———. The Protestant Ethic and the Spirit of Capitalism. Translated by Talcott Parsons. New York: Scribner's, 1958.

———. The Theory of Social and Economic Organization. Translated by A. M. Henderson and Talcott Parsons. Glencoe, Ill.: The Free Press, 1947.

Wilson, John A. The Burden of Egypt. Chicago: University of Chicago Press, 1951.

Wittfogel, K. A. Oriental Despotism: A Comparative Study of Total Power. New Haven: Yale University Press, 1957.

———. "The Marxist View of China (Part I)," *The China Quarterly,* XI (1962), 10–14.

Xenophon. The Constitution of the Spartans, in Greek Historians, vol. II, edited by F. R. B. Godolphin. New York: Random House, 1942.

Yang, L. S. Money and Credit in China. Cambridge, Mass.: Harvard University Press, 1952.

———. "Notes on Dr. Swann's *Food and Money in Ancient China*," *Harvard Journal of Asiatic Studies,* XIII (1950).

Works in Chinese

Arranged alphabetically by abbreviation. The Chinese characters for the titles are given in my dissertation, "A Study of Social Mobility in Ancient China, 722–222 B.C." (University of Chicago, 1962), pp. 336 ff.

BIHP   *Bulletin of the Institute of History and Philology*, Academia Sinica.
CCST   Ch'en Hou-yao. Tseng Ting Ch'un Ch'iu Shih Tsu Yüan Liu T'u K'ao. Revised by Chang Mao-lai. Chi Ku T'ang, 1850.
CCTS   Ku Tung-kao. "Ch'un Ch'iu Ta Shih Piao," in Huang Ch'ing Ching Chieh Hsü Pien, vol. XXXII. Edited by Wang Hsien-ch'ien. Nan Ching Shu Yüan, 1888.
CCYT   Hung, William, ed. Ch'un Ch'iu Ching Chuan Yin Te. Harvard-Yenching Institute Sinological Index Series, supplement no. 11. Peiping: Harvard-Yenching Institute, 1937.
CHS   Pan Ku. Ch'ien Han Shu. Annotated by Yen Shih-ku. SPPY ed.
CHSP   Wang Hsien-ch'ien. Han Shu Pu Chu. Changsha, 1900.
CHT   Chuang Tzu. Also known as Nan Hua Chen Ching. Annotated by Kuo Hsiang and Lu Te-ming. SPTK ed.
CICI   Chou I Cheng I. Annotated by Wang Pi, Han K'ang-po, Lu Te-ming, and K'ung Ying-ta. Shih San Ching Chu Su edition, 1815.
CKCC   Liu Chi-hsüan. "Chan Kuo Shih Tai Chih Ching Chi Sheng Huo," *Nanking Journal*, V, no. 2 (1935).
CKCH   Hu Shih. Chung Kuo Che Hsüeh Shih Ta Kang. Shanghai: Commercial Press, 1936.
CKCN   Lin Ch'un-p'u. Chan Kuo Chi Nien. Chu Po Shan Fang Shih Wu Chung edition, 1838.
CKCT   Ch'i Ssu-ho. "Chan Kuo Chih Tu K'ao," *Yenching Journal of Chinese Studies*, XXIV (1938).
CKFC   Ch'ü T'ung-tsu. Chung Kuo Feng Chien She Hui. 3rd ed. Changsha: Commercial Press, 1938.
CKHP   Wang Yü-ch'üan. Chung Kuo Ku Tai Huo Pi Ti Chi Yüan Ho Fa Chan. Shanghai: Ko Hsüeh Ch'u Pan She, 1957.
CKKT   Tung Tso-pin. Chung Kuo Ku Tai Wen Hua Ti Jen Shih. Taipei: *The Continent Magazine*, 1952.
CKNL   Li Ya-nung. Chung Kuo Ti Nu Li Chih Yü Feng Chien Chih. Shanghai: Huang-tung Jen-min Press, 1954.
CKS   Yang K'uan. Chan Kuo Shih. Shanghai: Jen Min Ch'u Pan She, 1955.
CKSH   Li Tsung-t'ung. Chung Kuo Ku Tai She Hui Shih. Taipei: Chung Hua Wen Hua Ch'u Pan Wei Yüan Hui, 1954.
CKT   Chan Kuo Ts'e. Annotated by Kao Yu and Yao Hung. SPPY ed.
CKTC   Ch'i Ssu-ho. "Chan Kuo Ts'e Chu Tso Shih Tai K'ao," *Yenching Journal of Chinese Studies*, XXXIV (1948), 257–78.
CKTH   Ch'i Ssu-ho. "Chan Kuo Tsai Hsiang Piao," *Shih Hsüeh Nien Pao*, II, no. 5 (1938), 165–93.

CKTL Wu Ch'eng-lo. Chung Kuo Tu Liang Heng Shih. Shanghai: Commercial Press, 1937.

CKTT Chang Hung-chao. Chung Kuo T'ung Ch'i T'ieh Ch'i Shih Tai Yen Ke K'ao. Appendix to Shih Ya. Peiping: Chinese Geological Survey, 1921.

CLC Han Yü. Ch'ang Li Chi. SPTK ed.

CLCI Chou Li Cheng I. Annotated by Sun I-jang. SPPY ed.

CSCM Hunan Po Wu Kuan. "Ch'ang Sha Ch'u Mu," K'ao Ku Hsüeh Pao, 1959, no. 1, pp. 41–60.

CSCY Chün Shu Chih Yao. Ed. and annotated by Wei Ching. SPTK ed.

CSKC Lo Fu-i. Chuan Shih Li Tai Ku Ch'ih T'u Lu. Shanghai: Hsin Hua, 1957.

CSKL Ts'ui Shu. Chu Ssu K'ao Hsin Lu, in Tung Pi I Shu, vol. III, edited by Ku Chieh-kang. Peiping: Ya Tung, 1936.

CSKY Ts'ui Shu. Chu Ssu K'ao Hsin Yü Lu, in Tung Pi I Shu, vol. IV, edited by Ku Chieh-kang. Peiping: Ya Tung, 1936.

CTCT Hsü Chung-shu. "Ching T'ien Chih Tu T'an Yüan," in Bulletin of Chinese Studies, IV, no. 1 (1944).

CTKS Liang Ch'i-ch'ao. Chu Tzu K'ao Shih. Shanghai: Chung Hua, 1936; Taipei reprint, 1957.

CTSW Lu Te-ming. Ching Tien Shih Wen. SPTK ed.

CTTC Huang Chan-yüeh. "Chin Nien Ch'u T'u Ti Chan Kuo Liang Han T'ieh Ch'i," K'ao Ku Hsüeh Pao, 1957, no. 3.

HCCT Ch'ien Mu. Hsien Ch'in Chu Tzu Hsi Nien K'ao Pien. Shanghai: Commercial Press, 1936.

HCHP Wang Ming-yüan. Hsien Ch'in Huo Pi Shih. Kwangtung: Chung Shan University, 1937.

HCHT Liang Ch'i-ch'ao. "Hsün Ch'ing Chi Hsün Tzu," in KSP, vol. IV (1933).

HCLH Li Chien-nung. Hsien Ch'in Liang Han Ching Chi Shih Kao. Peking: San Lien, 1957.

HFCS Ch'en Ch'i-t'ien. Han Fei Tzu Chiao Shih. Taipei: Chung Hua Ts'ung Shu, 1958.

HFCT Jung Chao-tsu. "Han Fei Ti Chu Tso K'ao," in KSP, vol. IV (1933).

HFT Wang Hsien-shen. Han Fei Tzu Chi Chieh. N.p., 1896.

HH Liu Hsiang. Hsin Hsü. SPTK ed.

HHPK Chung Kuo K'o Hsüeh Yüan. Hui Hsien Fa Chüeh Pao Kao. Chung Kuo T'ien Yeh K'ao Ku Pao Kao Chi, no. 1. Peking: K'o Hsüeh Ch'un Pan She, 1956.

HHWC K'ang Yu-wei. Hsin Hsüeh Wei Ching K'ao. Peiping: Wen Hua Hsüeh She, 1931.

HL Huan T'an. Hsin Lun. Quoted in TPYL. SPTK ed.

HMKT Shansi Wen Wu Kuan Li Wei Yüan Hui. "Hou Ma Kung Tso Chan Kung Tso Ti Tsung Shou Hu," K'ao Ku, 1959, no. 5, pp. 222–28.

HNT   Huai Nan Hung Lieh Chieh. Also known as Huai Nan Tzu. Annotated by Hsü Shen. SPTK ed.
HPSC   Hopei Wen Wu Kuan Li Wei Yüan Hui. "Ho Pei Shih Chia Chuang Shih Shih Chuang Tsun Chan Kuo I Chih Ti Fa Chüeh," *K'ao Ku Hsüeh Pao*, 1957, no. 1, pp. 87–92.
HSWC   Han Shih Wai Chuan. SPTK ed.
HSWT   Hu Shih. Hu Shih Wen Ts'un, vol. I. Shanghai: Orient Book Co., 1930.
HT   Hsün Tzu. Annotated by Yang Liang. SPTK ed.
HTCC   Wang Hsien-ch'ien. Hsün Tzu Chi Chieh. Changsha: n.p., 1891.
HTCH   Chang Hsi-t'ang. "Hsün Tzu Ch'üan Hsüeh P'ien Yüan Tz'u," in KSP, vol. VI (1938), 147–62.
ICS   I Chou Shu. Also known as Chi Chung Chou Shu. Annotated by K'ung Chao. SPTK ed.
KKCC   K'ao Ku Yen Chiu So. K'ao Ku Hsüeh Chi Ch'u. Peking: K'o Hsüeh Ch'u Pan She, 1958.
KKSH   K'ao Ku Yen Chiu So, ed. Hsin Chung Kuo Ti K'ao Ku Shou Huo. Peking: Wen Wu Ch'u Pan She, 1962.
KLC   Ch'un Ch'iu Ku Liang Chuan. Annotated by Fan Ning. SPTK ed.
KSP   Ku Shih Pien. Edited by Ku Chieh-kang, et al. Peiping and Shanghai: Pu She and K'ai Ming, 1926–41.
KSTK   Ch'ien Mu. Kuo Shih Ta Kang. Shanghai: Commercial Press, 1940; Taipei reprint, 1956.
KSYC   Wei Chü-hsien. Ku Shih Yen Chiu. Peiping: Hsin Yüeh, 1928.
KT   Kuan Tzu. Annotated by Fang Hsüan-ling. SPTK ed.
KTKK   Weng Wen-hao. "Ku Tai Kuan K'ai Kung Ch'eng Fa Chan Shih Chih I Chieh," in Ch'ing Tsu Ts'ai Yüan P'ei Hsien Sheng Liu Shih Wu Sui Lun Wen Chi, vol. II, pp. 709–12. Peiping: Academia Sinica, 1935.
KY   Kuo Yü. Annotated by Wei Chao. SPTK ed.
KYC   Ch'un Ch'iu Kung Yang Ching Chuan Chieh Ku. Annotated by Ho Hsiu. SPTK ed.
LC   Li Chi. Annotated by Cheng Hsüan. SPTK ed.
LCCW   Kuo Mo-jo. Liang Chou Chin Wen Tz'u Ta Hsi K'ao Shih. Tokyo: Bunkyodo, 1935.
LHSC   Liu Tsung-yüan. Liu Hsien Sheng Chi. SPTK ed.
LSCC   Lü Shih Ch'un Ch'iu. Annotated by Kao Yu. SPTK ed.
LSCI   Li Chün-chih. "Lü Shih Ch'un Ch'iu Chung Ku Shu Chi I," in KSP, vol. VI (1938), 321–39.
LSFH   Liu Ju-lin. "Lü Shih Ch'un Ch'iu Chih Fen Hsi," in KSP, vol. VI (1938), 340–58.
LTCT   Yang K'uan. Chung Kuo Li Tai Ch'ih Tu K'ao. Changsha: Commercial Press, 1938.
LTHM   T'ang Lan. "Lao Tan Ti Hsing Ming Ho Shih Tai K'ao," in KSP, vol. IV (1933), 332–51.

LWTC Fu Ssu-nien. "Lun So Wei Wu Tun Chüeh," BIHP, II (1930), 110–29.

LYHN Huang Chan-yüeh. "1955 Nien Ch'un Lo Yang Han Ho Nan Hsien Ch'en Tung Ch'ü Fa Chüeh Pao Kao," *K'ao Ku Hsüeh Pao,* 1956, no. 4.

LYYS Ts'ui Shu. Lun Yü Yü Shuo, in Tung Pi I Shu, vol. V. Edited by Ku Chieh-kang. Peiping: Ya Tung, 1936.

MOT Mo Tzu. Annotated by Pi Yüan. SPPY ed.

MT Meng Tzu. Annotated by Chao Ch'i. SPTK ed.

MTCT Ch'i Ssu-ho. "Meng Tzu Ching T'ien Shuo Pien," *Yenching Journal of Chinese Studies,* XXXV (1948).

MTHK Sun I-jang. Mo Tzu Hsien Ku. Shanghai: Commercial Press, 1936.

MTPC Chu Hsi-tsu. "Mo Tzu Pei Cheng Men I Hsia Erh Shih P'ien Hsi Han Jen Wei Shu Shuo," in KSP, vol. IV (1933).

MTST Ch'ien Mu. "Mo Tzu Ti Sheng Tsu Nien Tai," in KSP, vol. IV (1933).

PFS Hsü Chung-shu. "Pin Feng Shuo," BIHP, VI (1936).

SC Shih Ching. Also known as Mao Shih. Annotated by Mao Heng and Cheng Hsüan. SPTK ed.

SCCI Fu Ssu-nien. "Shih Ching Chiang I Kao," in Fu Meng Chen Hsien Sheng Chi, vol. II-B. Taipei: Taiwan University, 1952.

SCHI Ssu-ma Ch'ien. Shih Chi Chi Chieh. Annotated by P'ei Yin, Ssu-ma Chen, and Chang Shou-chieh. SPPY ed.

SCIC Jung Keng. Shang Chou I Ch'i T'ung K'ao. Peiping: Harvard-Yenching Institute, 1941.

SCTW Ku Chieh-kang. "Shih Ching Tsai Ch'un Ch'iu Chan Kuo Chien Ti Wei," in KSP, vol. III (1931).

SHCC Li Tao-yüan. Shui Ching Chu. SPTK ed.

SKCS Chi Yün, ed. Ssu K'u Ch'üan Shu Tsung Mu. Shanghai: Ta Tung, 1930.

SLCT Ch'en Chen-sun. Chih Chai Shu Lu Chieh T'i. Shanghai: Commercial Press, 1939.

SLSY Jan Chao-teh. "Shih Lun Shang Yang Pien Fa Ti Hsing Chih," *Li Shih Yen Chiu,* VI (1957).

SNKK Hsia Nai. "Shih Nien Lai Chung Kuo K'ao Ku Ti Hsin Fa Hsien," *K'ao Ku,* 1959, no. 10.

SPPY Ssu Pu Pei Yao.

SPTK Ssu Pu Ts'ung K'an.

SS Shang Shu. Annotated by K'ung An-kuo. SPTK ed.

SSCC Shansi Wen Wu Kuan Li Wei Yüan Hui. "Shan Hsi Ch'ang Chih Shih Fen Shui Ling Ku Mu Ti Ch'ing Li," *K'ao Ku Hsueh Pao,* 1957, no. 1.

ST Ma Kuo-han. Shen Tsu, in Yü Han Shan Fang Chi I Shu, 1883.

SY Liu Hsiang. Shuo Yüan. SPPY ed.

SYPF   Ch'i Ssu-ho. "Shang Yang Pien Fa K'ao," *Yenching Journal of Chinese Studies*, XXXIII (1947).

TCCI   Ch'un Ch'iu Tso Chuan Cheng I. Also known as Tso Chuan. Annotated by Tu Yü, K'ung Ying-ta, and Lu Te-ming. SPPY ed.

TCTC   Ssu-ma Kuang. Tsu Chih T'ung Chien. SPTK ed.

TMYC   Liang Ch'i-ch'ao. "Tu Mo Ching Yü Chi," in KSP, vol. IV (1933), 253–61.

TPYL   Li Fang, *et al.*, ed. T'ai P'ing Yü Lan. SPTK ed.

TS   Ku Chieh-kang. "(Lun Chuang Tzu Chen Wei) Ta Shu," in KSP, vol. I (1926), 282.

WSTK   Chang Hsin-cheng. Wei Shu T'ung K'ao. Changsha: Commercial Press, 1939.

WTIS   Cheng Cheng-to, ed. Wei Ta Ti I Shu Chüan T'ung T'u Lu. Peking: Chung Kuo Ku Tien I Shu Ch'u Pan She, 1952.

YCST   Lü Chen-yü. Yin Chou Shih Tai Ti Chung Kuo She Hui. Shanghai: Pu Erh, 1936.

YTL   Huan K'uan. Yen T'ieh Lun. SPTK ed.

Index

Index

38, 87–88, 175–76; and the manor,
107–9, 126
Fan family of Chin, 52, 73, 83, 87 f,
109
Fan Sui, 44, 50, 103
Feudalism, Chou, 2–3, 5–8, 53–55,
79–80; manorial system, 8–14,
107–15, 126–27; ideology and, 14–
22, 178; changes in, 83, 92–94, 176
Fu Ssu-nien, 183

Generals, Chan Kuo period, 75–77
Gods in ancient China, 14–19
Granet, Marcel, 8n, 69
Great Wall of China, 68n, 76

Han, state of, 93 f, 97; chancellors,
47–48; and war, 62, 67, 71
Han family of Chin, 33, 52, 82 f, 88
Han Fei, *Han Fei Tzu*, 72, 94, 96n,
105, 124–29 *passim*, 144 f, 189–90;
on rulers, 146; on family, 152–53;
against tradition, 156–57; on *chün
tzu*, 172–73
Han Shu, 109, 209
Han-tan, city, 135 f
Hospitable princes, the four, 41n,
46
Hou Chi, 16
Hou family of Lu, 81, 206
Hsiao jen, "small men," 162, 165,
173, 175. See also Artisans; Mer-
chant class; Peasant class
Hsien system, 68n, 83, 207
Hsin-ling, Lord, 41n, 50, 75 f
Hsü, state of, 57–60 *passim*, 203
Hsü Hsing, 103, 118
Hsüan, King of Ch'i, 103, 142, 147,
151
Hsün Tzu, *Hsün Tzu*, 113, 122–26
passim, 138, 189; on rulers, 143–
44, 148 f; on the *shih*, 150; on
chün tzu, 170–72, 173
Hu Shih, 187 ff
Huan, Duke of Ch'i, 3n, 53, 86, 117

Huan, Duke of Lu, 26, 28, 78, 173
Huan families of Lu, the three, 27,
32, 80 ff, 86, 90, 93
Hui Shih, 49
Hung, William, 185 f

I Ching, Hsi Tz'u appendix, 122
Industry, 121, 127, 130
Iron tools, 130–31
Irrigation, 131, 133

Jan Yu, 36–37, 101
Jung, barbarian state, 70
Jung Chao-tsu, 190

Kan Mao, 43, 74, 76, 103
Kao family of Ch'i, 33, 83 f, 86
K'ao Kung Chi, 127, 210
Karlgren, Bernard, 184, 186
Kato, Shigeshi, 108n
Ku, barbarian state, 60
Ku Chieh-kang, 188
Ku Tung-kao, 58n
Kuan Chung, 105, 173; *Kuan Tzu*,
114, 129, 209
Kung-sun Yen, 43, 49 f, 72, 103
Kung-tzu, family name, 26 f, 29, 40
Kuo, state of, 59–62 *passim*
Kuo family of Ch'i, 33, 83 f, 86
Kuo Hsiang, 188
Kuo Yü, 25, 124, 185–86

Land, 107–8, 110–12, 115. See also
Feudalism
Lattimore, Owen, 3n
Legge, James, 162n, 196, 208, 214 ff
Li, "propriety," 143, 146, 154, 171 f,
204
Li Chi, 211
Li Kuei, 48, 109, 202
Li Tsung-t'ung, 80
Liang Ch'i-ch'ao, 187, 189
Lineage systems, 32
Lin-tzu, city, 71, 137
Liu Hsiang, 191 f

Liu Ju-lin, 184
Liu Tsung-yüan, 186
Lo family of Sung, 85, 87, 91
Lo I, 40, 75, 103
Lu, state of, 24, 78, 101, 116, 184 f;
    ducal house, 6 f; 25–29 *passim*,
    78–82; Chi family, 25, 34, 36, 78,
    81, 87, 98, 109; three Huan fami-
    lies, 27, 32, 80 ff, 86, 90, 93; and
    Confucianists, 35–36, 36–37; *shih*
    class, 35–36, 89–90; and warfare,
    55–61 *passim*, 66–71 *passim*; taxa-
    tion, 108–9, 113
Luan family of Chin, 34, 52, 73, 83,
    87
Lü Pu-wei, 45, 129, 138 f, 191
Lü Shih Ch'un Ch'iu, 105, 133, 191,
    219

Manorial system, 8–14, 92–93, 107–
    15, 126–27, 138–39
Maspero, Henri, 8n, 108n, 185n
Mencius, *Mencius*, 72, 82, 100, 102,
    118, 138, 154, 188; on farmers, 11,
    113 f, 116, 126–30 *passim*; on com-
    merce, 12n, 128; on well-field sys-
    tem, 108, 196; on rulers, 142–43,
    147–52 *passim*; on *chün tzu*, 167–
    69, 173
Meng-sun family of Lu, 34, 78, 81,
    87
Merchant class, 11–13, 89n, 115 f,
    128–29
Ministers (*Ch'ing, tai fu*): relations
    with rulers, 5, 20–21, 57–58, 140–
    44, 151–54; hereditary power, 7–
    8, 22, 31–34, 86, 88–89; and wars,
    57–58, 60n, 80–86; selection of,
    79–80, 92–93, 94–95, 141–46; and
    the people, 90–91
Miyazaki, Ichisada, 81n, 108n, 134n,
    137
Mobility, social, 1–2, 53, 130, 144–
    45, 159, 175–80. *See also* Down-
    ward mobility; Upward mobility

Mohists, 140, 152, 167, 179, 186. *See
    also* Mo Tzu
Money, 12–13, 116, 122–25, 152–54,
    178, 211; usury, 113–14; salary sys-
    tem, 153–54, 208
Mo Tzu, *Mo Tzu*, 102, 108n, 110,
    124 f, 138, 154, 186–87; on rulers,
    141 f; on *chün tzu*, 166–67

Nan K'uai, 35, 81, 89
Nobility, hereditary. *See* Aristocracy

Pa, "overlord," 53, 118
Pai Kuei, 48 f, 128, 138
Pan Ku, list of, 25, 35, 38
Pao family of Ch'i, 83 f, 89n
Peasant class, 8–11, 104n, 107–10,
    112–15, 116, 126–27; and conscrip-
    tion, 71; relations with rulers, 90–
    91, 147–48
Pi, state of, 82, 90
"Presenting reports," 95
Professions, types of, 126–28

Radcliffe-Brown, A. R., 3n, 32
Rewards and penalties, 95 f, 153; in
    battle, 61, 72 f, 91, 111; of land,
    58, 73, 83, 111
Rituals, 21n; military, 19, 59, 61
Roads, 117–18
Rulers, 110, 147–49, 151; relations
    with ministers, 5, 20–21, 57–58,
    79–80, 94–95, 140–44, 151–54; and
    peasants, 90–91, 147–48; and ide-
    ology, 141–46 *passim*, 174. *See also*
    Aristocracy; Feudalism

Salary system, 153–54, 208. *See also*
    Money
Scholars and masters, 100–105, 112,
    118; mentioned by name, 25, 40,
    43, 46, 49, 102–3, 104. *See also by
    name, as* Confucius, *etc.*
Seven major states, 62, 88, 124, 177
Shang dynasty, 2, 14–15, 16, 18